Angevin England
1154–1258

A History of Medieval Britain

General Editor
Marjorie Chibnall

Advisory Editor
G. W. S. Barrow

This series will cover the history of medieval Britain from the Roman withdrawal in the fourth century to 1529. The books will combine the results of the latest scholarship and research with clear, accessible writing.

Already published

Anglo-Norman England, 1066–1166
Marjorie Chibnall

Angevin England, 1154–1258
Richard Mortimer

In preparation

The Age of Settlement, c.400–c.700
Philip Dixon

The Emergence of the English Nation, c.650–c.920
Richard Abels

Late Anglo-Saxon England, c.920–1066
Robin Fleming

England under Edward I and Edward II, 1259–1327
J. H. Denton

England from Edward III to Richard II, 1327–1399
Barrie Dobson

Lancastrian England, 1399–1471
Simon Walker

The Closing of the Middle Ages, 1471–1529
Richard Britnell

Medieval Wales, 1050 to the Death of Owen Glyn Dwr
Ifor W. Rowlands

Scotland, 400–1100
David Dumville

Later Medieval Scotland
Norman A. T. MacDougall

Angevin England
1154–1258

Richard Mortimer

BLACKWELL
Oxford UK & Cambridge USA

© Richard Mortimer 1994

The right of Richard Mortimer to be identified as author of this work has been asserted in accordance with the Copyright, Designs and Patents Act 1988.

First published 1994

Blackwell Publishers
108 Cowley Road
Oxford OX4 1JF
UK

238 Main Street
Cambridge, Massachusetts 02142
USA

British Library Cataloguing in Publication Data

A CIP catalogue record for this book is available from the British Library.

Library of Congress Cataloging-in-Publication Data
Mortimer, Richard.
  Angevin England, 1154–1258 / Richard Mortimer.
    p. cm.—(A history of medieval Britain)
  Includes bibliographical references (p.) and index.
  ISBN 0–631–16388–3 (alk. paper)
    1. Great Britain—History—Angevin period,
  1154–1216. 2. England—Civilization—1066–1485.
  3. Anjou, House of. I. Title. II. Series.
  DA205.M67 1994
  942.03—dc20   93–36482
                                                            CIP

Typeset in 11/12.5 pt Sabon by
Pure Tech Corporation, Pondicherry, India
Printed in Great Britain by Hartnoll Ltd.

This book is printed on acid-free paper

For Helga

Contents

List of Plates

List of Figures

List of Maps

Preface

This book is an attempt to see England as a whole, putting together areas of life and activity which are more usually treated separately, and then to view England in its British and European context. Several excellent full narrative accounts of the events of these years are available and I have not attempted to produce another one, not having the space to do it in detail; I have preferred a thematic approach, with the most important events briefly narrated where appropriate.

I could not have undertaken such an ambitious scheme without imposing on the kindness of friends who have generously lent their expertise. I must thank Paul Brand, Lindy Grant, Christopher Harper-Bill, Barbara Harvey, Ruth Harvey, Michael Herren, George Rigg, Ian Short and Jeffrey West, who have all read parts of the book and greatly improved it by their comments and suggestions. David Carpenter and John Gillingham have read long stretches of it, and I am deeply indebted to their friendly critical acumen and generosity with their time. Marjorie Chibnall, who suggested that I might write this book, has read all of it, some parts more than once, correcting many errors of fact, interpretation and syntax and providing a calming or stimulating influence as necessary. I am most grateful to them all. The conclusions, and the errors which no doubt remain, are my own responsibility. I owe a further debt of gratitude to Lindy Grant for her help with the photographs, and to John Davey and the staff of Blackwell Publishers for seeing the book efficiently through the press. But my greatest debt is to my wife, Helga Braun, who has created the conditions in which it could be written and whose patient support has been vital at every stage.

RICHARD MORTIMER

Part I

Politics and Government

I

The Background to Politics

On the Sunday before Christmas 1154, Henry II was crowned king of England in Westminster Abbey. He was 21 years old. His kingdom was only a part of his lands, the last to come under his control. During the previous five years everything he had aimed for had fallen into his lap, his efforts crowned with apparently easy success. His mother Matilda was the only surviving legitimate child of Henry I, who had tried to ensure that she inherited England and Normandy (see figure 1.1). Her claim to Normandy had been made good through conquest by her husband, Geoffrey count of Anjou, in the 1140s, but repeated efforts to gain England had been frustrated by king Stephen, who had seized the crown and royal treasure in 1135 and struggled ever since, with generally decreasing success, to make his kingship universally accepted. In 1149 Geoffrey ceded the duchy of Normandy to Henry, his eldest son, who shortly afterwards led an expedition to England. Gaining the recognition of king Louis VII of France, the overlord of Normandy, briefly posed a difficulty: allied with Stephen's son Eustace, Louis attacked Normandy in 1151, but a truce resulted and Louis accepted Henry's homage for Normandy at a ceremony in Paris. Later that year Geoffrey died, leaving Anjou for Henry.

The following year the young duke of Normandy and count of Anjou seized an opportunity to increase his lands enormously while simultaneously settling the question of his marriage. Eleanor, heiress of the large duchy of Aquitaine which covered most of south-western France, had been married to king Louis and had had two daughters by him. In a particularly clamorous case the couple were divorced on the convenient grounds of consanguinity. Since Eleanor took her rights with her wherever she went, the result was both a diminution in the power of the French king and the sudden reappearance on the marriage market

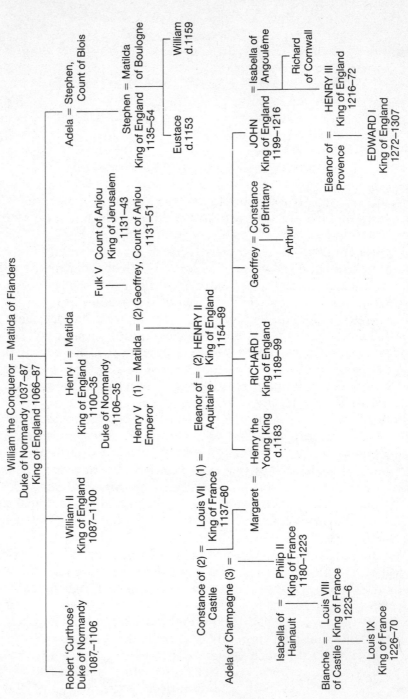

FIGURE 1.1 The ancestors, rivals and descendants of Henry II

of one of the greatest heiresses of the middle ages. In what must have been an exciting ride, Eleanor left Beaugency on the Loire near Orléans, where the divorce was settled, and avoiding attempts by count Theobald of Blois and Henry's brother Geoffrey to kidnap her, arrived safely at Poitiers in her own lands. Once there, she chose to marry Henry. The degree of collusion between the two was a point of discussion at the time, and long after. Eleanor was more closely related to Henry than to Louis; the divorce and remarriage were seen by some later churchmen as the fundamental sin which underlay and eventually poisoned their married life, finally bringing Henry to defeat and their children to disaster.[1] But this was a selective view with much benefit of hindsight; for years yet, Henry carried all before him. King Louis did not allow nearly all of western France to be united under one man's control without opposition; a coalition of virtually all Henry's neighbours was formed to attack him, but Henry held his own so successfully that in January 1153 he was able to cross again to England for the final act in the drama of his ascent.

Henry's and Stephen's armies met at Wallingford, which Stephen was besieging. It seems that some churchmen facilitated an agreement between the magnates on both sides, resulting in a truce. One chronicler says Henry took the agreement badly, complained of the negotiators' infidelity, but accepted it to keep them on his side;[2] another sees a more sinister motive behind the truce, barons who wished to keep the war going for their own benefit attempting to prevent a decisive victory for one side which might result in the restoration of a strong monarchy.[3] But what ultimately proved fatal to Stephen's kingship was his failure to arrange a credible succession in his own family. He attempted to secure recognition for his son Eustace, and he tried to force the archbishop of Canterbury, Theobald, to crown him. Theobald had been forbidden to do so by the pope, and avoided royal pressure by escaping abroad, but Eustace did not attract enough lay loyalty to make him a serious candidate. His early death in August 1153 cleared the way for the agreement, made in November, which ended the war and brought the Angevin dynasty to the throne. Stephen recognized Henry's hereditary right to the kingdom, but was to hold it for the rest of his life;

[1] Magna Vita ii, 184–5; Newburgh i, 281.
[2] Torigni, 173–4.
[3] Huntingdon, 287.

Henry was to succeed on Stephen's death. As well as the dynastic issue the agreement addressed the problems of landholding and order to which the long war had given rise: lands which had been taken away by 'intruders' were to be returned 'to their former legitimate possessors' who had held them in the time of Henry I, and castles built since his time were to be destroyed.[4] The treaty was ratified by an assembly of bishops and leading laymen at Winchester at the end of November 1153.

The king and his new heir showed enough restraint for the ensuing year to pass without a definite breach. In the summer Henry returned to Normandy and 'little by little and carefully' began to recover various ducal rights which his father had conceded to the great men of the duchy, as a local chronicler put it.[5] In the meantime, peace reigned in England 'for love and fear of Duke Henry', as it had when he was there. At the end of October Stephen died. Henry went to the port of Barfleur, but had to wait a month for a favourable wind. The peace in England remained unbroken despite the absence of a king; after the wars of the previous reign this attracted favourable comment. For the first time in over a century the succession to the throne, when it happened, was peaceful and uncontroverted.

Thus was created what historians, though not contemporaries, call the 'Angevin empire' (see map 1.1). It was a grouping of disparate lands, part of them held of the king of France, with no overall connection except in the person of their ruler and a common French culture, and even the latter varied with the region. It had been brought together by inheritance, conquest, marriage and luck. Already in the process of its creation certain significant features can be discerned. It was a highly personal entity, owing much to the personality of its ruler. His relations with the king of France were close but hostile; the French king was his feudal superior for his lands on the continent, and he was dependent on recognition at the outset of his reign. A further difficulty arose from the recent past: in both England and Normandy Henry followed regimes which had tried to buy support by allowing royal lands, rights and authority to slip into the hands of locally powerful lords, who had not only taken over royal rights and dues, but had annexed the possessions of their neighbours too. Much of the preceding 'anarchy' in England had been due not so much to an inherent baronial love of fighting as

4 Torigni, 177.
5 Ibid., 179.

Approximate boundary of Henry II's
lands in 1174 — — — — — —

MAP 1.1 Henry II's French lands

to attempts to solve disputes by recourse to violence. Justice and peace were interdependent: 'all the people loved him, for he administered justice fairly and made peace'.[6] The date chosen as the last time right prevailed, and therefore the touchstone of just possession, was 1135, the end of Henry I's reign. In any number of writs and charters Henry II stressed that right flowed from possession under Henry I, his grandfather – for his right to succeed Henry I was the core of his own legitimacy.

[6] *Anglo-Saxon Chronicle*, trans. G. N. Garmonsway, London 1972, 268 (E-text, 1153).

It is hard for us to imagine the attitudes and pressures which underlay the activities of people in the twelfth and thirteenth centuries, and all too easy to ascribe motives, policies and strategies to them on the basis of what looks sensible to us, or to deduce their motives from their recorded actions. Their daily world was almost unimaginably different from ours, and the way they were brought up and educated and their way of life created types of relationship and accompanying emotional tensions which we have to make an effort to understand. Though it is a wise warning that 'the historian who makes too big an imaginative leap into the mind of the past may end up as far from it as one who makes no leap at all',[7] we should still make the attempt. We have, and can reconstruct, some of their physical world, and imaginative literature provides a useful way into their

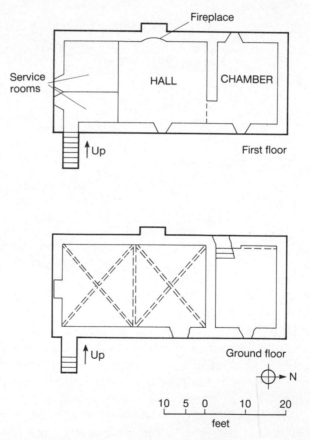

FIGURE 1.2 Boothby Pagnell manor house, c.1200: hall, chamber and service rooms
above a partly vaulted basement

[7] Reynolds, *Kingdoms and Communities*, 37.

PLATE 1 Boothby Pagnell manor house, *c.*1200; the square windows are later
(*reproduced by permission of RCHME Crown Copyright*)

thoughts and feelings. Two types of relationship mattered most: that of lord and man, and those which grew up in the family. The mechanics of domestic life played an important part in conditioning actions and attitudes, and it is with them that we shall begin.

The basic requirement in the medieval aristocratic house was for two rooms, hall and chamber, the latter smaller and less public than the former. There were two designs, one with hall and chamber laid end to end at ground level; the other, the 'first-floor hall' type, with the rooms raised over a vaulted basement which often duplicates the plan of the floor above (see figure 1.2 and plate 1).[8] These could be built on any scale, the same ideas applying to all buildings from the small manor house to the royal palace. The ground-floor hall could have aisles; the fireplace was often in the centre of the hall, with the smoke escaping, eventually, through a shuttered hole in the roof (see plate 2). This ancient arrangement, the only safe one in a wooden building, was used in stone halls too, down to the end

[8] P. A. Faulkner, 'Domestic planning from the twelfth to the fourteenth centuries', *Archaeological Journal* 222 (1965), 133–58, reprinted in M. J. Swanton, *Studies in Medieval Domestic Architecture*, London: Royal Archaeological Institute 1975, 84–117.

PLATE 2   Winchester castle: interior of the hall
*A large aisled stone hall built for Henry III, 1222–35. The circular object on the wall
is a fourteenth-century round table*
(courtesy of the Courtauld Institute of Art, Conway Library, London;
photography: Dr Lindy Grant)

of the middle ages and beyond. First-floor halls more commonly
had wall fireplaces. An arrangement found at Oakham castle in
the late twelfth century, and common later, was a two-storey
chamber block adjoining a ground-floor hall, with the most
luxurious room upstairs. Adjoining the chamber there was often
a separate small room housing a private lavatory. This room was

called by the French word *garderobe*, which gives the modern English 'wardrobe', implying an additional use as a storage area for personal belongings. One end of the hall would constitute the 'service' end, with two small rooms, the buttery and pantry, partitioned off by the entrance. The kitchen was a separate building, often reached by a passage between the buttery and pantry. The service rooms did not need to rise the full height of the hall, and sometimes the chamber was located above them leaving the other end of the hall free, as in the bishop's palace at Lincoln of *c.*1225. The two basic designs are still recognizable in the most impressive houses of the period, the great tower keeps of castles. At Castle Hedingham, Essex, the four rooms of the upper-floor hall plan are stacked one on top of the other, with the upper hall emphasized by a gallery with windows. At Middleham (Yorkshire) the hall and chamber are laid side by side, rather than end to end, and fortified with walls more than ten feet thick. The sophisticated plan of Orford castle, built in the 1160s, includes not only a hall and chamber, both with galleries, but no less than five private chambers, two with *en suite* gardrobes, a chapel, a kitchen, and what looks like a bathroom.[9]

This was the physical background common to the upper level of society, from the lord of a manor or two to the king, for the part of their lives lived indoors. The households of the aristocracy have many characteristics in common despite obvious variations of scale. Each compartment of the house had a responsible officer. The cook occurs quite commonly as a witness of baronial charters, and his status was apparently often high. The pantry, where the bread was kept, might be called the 'dispense' and its responsible officer the 'dispenser'. The butler, working from the buttery, was responsible for the provision of drink. The steward or seneschal (Latin *dapifer*) was responsible for the hall, and the chamberlain for the chamber. A household of any pretensions had a clerical staff, separate chapels being common in castles though less so in manor houses at this date, and they would also perform any writing duties. Great lords of the church had households of the same type as their brothers of the laity. A charter of archbishop Theobald dating from the early 1150s shows him accompanied by many clerics of his household, including Thomas Becket and John of Salisbury, Osbert his

[9] T. A. Heslop, 'Orford Castle, nostalgia and sophisticated living', *Architectural History* 34 (1991), 36–58.

cross-bearer, four of his nephews with their tutor, his chancellor and two monk-chaplains, and then the household officers:
butler, dispenser, chamberlain, seneschal, master cook, usher,
porter and marshal.[10]

The daily life of the aristocracy was not based on the family,
but on the wider group of the household, the *familia*. Households which ate together, whose knights might have to fight
together, and religious ones which prayed together, developed a
strong sense of corporate identity. The head of such an institution had to fulfil the expectations of his subordinates or face the
constant accusation, spoken or silent, of failure. It is easy to
underestimate the degree of influence exerted from below in a
hierarchical structure. The lord had to carry his followers with
him, especially if he was to undertake anything risky. A wise lord
took advice before acting. Hence the importance of counsel, and
councillors. Failure to seek advice might undermine the lord's
position and split him from his followers. As an exasperated
John of Salisbury said to archbishop Becket just before his
murder:

> 'You have always been like that. You always act and
> speak entirely on your own.'
> 'What would you have me do, Master John?' countered
> the archbishop.
> 'You should have summoned your council. You must
> realize that those knights simply want an excuse to kill
> you.'
> 'We must all die, Master John . . . I am ready to accept
> death for the sake of God and of justice and the church's
> freedom – far more ready to accept death than they are to
> kill me.'
> 'But the rest of us are sinners and not so ready for death,'
> answered John. 'I can see no one here who wants to die
> except yourself.'
> 'God's will be done,' said the archbishop.[11]

But the household might contain conflicting interest groups,
and wise counsel could mean telling the lord what he wanted to
hear. King William of Scotland assembled his council before
deciding on the invasion of England in 1173, and it is clear that

[10] *Stoke by Clare Cartulary*, ed. Christopher Harper-Bill and Richard Mortimer,
Suffolk Records Society 1982, i no. 136.
[11] From the life 'Anonymous I', Mats Becket i, 74.

this was a formal occasion with a great deal of reputation and 'face' at stake for those who dared speak. A split opened up between the household knights, who were eager for action, and those with lands, who had more to lose. The 'peace party' were braving the king's displeasure, and were compelled to say they would fight in order to avoid the charge of cowardice.[12]

Relations between masters and servants can be far from simple. Walter Map was speaking from experience, even if his tone was jocular, when he complained how difficult it could be to run even a small household. His servants cheated him and boasted of it among themselves, and loved spending his money. Servants were careful at first but spendthrift later. In bigger households, such as the king's, the supposed master could not even remember his servants' names, 'much less know their hearts, and no one can entirely control a household whose thought and speech – I mean the speech of their hearts – he knows not'.[13] Households could contain factions, individuals forming alliances to advance their mutual interests, as Becket himself seems to have done with some others when in archbishop Theobald's household.[14] On the other hand, a lord who knew how to gain and keep the loyalty of his household could create a formidable power-base for himself: 'they greatly increase in prowess and valour, those who have a good lord'.[15]

It is not easy to reconstruct how medieval houses were lived in. The public hall and the private chamber probably gives too simplified a view – the privacy of the chamber was only relative. In Béroul's Romance of Tristan, most people bed down in the hall, but the king and queen sleep in the chamber in the bed, while Tristan, a dwarf and at least one other person sleep on the floor of the chamber.[16] Archbishop Thomas Becket was wont to dine with his clerks, listening to a Latin reading while his household knights ate at a separate table. On the day of his murder the archbishop had dinner in the hall and then withdrew to the chamber. When his murderers arrived they found the servants having their own meal in the hall, having just served Thomas and his company. The steward greeted them, offered refreshments, and went to announce their arrival to the archbishop.[17]

[12] Jordan, ll. 378–406.
[13] Map, 21–5.
[14] William of Canterbury in Mats Becket i, 4.
[15] Marshal, ll. 11070–2.
[16] Béroul, 61–4.
[17] Barlow, Thomas Becket, 239–40 and refs.

Empty houses are dead places, and after a visit to a ruined castle it is easy to imagine medieval living conditions as devoid of what we regard as basic necessary comforts, even for the aristocracy. The vast rooms with tiny windows must have been dark, cold and draughty. But trying to imagine how a modern person would react to medieval life is pointless: for contemporaries there were plenty of opportunities for luxury and conspicuous expenditure, and an immense gulf between rich and poor. No doubt the rich felt comfortable enough if they compared their lives with those of the poor. At least baths were not as uncommon as is frequently supposed, though the Benedictine rule disapproved of them for the young and healthy and monastic culture was less enthusiastic than the laity. King John's bath tub and William, his attendant, travelled round with him: the king took at least eight baths over a period of four and a half months in 1210.[18] Some monasteries had elaborate water-supply systems, and the keep of Dover castle has water tanks and lead piping laid into the walls. King John's clothing, his furs and jewels comprised a large collection. His tableware was of gold, he slept in silk sheets, wore silks and rare furs, and even his horses had silk caparisons emblazoned with the heraldic lions of England in gold.

King John was indulging in conspicuous expenditure to underline his royal status, all the more necessary when his affairs were going badly. Other aspects of life reveal a more primitive world. Glass was rare in house windows, shutters fastened by wooden pins being the normal method of closing them. This means there was a choice between darkness, poor artificial light or completely open windows, so that the productive day was limited to the hours of daylight, and necessarily short in the English winter. 'I am afraid lest nightfall put a sudden end to our labours', as one conscientious teacher is supposed to have said.[19] Window seats are found from the later twelfth century. Tapestry wall hangings do not seem to have been normal in houses. Henry III chose schemes of painted decoration for his chamber at Westminster and elsewhere, and installed painted wooden wainscoting in a number of his houses. Rushes or straw were the normal floor-covering. In an agreement with Roger Follus, his otter-hunter in the 1170s, Henry II specified that the floor of his hospice at Aylesbury was to be covered with straw if he came in winter and

[18] Rot Mis, 115.
[19] Dialogue, 68.

with herbs in summer.[20] Rooms may have been swept out and re-strewn from time to time, but that did not prevent unpleasant substances from accumulating underneath in the meantime. This is mentioned as a particular feature of English life by Erasmus in the sixteenth century – he especially mentions bones, beer and the excrement of dogs and cats – and things are unlikely to have been better in the twelfth century.[21] When Eleanor of Castile was received in London in 1255 before her marriage to the young Edward, the walls of her room were hung with silk and tapestry 'like a temple', and even the floor was covered with them. Her Spanish attendants did this, and, wrote Matthew Paris, the English thought it highly ridiculous.[22]

With so few rooms there was nowhere in these households to be alone. The lack of privacy is striking, but in fact it was not regarded as desirable to be alone – the voluntary solitude of the hermit was a form of asceticism. It was unbecoming for a great lord or lady not to be attended by a crowd of followers of various kinds: even the Exchequer, that efficient centre of the royal bureaucracy, had extra staff in order to appear dignified, as the treasurer admitted.[23] The problem of finding somewhere private must have made plotting difficult, and also the expression of secret emotions: a story depicts the plight of a woman consumed by a secret love, but unable to weep even in the chamber because of the scandal it would cause.[24] Perhaps the emotionalism of medieval behaviour, on which historians often comment, was partly a result of having nowhere to let off steam in private.

A king especially would live his life in the centre of a crowd, which when swollen by litigants and people pressing for favours might become a heaving mob. Walter Map describes Henry II in the middle of a shouting, jostling crowd trying to get at him to transact their business; he is 'pulled hither and thither, pushed whither he would not', but shows no anger, listens patiently to everyone and simply 'retreats to some place of quiet . . . when he is hustled beyond bearing'.[25] The king at least would be able to enforce a relative privacy when there were confidential matters

[20] Acta, no. 119.
[21] Letter to Francis, quoted in N. Lloyd, A History of the English House, London 1931, 80.
[22] Chron Maj v, 513.
[23] Dialogue, 28.
[24] Map, 275.
[25] Map, 487.

to discuss: when trying a lawsuit in a monastic chapter house, Henry II ordered that no one be admitted unless summoned by name, and sat inside with a small group of men of his household.[26] When kings met to negotiate privately they often did so in the open air, away from their followers but still watched by them. But under ordinary circumstances for kings and lords to withdraw from the crowd and become less accessible was frowned on.

But houses were only part of the physical background lying behind aristocratic life and politics. Much of the time was spent travelling, and life on the road was an important part of the routine of both seigneurial estate management and of kingship. Clerical and baronial households travelled round their estates, and their journeys had to be arranged in advance. In 1215 the abbot of Westminster came to an agreement with Ivo of Deene, one of his Northamptonshire tenants, about the abbot's rights to hospitality at Deene. Ivo was to have a fortnight's written notice of the abbot's arrival and was to provide a day and a night's board and lodging at his own expense. If the abbot's household stayed longer, the cost was calculated and deducted from the rent Ivo paid for his holding. The abbot was to be preceded on the day of his arrival by his seneschal, chamberlain, pantler, butler, usher, cook and marshal, who would take over the house. They were to be 'honourably received' by Ivo, who would provide everything necessary for them, and give them 12 pence each.[27] Such men were very much working officers, and their everyday functions brought them into intimate contact with their lord. It is not surprising if the lord consulted them about his concerns, and came to rely on their advice.

Outdoor life must have been dominated by horses: *destriers* or war horses, palfreys for more normal riding, packhorses for transport, and those that pulled the carts. Feeding, stabling and looking after them was the job of the marshal. The king's marshal also cared for the arms and armour, organized household transport and was often responsible for escort duties. One of his functions was to arrange accommodation on the household's travels.[28] Another unmistakable presence must have been the huntsmen, and especially the hunting dogs and hawks. A great variety of dogs were bred for specific purposes, each kind with

[26] Battle Chronicle, 176–8
[27] Stenton, *First Century*, 70–1
[28] Jolliffe, *Angevin Kingship*, 202.

its own handlers, and the hawks required their own highly skilled trainers.

All the Angevin kings were regularly on the move; they might stay for a little while, perhaps a week or more, in some major centre or favourite hunting place, but eventually they would pack up and go. Quite apart from major expeditions of a more military nature than usual – to Toulouse in 1157, or Ireland in 1210, for example – travelling consumed almost the whole of their lives. The place-dates given at the end of Henry II's charters show that his journeys were concentrated on the old royal demesne lands in southern England and Normandy and in Anjou. Visits to northern England beyond Nottingham, the south-west beyond Dorset, and East Anglia were rare, while Brittany and the lands south of the Loire valley figure hardly at all. For the king to stay in his subjects' castles seems to have been very rare. Much of Richard's time was spent in warfare on the frontiers of his continental dominions. He paid only two brief visits to England, once for his coronation. For the first four years of his reign, John was preoccupied with the defence of his lands in France; when confined to England he prowled widely, regularly including the north for the first time. Henry III reversed the pattern, venturing less far into the Midlands, and staying in his palaces, especially Westminster, for longer periods than his predecessors. The Thames valley and the south-east now became what they remained until queen Victoria's reign, the central landscape of English royalty.

The road system of Angevin England was not much different from today, except for obvious later additions such as eighteenth-century turnpikes and modern motorways. The country had long been quite densely settled and was covered by a network of tracks which waxed and waned in importance as the settlement pattern altered. Roads were always liable to minor changes in the detail of their course, but the basic outline remained the same. Thus the road from Winchester to Oxford and Northampton and on to Stamford, one of the most important routes of medieval England, was more or less the modern A34 and A43.[29] The distinction between major through roads and minor local ones may not have been as great as it is now; sometimes there were several parallel tracks or alternative ways which would diverge and reunite. Medieval roads were not surfaced, except where something remained of Roman roads. Most roads must

---

[29] Christopher Taylor, *Roads and Tracks of Britain*, London 1979, 115–19.

have been rutted and holed and especially difficult in wet weather, though they may not have been as bad as in later centuries when traffic was heavier, carts more numerous and the roads still not surfaced.

It is not possible to tell exactly how much of his time the king spent in his castles and palaces, and how much on the road, but it is clear, if only from the distances covered, that travelling must have been one of the main occupations of everyone connected with the court. Perhaps we tend to think of kings as typically engaged in presiding over assemblies in castles and palaces, and to some extent this is justified; but always in the background lay the need to pack up both luxuries and necessities, load them into carts and on to horseback, and trundle off to the next stopping place. Packing was a developed art. King John's robe was put into a leather case, his fine cloth into sacks, and his crossbows into containers of felt and cowskin.[30] With the king went his stores of arms and armour, his hunting horn and his backgammon table. A certain amount of John's collection of plate and jewels, like his treasure in coins, was kept in regional centres and brought out on his arrival, but much was carried round with him, so much that it was itself a significant proportion of his wealth. And not only the king's personal luxuries were carted round, but also the equipment of each of the departments of the household – the kitchen, the chapel, the stables and so on, as well as the chamber. The chamber goods in John's reign went into a 'long cart', the largest available, which needed three smaller one-horse carts to replace it if it broke down. The kitchen needed one or two small carts, the butlery and associated offices one more, while the chapel, the forge and the armaments went on pack horses. Peter of Blois, for a while one of the members of this band of nomads, has left a famous description of the miseries of the travelling life, the unpredictability of the king on whom everyone depended, the uncertainty of finding any suitable accommodation, and the sheer chaos which might result.[31]

But each stage of royal travelling ended in some more convenient place, with a castle or large house to shelter the people and horses. The journeying was not random, and neither was it undertaken, at least in the king's case, out of a need to consume the produce of a scattered estate. The king's itinerary was planned six or more weeks in advance, his subjects informed and

---

[30] Jolliffe, *Angevin Kingship*, 264 n2.
[31] Peter of Blois i, 50–1.

provisions collected in readiness for the wagon train's arrival. For the Christmas feast to be held at Oxford in 1205, for example, Robert de Berners went down in early November to start the preparations; the kitchen and the king's lodging were put in order, the sheriff was told to deliver 250 cartloads of firewood and 20 of charcoal, and large quantities of cloths and furs were bought.[32] The royal feasts on major festivals were an immense undertaking, and certainly not devoid of luxuries. For John's Christmas feast at Winchester in 1206 he ordered 20 oxen, 100 pigs, 100 sheep, 1500 chickens and 5000 eggs.[33] Henry III spent Christmas 1236 at Marlborough, and the provisions included 40 pounds of dates, six 'frails' of figs, four boxes of pressed grapes and five or six packets of good ginger.[34] Wine, mostly from western France, was consumed in vast quantities, and required an entire administration to supply it. A typical order, from 1233, called for 15 tuns (barrels) of Gascony wine and five of Anjou to be taken to Woodstock, five of Gascony and three of Anjou to Oxford, and three of Gascony and two of Anjou to Reading.[35] There was nothing mean or small-scale about the king's constantly moving court. An itinerant life was quite consistent with royal dignity and at least intermittent display.

The aristocratic diet need not have been monotonous. Everything suggests that it was strongly carnivorous throughout the middle ages and beyond. A great variety of fresh meat was available round the year, venison from parks – enormous quantities of deer bones have been found at Okehampton and Barnard castles – doves from dovecots, rabbits from the artificially created and managed warrens which were becoming common in the twelfth century, and fish from fishponds. Wild birds were an important component of the diet; the number of species and quantity of bones found archaeologically in medieval contexts is 'considerably greater than in any earlier period since the advent of farming'.[36] Species excavated or known to have been sold include swans, cranes, rooks, pipits, larks, crows, jackdaws and plovers, as well as wild ducks and, of course, quantities of blackbirds which were presumably baked in a pie.

[32] Jolliffe, *Angevin Kingship*, 222; Rot Litt Claus i, 56–60.
[33] Rot Litt Claus i, 75.
[34] Cal Lib Rolls 1226–40, 247.
[35] Ibid., 214.
[36] Annie Grant, 'Animal Resources' in Astill and Grant, *The Countryside of Medieval England*, 170.

MAP 1.2 King John's journey, February–March 1205

The work, trouble and expense involved in royal journey-ing must have been compensated by real advantages. It was one way of reconciling an extremely personal government with a number of static communities. The constant journeying enabled the king to keep in contact with his various provinces; it also helped to accustom them to his rule. As the king and his household rode and lumbered from region to region, the local notables and royal officials would come to meet him and trans-act their business. They can be seen coming and going in the charter witness lists, and the effects traced in the administrative documents. In February and March 1205, for instance, John did a circuit round most of England while waiting for a fleet to be assembled for his intended crossing to Normandy (see map 1.2).[37] Beginning at Woodstock, the king moved north by stages through Northampton to Nottingham, where he met the earl of Chester, William de Ferrers and other Midland lords. Moving north, he was met at Tadcaster by the sheriff of Northumberland, and at York, where he stayed for three days, by the bishop of Durham and most of the major northern barons. The business dealt with at York concerned, among other things, archbishop Geoffrey's quarrels with his suffragans and cathedral chapter, and the grant of the honour of Richmond to the earl of Chester. For these important matters the king had the opportunity to consult the local interests most affected by them. The court then turned south, back to Nottingham and then Kenilworth, shedding its northern attenders on the way. The westernmost point reached was Worcester, where the king stayed for three days in the company of the earl of Hereford and other Marcher lords, concerned with Welsh and border affairs. Within a few weeks the king had met many of the most important people in the country and dealt with a great variety of business of lesser and greater significance. Whether the king listened to them or not, some at least of the local notables had been present when decisions were made and had got to know something of the man who made them. This is part of the practical background of politics in the Angevin period: frequent changes of scene, people coming and going, constant variation in matters arising and people discussing them.

The king's moving household, with the people it met in the places it travelled through, constituted the royal court. It may seem difficult to reconcile the centre of literary and intellectual patronage of some historians with the dry administrative machine of others, and to fit them both into this unfamiliar world of packhorses and muddy roads. The multiplicity of the court struck contemporaries too. Walter Map wrote from personal experience, 'In the court I exist and of the court I speak, and what the court is, God knows, I know not . . . When I leave it, I know it perfectly; when I come back to it I find nothing or but little of what I left there . . . The court is the same, but its members are changed.'[38]

The formal tie which bound man and lord together was homage and fealty. 'For mere lordship no homage is done except to the king': the lord must grant some sort of property. The homager

---

[37] Jolliffe, *Angevin Kingship*, 155–60; Rot Litt Claus i, 19–23, Rot Litt Pat, 50–1, Rot Chart, 141–5.
[38] Map, 3.

swears to 'bear faith to the lord' in respect of the gift, to preserve his earthly honour in all things saving the faith due to the king and his heirs.[39] Fealty, on the other hand, created a subordinate relationship without apparently necessitating a grant. This was a society of lords and men based on personal dependence, knights on lords, greater barons on the king, but subordination did not imply powerlessness in theory any more than in reality. 'The bond arising from lordship and homage should be mutual.'[40] In cases where homage had been done to several lords, there had to be a chief or 'liege' lord, of whom the main estate was held.

The original and basic duty of the followers was to fight if required, and the aristocracy long cherished the comradely sentiments of the war-band. Its style was military: contemporary lords are depicted as knights on their seals and their tombs. Jordan Fantosme's heroic poem of the war of 1173–4 presents a world of knights and lords, vassals and fighting: 'at the end of the battle he will be praised who smites best with the sword and does the most fighting'.[41] Though reality was more complicated, the aristocracy liked to see itself as a society of heroic soldiers.

Angevin England, in fact medieval England generally, was a violent society. Men were expected to have weapons and to know how to use them. Physical punishment was normal – husbands beat wives, parents beat children, confessors beat penitents, monks beat each other for their spiritual good, courts ordered floggings and mutilations as well as executions. It is not therefore surprising that violence was learned young and readily adopted in conflicts of all kinds, and murder and violent crime were rife. When the itinerant justices visited Lincolnshire in 1202 they tried crimes which in all probability had been committed since previous visits in 1201 and 1200. These included some 114 homicides, 89 robberies, generally with violence, 65 woundings and 49 rapes.[42] In the 20 years from 1241 to 1261 there were at least 58 cases of homicide in Oxford, a town with an estimated population of 8000: Robert Grosseteste's and Roger Bacon's Oxford had a murder rate far higher than twentieth-century American cities.[43] Much of the mayhem was the result of

[39] Glanvill, 104.
[40] Ibid., 107.
[41] Jordan, ll. 1866–7.
[42] Poole, *Obligations*, 82–3; Doris M. Stenton, *The Earliest Lincolnshire Assize Rolls*, Lincoln Record Society 22, 1926.
[43] Given, *Society and Homicide*, 38–9, 85–7.

brawls involving gangs of men, often relatives or members of a household. There are instances of highway banditry by such gangs – the forested stretch of the road from London to Winchester round Alton was haunted by a band over 50-strong in 1249.[44] The Robin Hood of later legend was not a historical figure, but there were plenty of robbers and outlaws who were genuine enough.

A sample from thirteenth-century eyre rolls shows that nearly 20 per cent of murder victims and only 8.6 per cent of the accused were women.[45] Women sometimes ended as more or less accidental victims while trying to calm arguments. Men and women accused of homicide stood a roughly equal chance of acquittal, but if convicted, women were twice as likely to be executed. Those accused of murdering women were noticeably less likely to be acquitted than those accused of killing men – there seems to have been strong disapproval of violence by and against women, while that among men was normal.

Wars in the Angevin period were generally indecisive, though not for lack of effort. The view that medieval warfare was devoid of strategy and even tactics, without thought or skilled generalship, has long since been abandoned, at least by medieval historians [46] Warfare was conducted by professionals. It was among the main occupations of a large section of the ruling class, and its methods were the outcome of much practical experience. Some theoretical work was available; the late Roman treatise of Vegetius on warfare was quite well known, but it was not necessary – contemporaries were perfectly capable of intelligent observation and advice. Gerald of Wales noted the military methods of the Welsh, and wrote chapters on both how they could be conquered and how they could best resist. Most discussion of military matters must have taken place among the aristocracy and gone unrecorded, though echoes of it are sometimes to be found in vernacular literature.

War was only one of several ways of conducting a conflict, and it was commonly combined with the others. It began and ended in politics. It was part of a process made up of negotiation and truce, threats, cajolery and jockeying for position. It was seldom continuous. Most of the fighting in which the Angevin kings were involved was border warfare with the Capetian kings of France. There were only two major outbreaks of fighting in

<hr>

[44] Ibid., 113.
[45] Ibid., 48.
[46] Verbruggen, *Art of Warfare*, 185–300; Smail, *Crusading Warfare*, 123–30.

England, in 1173–4 and 1214–17, and although these were civil wars, the techniques involved were largely the same as those used against the French. The wars against the Celtic peoples presented rather different problems.

Henry II ruled the second largest state in western Christendom for 35 years without fighting a single major battle; Philip II conquered vast areas of France but fought only one major battle. There is no doubt that battles were deliberately avoided, and were allowed to happen only under special circumstances. The main factor in a battle was the massed charge of heavily armoured knights, but using this weapon presented a commander with a risky decision, as the charge had to be carefully timed and directed and, once launched, could easily slip out of control.[47] Though a battle might be decisive, its outcome was unpredictable, and effective victory could be won with less risk in other ways.

The underlying situation was the superiority of defence over attack. Despite the increasing sophistication of siege techniques in the twelfth century, a well-supplied and defended castle could hold out for years, even against determined assailants. This superiority nevertheless had limits. Castles and fortified towns occupying the nodal points of the road network may appear to have commanded space and dominated the strategic situation, but this was much more true in peacetime than in war and fluctuated according to circumstances. The castle itself could not block the path of an army or prevent invasion. Part of the castle's role was to act as a secure base for raiding and the enforcement of obedience. The area controlled by the garrison might shrink to the perimeter walls of the castle when under attack, but as long as the castle remained untaken the garrison's control could be re-established over a wide area when the enemy withdrew. Castles functioned as 'repositories of lordship';[48] to retain them and compel the invader to withdraw was to emerge with effective victory, while the only way to capture territory was to capture castles and towns. It was rare for a siege to be pushed to the bitter end: much commoner was a period of truce to be followed by surrender if the castle was not relieved.

A medieval army lived mostly off the land and supplied itself by ravaging.[49] The plunder of the invaded area provided rewards

---

[47] Smail, *Crusading Warfare*, 114, 137.
[48] Ibid., 214.
[49] J. Gillingham, 'Richard I and the science of war in the middle ages', in Gillingham and Holt, *War and Government*, 78–91.

for the soldiers – plunder being the main incentive to join an army, especially for the infantry. Ravaging might also deprive the defenders of supplies, and by dislocating agriculture in the neighbourhood would reduce the value of the lordship. 'Destroy your enemies and lay waste their land: let it all be consumed in fire and flames! Do not leave them anything for breakfast outside their castles! Then assemble your men and lay siege to their castles! This is the way to begin to fight, in my opinion: first lay waste the land, then destroy your enemies!'[50] Pity for the effect on the local peasantry was not a deterrent to warfare. The defenders' aim was to threaten the ravagers, forcing them to stay together and thus reducing their effectiveness. Though supply was often a major problem, particularly during sieges, an army operating in enemy territory did not generally require supply lines. The net result of these factors was that campaigns consisted of raids, skirmishes, sieges and attempted surprises, a confused pattern which looks aimless but was not so in reality, which is bewildering to follow and usually tedious to narrate.

If the massed charge of mailed knights was an unusual event, in what did their superiority consist? It is possible that the charge of smaller numbers of knights was still crucial, but it was never possible to take a castle with a cavalry charge and even in pitched battles knights occasionally fought dismounted. The superiority of the knight was in his equipment and training, his greater likelihood of survival because of his armour, and his self-confidence. In the end it was social and political as much as military.

Walter Map tells a story from the Welsh Marches which illustrates this. While some Welsh raiders were watching a house, intending to attack it, they saw a travelling knight received there as a guest. They hesitated, but decided to attack in the night. The guard dogs came at them but, seeing their numbers, left the yard and barked outside. The knight, who was sleeping in the hall under the big windows, guessed from the barking that an attacking band had come, 'and in haste and silence he threw on his coat of mail, and spear in hand took his stand in the middle of the floor opposite the windows, listening, and was aware of their numbers though they kept as quiet as they could'. The first man through the window received a spear in the heart and was thrown out backwards. The next, his brother, swore, pushed him aside, and was thrown back with the same wound. The Welsh then took up their dead and fled.[51]

[50] Jordan, ll. 443–50.
[51] Map, 197–9.

Knighthood was an honourable status: the young Henry II was knighted by his relative, king David I of Scots, and the knighting of his sons were significant moments in their careers. Lords were entitled to take a levy from their tenants to defray the costs of knighting their eldest sons.[52] The symbol of knighthood was the belt: the young king Henry asked William the Marshal to knight him, which he did by buckling a belt on him and kissing him.[53] The verse biography of William the Marshal presents him as the ideal young knight, brave, generous, the best fighter and the most honourable of men. It was felt that knights should not demean themselves by engaging in trade.[54] The honourable status of knighthood, or rather the adoption of knighthood as an honorific title by the wealthy, gathered pace during the twelfth century, until in the thirteenth the witnesses of charters who wished to underline their status called themselves *miles*, knight. Not that these people necessarily engaged in the sordid business of actually fighting: for one thing, age might have blunted both fervour and capacity; for another, there may have been long periods when no fighting was required. Calling up the knights of the countryside was not the best way to raise an army. And after all, some may have preferred not to fight. However military their image of themselves, many knights were not fighters. When a knight's creditors foreclosed on him and his belongings were sold, he was to be left a horse – unless he was a fighting knight, who 'ought to be counted among the active ones' (*strenui*) in which case he was to be left his armour and several horses.[55] While this was increasingly true at the lower levels, the magnates and their households might well be called upon to fight in person.

The flower of virtues for a knight, strenuous or otherwise, was loyalty. Written all over the vernacular literature is the knight's supreme duty, to his lord. It was Henry II's trusty *barnage*, his 'barons', who won the war of 1173–4 for him, as described by Jordan Fantosme. Jordan's poem rings with challenges and boasts of loyalty. If anyone counsels you against war, count Theobald is supposed to have said to king Louis, 'you see me here in your court, ready to pledge my gage that he is false to you and seeks your shame!'[56] The lord's household appears as a

[52] Glanvill, 122.
[53] Marshal, ll. 2071–96.
[54] Dialogue, 109.
[55] Ibid.
[56] Jordan, ll. 457–8.

world of honour, shame and *macho* posturing. Great oaths were sworn – it seems individuals had their own favourite oaths: Philip of Flanders by the Precious Wound of Christ, Walter fitz Robert by the Holy Lance.[57] In such a world it would be easy to get into situations from which it was impossible to back down.

Treachery, the opposite of loyalty, was therefore a serious and wounding charge which was likely to be remembered. Henry III in a temper used it too readily. Roger Bigod, earl of Norfolk, once tried to intercede for a relative of his wife's, who was out of favour. Henry flew into a rage and called the earl a traitor.

> 'You lie,' said the earl, 'I have never been a traitor nor shall I ever be! If you are just, how can you harm me?'
> 'I can seize your corn and thresh it and sell it,' retorted the king, 'and thus tamed, you will be humbled.'
> 'Do so,' answered the earl, 'and I will send back your threshers with their heads cut off!'[58]

Alongside personal honour and loyalty went display. Rank was expressed in simple, visible terms. The greater a lord, the more he spent. This was a 'culture of ostentation'[59] in which a king had to impress his subjects and a lord his tenants and equals, and even the members of his household, by obvious symbols of wealth and importance – the splendour of rich fabrics, costly jewels and plate, grand settings in fashionable buildings, and above all a retinue clothed, armed and horsed in appropriate style. Loyalty was procured by open-handed generosity – it was not expected to well up unencouraged, and would not last indefinitely if it went unrewarded. William the Marshal, good lord that he was, was due to distribute robes of scarlet and vair to his knights at Whitsun, and on his deathbed roundly cursed the priest who suggested he should sell the robes and spend the money for the salvation of his soul.[60] The fine sentiments of loyalty were what the aristocracy liked to hear about and be told they possessed, but in practice loyalty could be combined with wiliness, ruses and a fairly single-minded pursuit of self-interest. In Jordan Fantosme's poem Roger de Stuteville goes to ask the king of Scots for a truce when besieged in Wark castle rather than continue to defend it, but he sheds bitter tears

---

[57] Ibid., ll. 97, 1044.
[58] Chron Maj v, 530.
[59] Duby, *William Marshal*, 19.
[60] Marshal, ll. 18685–18706.

to think how his lord, Henry II, is not able to help his loyal
vassal. He begs the Scottish king not to dishonour him by taking
the castle: 'I greatly love your advancement, as long as it doesn't
impede mine.'[61]

A good deal of class feeling accompanied these attitudes. 'My
soul naturally loathes slaves', wrote Walter Map.[62] Rustics were
held to be incapable of finer feelings: 'goodness is the daughter
of nobility'.[63] William of Canterbury, the monk responsible for
recording the miracles at Becket's shrine, assumed all beggars
were liars, while the nobility told the truth.[64] If these feelings
were reciprocated by the lower orders, they have not found their
way into writing.

As well as the vertical ties of lordship, the horizontal bonds of
family relationship tied men and women together. The broader
kin of cousins, second cousins and in-laws often functioned as a
mutual benefit society, particularly visible among those rising in
the royal service, who employed each other, did each other's
dirty work and defended each other's cause as occasion arose.
They constituted an insurance against disaster, providing several
simultaneous careers, so that if one member fell another could
still be useful; but they might all fall together too.[65] A distant
relative might step in to acquire the wardship of a minor or the
marriage of an orphaned daughter, forestalling a more predatory
stranger. The kin group has often been invoked to explain political groupings, for example the concentration of relatives of the
house of Clare among the 25 barons of Magna Carta.[66] Yet it
was not so much the fact of descent, sometimes remote, from a
common ancestor which bound them together as more recent
ties largely created through marriage. The marriage of a baron's
parents, his own, and those he arranged for his children provided
three generations of connections which could be turned to account. Marriages were arranged for dynastic purposes, with an
eye to lands and alliances. A lord, including the king, would
expect to agree to, if not arrange himself, the marriages of his
tenants; those of heiresses and the remarriage of widows espe-

[61] Jordan, ll. 477–519.
[62] Map, 423.
[63] Ibid., 417.
[64] Mats Becket i, 524.
[65] R. Mortimer, 'The family of Rannulf de Glanville', *Bulletin of the Institute of Historical Research* 54 (1981), 1–16.
[66] Painter, *Reign of King John*, 290–2; cf. Holt, 'Feudal Society and the Family' iii, 2–3.

cially would be overseen by their lords. The lord's control of marriage was a crucial factor in his control of his fee: by it he could exert patronage, reward his followers and influence the personnel of his honour. But it was in the twelfth century that the church began to insist that the consent of man and woman was sufficient for a valid marriage – consent of family and lord, and a public ceremony, were unnecessary. At the same time, divorce was becoming harder to obtain. Love, like hatred, existed both inside and outside marriage; at least a minimum of sexual co-operation was necessary to produce children. Emotional matters thus could, and did, complicate the calculations of arranged marriages.[67]

Marriage gave women great importance, but it was as the potential bearers of children, the source of future heirs, not in their own right. The position of women was undoubtedly very restricted. Perhaps individual strong characters could break through the barriers, such as the countess of Leicester who appears, at least in heroic poetry, as her husband's chief councillor; but legally 'a woman is completely in the power of her husband'.[68] On marriage a woman received a dower from her husband and a marriage portion from her father. Dower could be specified lands or, if unspecified, it was taken to be one-third of the husband's estate. She could not give it away or sell it in her husband's lifetime. If the couple had a child and the wife died first, the husband kept the marriage portion for his life; but if there was no child it would return to the wife's family on her death. On marriage the wife's moveable property became her husband's, and she could not make a will without his consent. The husband should only alienate his wife's land with her consent, but if he did so without it she could recover it if she was widowed.[69] Widowhood was the life most favourable to the rights of aristocratic women. As long as they escaped remarriage they could administer their own dower as they wished, and wealthy widows are found paying the king not to be remarried. At lower social levels economic necessity may sometimes have given women a larger role. Villein widows are sometimes found in possession of their late husbands' holdings, presumably having been left with young children. In town women are found running businesses, appearing as potters, tilers, even blacksmiths, though

[67] John Gillingham, 'Love, marriage and politics in the twelfth century', *Forum for Modern Language Studies* 25 (1989), 292–303.
[68] Jordan, ll. 974–90; Glanvill, 60.
[69] Pollock and Maitland, *History of English Law* ii, 399–436.

they were especially prominent in the textile industries.[70] Upper-class ladies too were encouraged to take an interest in textile crafts. The distaff, a symbol of womanhood, was an implement used in spinning before spinning wheels became normal.

Small children might travel with the household, or be left in a monastery or at an estate. Young royal children had their own households, with other young noble companions. Lower down in society, parents with fewer estates would travel less and so be closer to their children, but the general practice at the upper social levels was for children to be sent away to another household where they were educated in the ways of the world. The young William the Marshal, a younger son of a baron, was sent to a Norman relative, the chamberlain of Tancarville, in whose household he was an *eskuiers* for eight years; the chamberlain knighted him when he was ready for it, made use of his services in war, and turned him out when the war ended.[71] The households of bishops and leading churchmen, such as Robert Grosseteste, bishop of Lincoln, were often favoured as houses of virtue and learning. The court, the royal and, by extension, other noble households, became models for behaviour, and the equivalents of the words 'courtly' and 'courteous' occur from the later twelfth century.

When it came to questions of property the significant unit was the 'nuclear' family of husband, wife and children. Primogeniture, the succession of the eldest son to the whole patrimony, was normal by the middle of the twelfth century, and though occasionally the king could arrange matters differently, the theory was that 'only God, not man, can make an heir'.[72] The father was not able to give any of the patrimony or the wife's inheritance to a younger son without the heir's consent; but consent must have been forthcoming, or dispensed with, as numbers of younger sons are found holding land of their brother. With land the father himself acquired, much but not all could be used to endow younger sons and daughters. Alan de Audri, a small tenant of the earl of Huntingdon, settled seven virgates on his younger brother David, but David preferred to go to Scotland with the earl who gave him a knight's fee in his lordship of Garioch.[73] It was not so much that younger brothers were routinely turned out of the family home to seek their fortune, as that

[70] Blair and Ramsay, *Medieval Industries*, 186–8, 193, 204, 316.
[71] Marshal, ll. 745–9, 772.
[72] Glanvill, 71.
[73] Stringer, *David of Huntingdon*, 83–4.

staying might involve poverty and ultimately loss of status. As for the father's moveable property, the widow and the heir should have one-third each, and the remainder could be left as the dying man wished, with a presumption that it would be used in charitable works for the benefit of his soul. If the defunct had no sons but more than one daughter, the estates were customarily divided equally between them. But a daughter could not succeed to estates and run them herself: the family or the lord would see to it that she was married, and the lands passed to her husband and her son.

Not that the transfer of property between generations therefore moved smoothly: arguments occurred about marriage portions, about divisions among co-heiresses, and between uncles and nephews and collateral branches.[74] Though it was clear that the paternal inheritance should descend to the eldest son, brothers might still fall out about the father's acquisitions, in which younger sons could expect a share. Quarrels between paternal uncles and nephews were particularly fraught in this period, the Percy, Quency and Braose families being affected as well as the clamorous Mandeville case. John's accession to the throne over the claims of his nephew Arthur created a temporary preference for the claims of uncles, which was reversed later in the thirteenth century. In all cases of inheritance acts of power by the king could overturn expected practice, but could well leave a residue of resentment and long-remembered claims. The medieval aristocracy had very long dynastic memories, and distant claims resurface after generations. Family conflict, largely about property, is an important source of friction giving rise to political action. One relationship which caused relatively little trouble was that between father and heir. To this the greatest exception was the royal family.

Henry II's struggles with his sons are a famous and dramatic example of family conflict and have attracted much literary and historical attention. Yet Henry's wishes for his sons were clear as early as 1169, and fitted into the pattern of arrangements normal in the aristocracy at the period (see figure 1.1). The eldest son, Henry, was to take the patrimony – England, Normandy and Anjou, the lands Henry had inherited from his parents. The younger brothers were to have lands acquired by other means. Richard, the second son, would have Eleanor's Aquitaine, and Geoffrey, the third son, would take Brittany – he was already

[74] Holt, 'Feudal Society and the Family' iii, 18–20.

betrothed to duke Conan's daughter and heiress, Constance. The youngest son, John, then aged two, was not yet provided for. Henry II fell seriously ill in August 1170 and made a will repeating these provisions.[75] By this time Geoffrey had received the homage of the barons of Brittany, and Richard had been recognized as the future lord of Aquitaine at meetings in the duchy. This is part of the context of the coronation of the young Henry as king of England by the archbishop of York at Westminster abbey on 24 May 1170: often seen as a provocation of archbishop Thomas Becket, which it was, it was also the centrepiece in Henry's arrangements for the future of his lands. He was taking a leaf out of the Capetians' book in associating his heir with himself in his lifetime, as indeed Henry's own father Geoffrey had done with Henry himself.[76]

But the ruler's intentions were only part of the story. The complicating factors were the attitude of the overlord, the king of France, who took every opportunity to undermine Henry, the impatience of the sons to exercise real power once their portion was known, the unwillingness of the father to allow the creation of a rival centre of power, and the absence of a proper endowment for the youngest son. The position was eventually simplified by the early deaths of two of the sons.

Trouble came in February 1173 when a marriage was arranged between the five-year-old John and the daughter of count Humbert of Maurienne. Henry had to endow John with an estate. He proposed the three castles in Anjou which his own brother had once held: Chinon, Loudun and Mirebeau. But Anjou was part of young Henry's future lands, and he angrily refused to consent. His indignation was fuelled by resentment at his lack of real power: though a crowned king, aged 18, he had no lands of his own and did not even control his own household. He demanded England, Normandy or Anjou, a claim which one chronicler believed Louis of France had encouraged him to make.[77] The young king slipped away and fled to Paris; the 15-year-old Richard and the 14-year-old Geoffrey soon followed, but queen Eleanor, who quite likely played a part in encouraging the younger brothers to join the rebellion, was arrested before she was able to escape. All Henry's closest family of an age to rebel had abandoned him. Only his illegitimate son Geoffrey, then bishop-elect of Lincoln, supported him. What now followed was

[75] Gesta i, 6–7.
[76] Le Patourel, *Feudal Empires* VIII, 'The Plantagenet dominions', 297.
[77] Gesta i, 34.

the first of several armed conflicts with his sons, with the king of France consistently on the sons' side, which eventually brought Henry to defeat just before his death. But the rebellion of 1173 was the most threatening of all because, as well as his sons and king Louis, it involved the most serious baronial uprising in England and Normandy between 1154 and 1215, other risings in Brittany, Maine and Aquitaine, and a war with the king of Scots and the count of Flanders. The fighting was general in Henry's dominions, but the scattered and unco-ordinated rebels were no match for Henry's efficient military machine. Henry repelled the French and suppressed the continental rebels while his lieutenants in England defeated an invasion by the earl of Leicester and captured the king of Scots.[78]

The peace settlement was largely free of vindictiveness. The rebel brothers were assigned revenues, and the young Henry had to agree to John being provided with land. Queen Eleanor, who was not mentioned in the peace, remained in custody for as long as Henry lived. The elder king's overwhelming victory in the war led only to his attempting to put the pre-rebellion status quo on to a more sustainable basis by conceding some of his sons' demands. Perhaps the father saw no realistic alternative to forgiveness, unless he was to imprison his three eldest sons for the rest of his life. Richard was sent to Aquitaine to put down his former supporters. This he did with speed and efficiency, acquiring a formidable military reputation: Richard had a job to do which fully absorbed him. The young Henry, however, had no occupation but the fashionable distraction of the tournament. In 1181 Geoffrey was married to Constance and immediately began to take effective control of Brittany. Perhaps it was the sight of yet another brother ruling a lordship which drove young Henry to his final acts of desperation, fleeing to the French king's court, and allying with rebels in Aquitaine whom he soon abandoned. As part of the father's plans to patch up a peace he required Richard and Geoffrey to do homage to the young Henry. Richard refused. In the war that followed the young Henry was left with nothing to pay his men, and he plundered and stripped churches and shrines. Accordingly it seemed like a judgement when he was struck down by a sudden sickness and died in June 1183.

It has often been pointed out that while the facts of the younger Henry's life contain nothing but 'deeds of the meanest

[78] See below, pp. 86–90.

ingratitude, selfishness, cowardliness and treachery',[79] he was the only member of his family who was widely loved and admired in his lifetime: 'of all Christians he was the beauty and the flower, the valour, the fountain of generosity'.[80] The apparent paradox of the young king's popularity is a warning that deducing character traits from the recorded actions of individuals risks being seriously misleading, and is certainly a poor basis for moral judgements. His death left the kingship open for Richard, and that of Geoffrey in 1186 cleared the way for the eventual succession of John.

Kingship was the ultimate form of lordship. Its sacramental aspects were now discouraged by the church, but it retained its power as a focus of secular loyalty. As the supreme lord of the kingdom the king received the fealty and homage of all the important landholders, but in return, as was the way with lordship, he had duties towards his men. Henry II and Richard do not appear to have attempted to dramatize their own royalty, though they indulged in the conspicuous expenditure that was an attribute of power. It was Henry III who went furthest in fostering the image and ideology of monarchy, particularly as his troubles increased – there is a fairly neat inverse relationship between the reality of declining power and the growth of Henry III's pretensions. He had the *Laudes regiae* sung before him, touched for the 'King's evil' like Louis IX, spent a fortune developing Westminster abbey as the shrine of Edward the Confessor and the coronation church, and indulged in ritualized works of charity such as feeding large numbers of paupers. After 1240 he provided on average 180,000 meals a year for the poor, but in 1244, when he returned defeated from France, he compensated by providing nearly 260,000.[81] It is easier to chart the form taken by Henry III's increasing personal grandeur than it is to say how many people, and who, were impressed by it.

This was very much a world of personal lordship. The personality of the king had a considerable impact on day-to-day events. The quarrels between Henry II and archbishop Thomas Becket, and between John and many of his barons, were deeply affected by the personalities of the participants. Nor is the history of political events without long-term consequences in other areas. Richard I's capture and ransom had important effects on the history of taxation; John's failure to take control in Ireland in

---

[79] Kate Norgate, *England under the Angevin Kings*, 2 vols, London 1887, ii, 221.
[80] Marshal, ll. 5602–5.
[81] Stacey, *Politics, Policy and Finance*, 240.

1183 closed off one possible avenue of development in the complex affairs of that island. Royal personalities therefore have consequences that work their way through many historical processes. What those personalities were like, though, is notoriously hard to fathom. The flattery and political bias, not to mention mutual contradictions, of contemporary descriptions help Henry II to remain enigmatic despite acres of modern commentary and the best efforts of dramatists and scriptwriters. The long and remarkable career of Eleanor of Aquitaine as a central character in the dramas of the age has attracted much attention; a wide-ranging cultural influence has often been attributed to her. Assessments of her role and personality are seriously hampered by many of the chroniclers' attitudes to women especially when they exercise power, the variety of evidence which bears on her life, not all of it systematically collected, and a tendency among modern writers to romanticize her.[82] Contemporaries were less forthcoming about Richard; for many modern historians he is sufficiently described as a soldier, which he was, but he must have had other areas of competence, too, in administration and diplomacy.[83]

With John there is more to work on. We can see his liking for domestic luxury, his interest in the details of administration and lawsuits, his tortuous deviousness. He was 'mercurial, inventive, cunning and unreliable'.[84] He would occasionally get lost in his own intrigues. He ordered Hubert de Burgh, the jailer of the important political prisoner Guy de Lusignan, to allow no one to speak to Guy unless accompanied by one of three members of John's household; but unfortunately John forgot who the three were, and had to order Hubert to admit the man he was sending anyway.[85] We can also see his crippling tendency to lose his nerve, perhaps panic, at crucial moments. Worst of all for a medieval king, 'he was unable to command respect'.[86] When he succeeded to the throne Richard's French allies gave up the fight against the king of France and went on crusade, 'seeing they were destitute of aid and counsel by the death of King Richard'.[87]

[82] See Jane Martindale, 'Eleanor of Aquitaine', in Janet L. Nelson, ed., *Richard Coeur de Lion in History and Myth*, Kings College London Medieval Studies viii, London 1992, 17–50.
[83] J. Gillingham, 'The unromantic death of Richard I', *Speculum* 54, (1979), 18–41.
[84] Holt, *Northerners*, 175.
[85] Rot Litt Pat, 17.
[86] Powicke, *Loss of Normandy*, 190.
[87] *Oeuvres de Rigord et de Guillaume le Breton*, ed. H. F. Delaborde, 2 vols, Société de l'Histoire de France, Paris 1882–5, i, 24.

Henry III is also comparatively visible to us, thanks to the voluminous administrative records of his reign and some contemporary descriptions. He has been characterized by many modern historians, who see him as impulsive, prone to enthusiasms, lacking any steady purpose or even a sense of political reality.[88]

[88] E.g. Powicke, *Henry III and the Lord Edward*, 156; Stacey, *Politics, Policy and Finance*, 35; Prestwich, *English Politics*, 11; Carpenter, *Minority*, 390.

2

The King's Government

Government is about controlling people – settling disputes
between them in a way that preserves the structure of society, and extracting revenue from them to support the perceived
needs of those at the top. England in the Angevin period witnessed
a huge increase in the tools available for government, and an even
more dramatic explosion in the quantity of records created, and
surviving, which can be used to shed light on it. It was a very
creative age in methods of government. What were the implications
of this creativity for the distribution of power? New forms of
taxation were invented, new administrative methods developed,
a whole legal system with its own intellectual culture grew up.
Who were the beneficiaries? Were they also the architects?

Much of government is local government. The forms government took were frequently expressions of local communities –
the shires and their subdivisions the hundreds, the towns, the
individual manors, and the honours, the great baronial estates
and their tenants. Each of these combined a segment of the
population defined by a certain status. Each involved people
with common interests and a common sense of solidarity. They
had grown up over a long period: most shires and hundreds had
two centuries behind them when Henry II came to the throne,
and even if they had started as creations of tenth-century royal
power they had developed a momentum of their own. Manors
were old and deep-rooted enough to have acquired customs
that were the only check on the power of their lords. Honours were
more recent, post-Conquest institutions, but they were backed
by the formidable power of their owners, the military aristocracy. Each of these units was centred on its court, which was
both the government and meeting place of its community.

The king's court was partly an honorial court assembling his
tenants, the baronage and greater churchmen of England; but the

feelers of royal power reached down to lower levels too – the king's peace covered everyone and everywhere in the kingdom, at least potentially. Serious crimes were committed not only against the victim but also against the king and his peace. This gave the king an interest in small-scale local affairs. His capacity for intervention grew significantly in this period. The development of government, especially royal government, can be seen as part of a dialogue between royal and communal institutions, between political centre and periphery, which outlasted the middle ages. But protecting his peace, providing for disputes to be settled without upsetting the stability of the structure which held him up, was only one of his interests: he also needed resources, essentially money and soldiers. Here he was responding to pressures being exerted on him, both political and economic.

The king had large expenses to meet. Henry II personally was not given to pomp and show, but that did not mean that his household was cheap to maintain; and of his successors John and Henry III were much more inclined to indulge their taste for luxury. But it was not simply a matter of personal choice, significant though that might be: the king had a position to maintain, a positive duty to stand head and shoulders above his subjects in every area where they could judge him. He had an army of servants as well as one of soldiers – the categories overlapped to a great extent – and they all had to be rewarded somehow.

Religious foundations were also an essential part of the royal ostentation, significant with the Angevin kings even if less than with some others. It is unfortunate that Henry II's Waltham abbey, on which he spent at least £1500, and John's Beaulieu have not survived, but we still have the greatest of all these works by far, Henry III's Westminster abbey, built on the grandest scale with the most lavish ornamentation (see plate 7). The financial effort virtually bankrupted Henry and contributed directly to his later political problems. The cost is difficult to assess, but an estimate in 1261 was nearly £30,000.

But it was military spending that ran away with the largest sums, not only during emergencies such as the rebellion of 1173–4, the cost of suppressing the English part of which has been estimated at something over £3000, but in every year when there was war somewhere in the Angevin dominions, and that was nearly every year.[1] Peace could be expensive too: in 1200

---

[1] Beeler, *Warfare in England*, 183.

John agreed to pay the French king 20,000 marks (£13,333) as a
relief for succession to his French fiefs. There were soldiers to be
paid, garrisons to be supplied, and castles to be built and maintained. Building seems to have been the greatest military expense: from 1155 to 1215 the kings spent at least £46,000 on
castles.[2] Henry II's greatest work is the keep and inner curtain
wall of Dover castle, built in the 1180s at a cost of over £6500
(see plate 8). Richard I spent most money and care on his new
castle in Normandy, Château Gaillard on the Seine covering the
approach to Rouen from Paris. The scene of John's main castle-
building was the north of England, which was the source of
much of the opposition to his rule; amongst other places he
strengthened Scarborough castle at a cost of over £2000. Dover
had justified Henry II's expenditure by successfully withstanding
a long siege, and Henry III continued to build massively there
after he came of age. The unfortified royal palaces had always
been as fine as the age could make them: John spent on them
nearly one-quarter of what he spent on castles. Henry III spent
some £10,000 on the palace of Westminster alone.

A fundamental fact in the history of this period is that it was a
great age of inflation, the worst period being between 1180 and
1220. The impact on the financial position of the monarchy was
bound to be serious. It cost Henry II 8 pence a day to hire a
knight; John had to pay 2 shillings – three times as much. The
figures for Henry II's expenditure are thus not directly comparable to Henry III's; but every extra penny had to be raised,
and the implications for the royal administration were far-
reaching. The difficulties were compounded because the height
of the period of inflation coincided with the crisis of political
relations between the Angevin kings and Philip Augustus of
France. The more-or-less continuous wars which eventually led
to the expulsion of the Angevins from most of their continental
domains and even an invasion of England were to a large extent
contests of finance and administration: who could bring the
greater resources to bear at the point of conflict.

The greatest need of these kings, then, was for a reliable army
and money for military expenditure. The king had a military
household which served as the nucleus of larger armies: John
had at least 50 knights constantly available, a number which
could be expanded to several hundred by the knights bringing in
retainers or by hiring others. Henry III in 1228 was paying 70

[2] Brown, Colvin and Taylor, *History of the King's Works*, 51–159.

household knights as well as mounted serjeants.[3] Another source of knights was the contingents owed to the king by the great landholders in return for their estates. That the large quotas of knights due to the king, the *servitium debitum*, established under the Norman kings could no longer be demanded in practice, for whatever reasons, was recognized as early as 1157 when Henry II called out only every third knight, the others 'helping them'.[4] In 1194 Richard called out one-third of the knight service, in 1198 one-tenth, and John in 1205 again a tenth.[5] By the middle of Henry III's reign what amounted to a new *servitium debitum* had been created at a fraction of the former quota.

How did the landholders obtain their quotas of knights? It seems unlikely that they used their own knightly tenants performing military service in return for their lands: by John's reign the knights of the honour of Hastings, for instance, owed no service outside the Rape of Hastings except at the lord's expense.[6] The households of the lords are a more likely source of military manpower. The higher aristocracy frequently served in person in the king's forces in England, Wales and France, though royal demands for service on the continent encountered growing opposition under Richard and John. They could negotiate a fine with the king if they did not wish to serve in person. Military service was a matter for bargaining on each occasion when it arose. There was an obligation to provide knights, but what it meant in practice was negotiable. By the reign of Henry II the tenants-in-chief were supplying both some knights and the monetary substitute for the *servitium debitum* known as scutage. If the tenant-in-chief performed his service in person with what the king accepted as a reasonable contribution of knights, no money would be demanded of him and he would be allowed to collect and keep scutage from such of his own tenants by knight service as had not joined his contingent. But the king did not succeed in raising the level of scutage and fines to the point where they would cover the cost of the equivalent mercenary force; hence the kings always preferred their tenants-in-chief to perform service in person, at least when they trusted them.

Many kinds of people served in armies for a variety of reasons, and categorizing them too rigidly is unhelpful. The king had

[3] S. D. Church, 'A question of numbers: the knights of the household of King John', in Coss and Lloyd, *Thirteenth Century England* iv, 151–65; Carpenter, *Minority*, 317.

[4] Torigni i, 307–8.

[5] Mitchell, *Studies in Taxation*, 302.

[6] Sanders, *Military Service*, 55.

different military needs: garrisons, siege troops, lightly armed foragers and raiders, as well as heavy cavalry. For garrison service the old system of 'castle-guard' was still functioning, though it was often commuted for money and men hired instead. Other needs could be met by a mixture of the royal household, tenants-in-chief serving at their own cost for a period, perhaps staying on longer at the king's expense, and, most important, hired soldiers. Not all these 'mercenaries' were comparable to the famous professional bands widely used on the continent, by Frederick Barbarossa and the French kings as well as Henry II. They had been used in England in Stephen's reign, and John also alienated support by importing them. They attracted a great deal of hatred and were condemned by the church but their professionalism and reliability, as long as they were paid, ensured their continuing employment.[7] Little is known about the bands in detail, though the presence of long-serving and trusted captains such as Richard I's Mercadier and John's Gerard d'Athée implies a degree of permanent organization. A band of mercenaries, horsed or on foot, was never cheap: their use added to the financial strain of warfare, and further increased the advantage of lords with large cash resources.

The thirteenth century saw the gradual emergence of broadly based methods of recruitment. It was not only those of knightly status who were armed. The Assize of Arms of 1181 specified the kinds of weapons to be owned by men of given levels of wealth down to the owners of rent or chattels worth 10 marks. The Assize paved the way for later measures: a writ of 1242 which enforced the watch and ward regulations recognized a more elaborate gradation of military classes, including mounted men at arms worth £15 a year and archers, set at 40-shilling landholders. By this date there was a growing tendency to summon stated numbers of men from a given area, often the hundred: the way was open for the later commissions of array which organized the armies of the fourteenth century.[8]

Royal finances

To meet the needs of war and ostentation a wide variety of sources of income was available, and it was significantly extended under

---

[7] Verbruggen, *Warfare*, 118–30.
[8] Gesta i, 261; EHD ii, 416–7; Cal Cl Rolls 1237–42, 482–4.

the Angevin kings. Royal income fell broadly into two types, regular and occasional, the regular being what came in every year, while the occasional sources, less frequent, could be used to raise funds for some specific purpose. Regular sources of income included the royal demesne lands, the forests, and profits derived from the king's position as the supreme feudal lord – the profits of courts, custody of lands normally held by great lords but which through wardship, escheat or vacancy happened to be in the king's hands, and 'relief' payments on the succession of heirs together with the right to arrange the marriage of heirs while still under age. Sources such as wardships and vacancies depended on the deaths of individuals and were therefore unpredictable, and the judicial revenue fluctuated, but the net result was a continual if varying income. These sources normally accounted through the exchequer and were enrolled on the pipe rolls. Occasional sources comprised the various forms of taxation: the geld, still taken early in Henry II's reign, and the carucage introduced under Richard I; scutage and 'aids', taken for specified purposes and assessed on the knight's fee; the proportional taxes on moveables and revenues; and tallage, a tax on the royal demesne lands. While some of these sources might go through the exchequer and the resulting income be found on surviving rolls, a separate office was frequently set up to handle the money. Written accounts from such offices have survived far less fully than the pipe rolls, which means that the total royal income is usually not known.

A fundamental resource of the monarchy was its landed estate, or 'demesne', which had been inherited from earlier kings. One use of the demesne was as a source of lands to grant as gifts and favours to buy or reward the loyalty of the recipient. This had happened frequently in the reigns of Henry I and especially Stephen; if it succeeded in encouraging loyalty to the king it was not necessarily a source of weakness, though the loyalty might not be passed with the land to the next generation. Henry II aimed to recover the lands thus granted, and he was himself reluctant to give land away on a permanent basis, though John and Henry III were more willing.

The normal way of exploiting the demesne was to let it along with the county and hundred courts in each county to the sheriff, who paid an annual lump sum, or 'farm', for them. Anything he could collect above the farm was then the sheriff's profit. The highest farm was that of Lincolnshire at nearly £1000, the lowest Sussex, at £40, and Rutland, £10. The farms of the counties had become fixed at the level of Henry I's reign, but rising prosperity and rising prices meant that the profit in the hands of the sheriff rose while royal income from this source stood still. Three ways of tapping the sheriff's profit were developed: charging him more, either by making him pay for office or by increasing his farm by an 'increment'; turning the farmer into a custodian, making him account for income and expenditure and transferring all the profit to the exchequer; or taking lands out of his control altogether, letting them for higher sums to another 'farmer'. Increments were first charged under Henry II and rose to very high levels under John; despite condemnation of the practice in Magna Carta it was reintroduced under Henry III. The second way of managing the demesne, direct exploitation by royal officials, was more difficult to achieve as it might compel royal agents to forgo opportunities for profit. King John tried it in 1204, using the sheriffs themselves as the officials; though in some counties it survived until the end of John's reign, the experiment eventually foundered on the hostility of the sheriffs, the political need for a strong royal agent in the counties and administrative difficulties in the exchequer.

Other land in the king's hands came from the aristocracy as a result of 'escheat' through lack of heirs or forfeiture for rebellion, and from the church during a vacancy in a bishopric or abbacy. These estates preserved their own identity and were often let out separately. Such estates could be used as a form of reward for royal servants if the sum the king accepted was substantially less than the lands could be made to yield. It was a common complaint, so presumably a common offence, that the men in charge of them ran them mercilessly for short-term gain, selling off the stock and timber and causing damage that would need years to repair. This was a way of rewarding servants that could also be profitable to the king.

In 1236 the management of the royal landed revenues was overhauled: the demesne was painstakingly surveyed and let out piecemeal, escheats were removed from the hands of the sheriff and entrusted to new officials called escheators, while the sheriff had to account at the exchequer for each item instead of paying in a lump sum.[9] One effect of this was to make the office of sheriff less profitable, and thus unattractive to the kind of men who had filled it in the past; now substantial men from the local gentry took it on, men with a reputation to lose and the interests

[9] Warren, *Governance*, 192–5.

of their neighbours more at heart. Though not long-lasting, this reform was popular, and was reintroduced by the baronial administration in 1258.

A further source of landed income was the royal forest. These areas had their own law and their own administration under the chief forester, accounting directly to the king. The extent of the forest in the twelfth century varied in proportion to the strength of the king: thus Henry I had added to it, it shrank under king Stephen, while under Henry II, who intended here as elsewhere to restore the situation obtaining under Henry I, it reached its maximum extent. It is possible for the first time to gain a good idea of its size in the thirteenth century.[10] It was widely scattered, but the largest concentration was in Hampshire, Wiltshire, Dorset and Somerset. Most of Essex was royal forest, there were concentrations in Nottinghamshire, south of Northampton, and between Cannock Chase and Feckenham forest in Worcestershire. The forest was not all woodland: it included large areas of moor, heath and upland, and some quite thickly settled regions. Nor was it by any means all royal demesne – many lords and churches held land within the forest, and this lies behind much of the opposition to it.

Its defining characteristic was the application of the forest law, defined in the Assize of the Forest promulgated in 1184 and expanded in the forest assize of 1198.[11] The activities which could be carried on in the forest were restricted and offences classified into two types: those against the animals themselves and those against the 'vert' – the trees and undergrowth which protected them. The Assize of the Forest forbade anyone to have bows, arrows or dogs within the forest, though customarily dogs could be kept if their toes were clipped, or 'lawed', to prevent them from chasing the deer. The chief offences against the vert were cutting down the woods for cultivation ('assarting'), encroaching on the forest (making 'purprestures'), and the most prevalent offence, 'waste', cutting timber.[12] Landholders could therefore not hunt deer on their own land or cut down their own woods if the area had been declared royal forest, but in practice assarts were allowed to remain if a rent was paid for them. The law was enforced at the forest courts, presided over by special justices. There was a permanent network of foresters and each forest had its own warden. In each county with royal forest 12

[10] Young, *Forests*, map on 62–3.
[11] Holt, 'Assizes'.
[12] Dialogue, 61.

knights, later known as 'regarders', were chosen to guard the venison and the vert, and a further four knights arranged the pasturing ('agistment') of the forest, collecting the resulting 'pannage' dues. The royal forests over all England were the responsibility of the chief forester, who from time to time would carry out 'eyres', journeys round the forests trying cases and collecting dues. The value of the forest was primarily financial. The kings certainly did use some of the forests for hunting, but others, especially those in the north, were hardly visited at all. The sums produced by administering the forest law were large but intermittent: a smaller but continuous stream came from rents paid by the foresters, pannage and the sale of various products such as hides, peat and salt as well as timber.

The forest law was also useful as an instrument of oppression and vengeance, as was clearly revealed in the eyre of 1175. During the war of 1173–4, when Henry II was in a tight corner, he ordered the suspension of the forest laws; but once the rebellion was crushed the king refused to honour his commitments and insisted on offences being tried retrospectively. Even the chief justiciar, Richard de Luci, protested at this but the eyre went ahead and netted for the king an enormous sum, at least £12,000.[13] It seems to have been the arbitrary nature of forest law as well as its ruthless application by the foresters that made it particularly hated. Even the author of the *Dialogue of the Exchequer*, a great admirer of Henry II's strong kingship, admitted that 'what is done in accordance with forest law is not called "just" absolutely, but "just according to forest law" '.[14] Under John the area of forest once again began to diminish. It had been found that the sale of exemptions could be profitable. Local communities and religious orders were prepared to pay to take whole areas out of the forest law – the Templars were declared free of forest customs at the beginning of John's reign, and in 1204 the counties of Cornwall, Devon and part of Essex were 'disafforested', Devon alone paying 500 marks.[15]

The king had a right to take a 'relief' from each tenant-in-chief on his succession to his lands, as the barons in turn could from their tenants. The amount charged was a matter of bargaining between king and baron. John notoriously used this right to put pressure on men he did not trust, charging enormous reliefs which they would not be called on to pay until they offended him

[13] Young, *Forests*, 23–4, 39.
[14] Dialogue, 59–60.
[15] Young, *Forests*, 20–1.

in some way. The result was the fixing of a standard, comparatively low, relief in Magna Carta: £5 for a knight's fee, £100 for a barony. As well as custody of the lands of minors, the king also had custody of the minors themselves and the right to arrange their marriage. This could be turned to profit by selling the marriage to, for example, a rising royal servant who would be pleased to marry the heir or heiress into his own family. Sums of money were also offered and accepted for royal favours of all kinds – in other words, the king could be bribed if the offer was large enough. Such offers covered almost the whole range of royal activities: judicial processes, confirmation of charters and rights, military service, and appointments to offices, to name only a few.

The demesne, the forest and the incidental benefits of escheats, wardships and reliefs accrued to the king by virtue of his overlordship. The same is true of the profits of jurisdiction. As well as instruments of political discipline, courts could be a source of profit for whoever held them. The king's courts were the most profitable of all. Those who attended the royal courts of justice could expect to leave poorer than they came. Writs had to be paid for and the goods of convicted felons were sold; but the largest source of cash was the 'amercements', which differed from fines in being arbitrarily fixed by the judges. Amercements were levied on whichever party to a suit lost, on appellors in criminal pleas who withdrew their appeal or failed in it, on jurors who gave false verdicts, on local officials, on anyone who attended or failed to attend the court, for a plethora of ingenious reasons. The profits of the courts were derived directly from people well down in the social scale, usually in small quantities from each but cumulatively considerable, and useful when every little helped.[16]

The royal demesne was a static or diminishing entity, and such windfalls as escheats and wardships could hardly fill the chests emptied by inflation and war. To do so the king, or his advisers and lieutenants, turned to taxation. Early in his reign Henry II continued to take the geld, the Anglo-Saxon land tax that had been the first 'system of national land taxation' in western Europe.[17] Though it was never formally abolished, the geld was allowed to fall into abeyance: it was last taken in 1161. There had been no new general reassessment of geldable land since the

[16] See e.g. Carpenter, *Minority*, 99.
[17] J. A. Green, 'The last century of Danegeld', *EHR* (1981), 241.

Norman conquest and its incidence was riddled with anomalies. It relied on the co-operation of landholders for its collection, and though administratively convenient it is likely to have been unpopular.

Scutage was assessed on the knight's fee, and was based on the list of fees drawn up in 1166 known as the *Cartae Baronum*. This takes the form of responses by each tenant-in-chief to a set of questions: how many knights were enfeoffed on your estate in the time of Henry I? how many have been enfeoffed since? and how many remain 'on the demesne'? that is, those the tenant-in-chief would have to supply if he had enfeoffed fewer than he owed to the king as his quota.[18] The inquiry was held for a number of possible reasons including a desire to extend taxation to the extra fees which many lords had granted above the number of the *servitium debitum*. When the government attempted to charge scutage on these extra fees the bishops and abbots refused to pay the extra, and eventually won their point. A compromise was reached with the lay barons, but the outcome was still advantageous for the royal finances as the new taxable base was generally higher than the old quotas had been.[19]

Scutages were relatively infrequent under Henry II (seven in 35 years) but became more regular under Richard (five in ten years), rising for a while to an annual tax under John (ten in 15 years, annually between 1201 and 1206), the rate per fee also increasing.[20] Both the occasions and the rate for taking scutage and aids were a grievance in John's reign, for Magna Carta provided that they should only be taken by consent and aids at a 'reasonable' rate (clause 12). Scutages continued to be taken throughout the period, though less frequently and less profitably.[21]

It seems to have been the need to raise a huge sum of money very quickly in 1193–4 to pay for Richard I's ransom that forced a rethink of the way the government raised revenue. The expedients adopted then were of crucial importance for the future: the basic type of later medieval tax, the proportion of movable wealth, was now used by the king's government for the first time, while the carucage, a land tax based on the carucate of 100 acres of assessed ploughland and bearing a resemblance to the geld, was introduced. These were both taxes on property irrespective

---

[18] For the *Cartae Baronum* see Red Book; the archbishop of York's Carta, giving the questions, is translated in EHD ii, 906–8, Keefe, *Feudal Assessments*, 7.

[19] Keefe, *Feudal Assessments*, 41–89.

[20] Ibid., 30 table 2.

[21] Mitchell, *Studies in Taxation*, 313–40.

of tenure: they were levied at a uniform rate on a revisable property assessment, and payment was therefore proportional to wealth – in theory, at least. The ransom carucage was taken on the hides and carucates of the Domesday assessment, but on the next occasion, 1198, when money was raised to support Richard I's war in France, a new national assessment was made.

An easier way to raise larger sums of money was the proportion of revenue or movable wealth; in this method has been seen the origin of modern taxation.[22] The basic idea was already familiar: it was that of the ecclesiastical tithe, ideally one-tenth of the annual increase of crops and livestock payable to the parish church. It was first applied as a country-wide tax for other than local purposes in 1166 when a general tithe was taken for the relief of the Holy Land. Six pence was levied for every £1-worth of personal property, payable over five years. The expedient was repeated in 1188, in the so-called 'Saladin Tithe', when the whole country was tithed to support the forthcoming crusade to recover Jerusalem, recently captured by Saladin. Each man swore to the value of his personal possessions before a commission of local and royal representatives. The same method was adopted to help raise king Richard's ransom: the rate was one-quarter of all revenues and movables, and in 1203 John took one-seventh of the the revenue.[23] Much better documented is the thirteenth on revenues and movables taken in 1207, which is usually regarded as a landmark in royal taxation and the origin of the later medieval lay subsidies. The rate was 1 shilling in the mark (the mark was worth 13 shillings and 4 pence) and the assessment was made on oath before specially appointed justices. The amount raised was about £60,000, and was allocated to no specific purpose or campaign but simply to the king's future needs.[24] All sections of society were subject to it, and it aroused a good deal of opposition. Most of the higher clergy bought themselves off for a lump sum, and so escaped assessment. The next such tax was not until 1225, when one-fifteenth was taken from all sections of the community, including merchants and the clergy. The occasion was Louis VIII's invasion of Poitou. Thereafter royal demands for this kind of taxation were frequent, though the last time such a tax was granted by the lay barons was in 1237. They were regarded as 'aids'; the consent of

[22] Mitchell, *Studies in Taxation*, 5.
[23] Ibid., 62–3.
[24] Ibid., 84–92.

the tenants was necessary, and Henry III's barons learnt to refuse.

Another landmark in royal fund-raising was the introduction of customs dues on imports and exports, which ultimately became a crucial component of royal finances. In 1202 John introduced duties at one-fifteenth of goods passing through the ports. Operated by custodians who were themselves merchants and financiers, the levy raised nearly £5000 in 1202–4 but was later abandoned.[25]

Any lord had the right to take tallage from the villeins of his demesne. This seems to have become an annual payment, and came to be one of the legal tests of villeinage. The king, however, took tallage from freemen as well as villeins on his demesne, notably from the towns, and from escheated honours and lands in wardship. The amount involved was decided by bargaining between assessors and taxpayers. Richard and John took it very frequently but it never became an annual levy, commonly being taken to coincide with scutage and linked to some specific need.[26] In effect like tallage, equally crude and certainly resented, was the practice of taking 'gifts' from the wealthy: in 1159, for instance, Thomas Becket netted over £3000 for the king in 'gifts' from the bishops and abbots, for which many in the English church never forgave him.[27] John, especially, when offended for whatever reason, charged large sums to regain his 'benevolence' or remit his ill-will.

There was one other way of raising ready cash: borrowing. Early in Henry II's reign the chief royal creditor was the Flemish merchant and moneylender William Cade, but if he represents a more numerous Flemish financial interest they were soon replaced by the Jews. The heyday of the medieval English Jewish community covers the latter half of Henry II's reign and those of Richard I and John. The king could tallage the Jews, who were under royal protection and completely at his mercy; but they were also a source of loans, repaid out of the farm of the shire or other county revenue. Groups of prominent Jews formed companies to advance large sums – one consortium in 1177 lent over £3000 in one payment. But the favourite method of tapping Jewish wealth was to sieze their goods and bonds on their death. The king could confiscate any Jew's property on his death, and

[25] Painter, *Reign of John*, 136–9.
[26] Mitchell, *Taxation in Medieval England*, 244–6, 286–7, 330–1; Hoyt, *Royal Demesne*, 107–24.
[27] Barlow, *Becket*, 59.

the temptation to abuse this right grew stronger as time passed and the strain on the royal finances worsened. The normal procedure was to take one-third of the fortune.[28] The richest and most famous of all the great Jewish capitalists was Aaron of Lincoln, who advanced money to a wide variety of debtors, including the king of Scotland, the archbishop of Canterbury, a clutch of bishops and at least four earls, on the security of lands and goods. He thus came to have large landed interests looked after by a network of local agents. On his death in about 1186 a special branch of the exchequer was opened to collect sums owing to him, amounting to some £15,000. They were enrolled on the pipe rolls year by year, but by 1205 only about half the total had been collected.[29]

It was probably the loss to the royal revenues caused by the riots of 1190[30] that led to tighter supervision of Jewish activities. From 1194 all contracts and bonds recording loans and business transactions were to be drawn up in duplicate and one copy deposited in a chest at one of a number of designated centres under the control of the newly established exchequer of the Jews. Thus whatever happened to the Jew, the royal administration would know who owed him money. Special justices presided over this exchequer, which soon developed judicial functions. Knowing so much more about the Jews' activities the royal administration was in a better position than before to turn the screw on them, an opportunity which king John did not allow to slip. In 1210 all the Jews of the kingdom were arrested and their charters seized, bringing considerable evasion of the exchequer to light. Many Jews were in effect expelled, and confiscatory fines imposed on others. In Henry III's reign heavy tallages succeeded each other frequently, while forgiving debt to the Jews was a useful form of royal favour. Subjected to harsh and arbitrary treatment, the Jews were a wasting asset by the middle of the thirteenth century, their place increasingly taken by merchants from Italy and from Cahors in southern France.

There are a number of reasons why attempts to work out the wealth of the Angevin kings are problematic and the results potentially misleading. One, already mentioned, is that our evidence certainly does not cover all sources. Another is the problem of what to include in the calculations. Interpreting medieval financial documents requires a high degree of technical expertise –

[28] Roth, *History of the Jews*, 101–2.
[29] Ibid., 14–17.
[30] See below, pp. 176–7.

it is never a question of simple addition. The results are necessarily tentative and controversial.[31] The crude figures need to be related to purchasing power. Nevertheless, the pipe rolls provide a minimum of knowledge about some aspects of royal finance as long as they are not pressed for a spurious precision. The thin and miserable pipe rolls of the first years of Henry II's reign show a great diminution of royal revenue when compared to the one surviving roll of Henry I's reign. The kinds of revenue discoverable from the pipe rolls show an overall increase from £10–15,000 early in Henry's reign to something around £20,000 later in his reign. Government revenue from ordinary sources reached over £30,000 early in John's reign, but collapsed to about £8000 in the early years of Henry III's minority; it had risen to £16,500 by 1225.[32] There was serious inflation between 1200 and 1220, so the lower figures for Henry III's reign represent a major loss. The total of farms, increments, fines and escheats for 1201 and 1205 have both been estimated at about £26,000.[33] The judicial eyres were great fund-raisers, that of 1246–9 having reputedly raised £22,000.[34] The geld of 1162 raised over £3000, the carucage of 1220 over £5000, but the land taxes, indeed any other sources, seem trivial compared to the sum of £60,000 raised by the thirteenth of 1207. The fifteenth of 1225 raised nearly £40,000.[35] This explains the king's preference for that form of taxation, the political necessity of obtaining consent to it, and the difficulty of doing so.

Law

Some of the most radical and far-reaching developments of this period occurred in legal administration. It was now that many of the distinctive features of the English legal system crystallized: the method of initiating suits by standard writs, the use of juries to ascertain facts and apportion guilt, judges who made the judgments rather than merely presiding or enquiring, regular record-keeping on rolls; it also saw the groundwork of institutions laid down which continued for centuries: the itinerant

[31] See J. C. Holt, 'The loss of Normandy and royal finances' in Gillingham and Holt, *War and Government*, 92–105; Gillingham, *Angevin Empire*, 72–83.

[32] Holt, *Magna Carta*, 39; Carpenter, *Minority*, 109–116, 413–17.

[33] Mitchell, *Studies in Taxation*, 16.

[34] Warren, *Governance*, 223.

[35] Ibid., 147–50; Carpenter, *Minority*, 381.

justices and the courts of king's bench and common pleas. From this period date the two earliest systematic treatises on English law, which go by the names of two celebrated judges, *Glanvill* and *Bracton*. It was also the period when litigation of any importance was increasingly drawn into the king's courts. This was the ultimate effect of royal supervision of the older non-royal courts, a duty which Henry II and John especially took very seriously. The work of local courts was transformed, not superseded.[36]

The most basic court was that of the manor, where the lord's bailiff dealt with matters arising from the everyday life of the tenants: labour services not performed or done badly, tenements changing hands, grants of permission to marry, cases of assault between tenants, breaches of manorial custom or the lord's peace.[37]

By the time of the Norman conquest England was already divided into shires, which later acquired the French name of counties, and shires in turn were subdivided into lesser regions called hundreds in the south and the west Midlands and wapen-takes in the east Midlands and Yorkshire. The court of the hundred or wapentake dealt with disputes between tenants of different manors, often about boundaries, pastures and agricul-tural business, but also such matters as brawling and assault of a less-serious nature, pleas of debt, arrears of rent and breaches of verbal agreements.[38] Judgments were given by the suitors to the court. They were usually presided over by a bailiff appointed by the sheriff; but many hundreds were in the hands of lords who appointed their own bailiffs, the bailiffs still being responsible to the sheriff for conduct of the king's business. The hundred was also the basic unit where the orders which passed down the political-judicial hierarchy finally had to be executed: it was often the hundred bailiff who served royal writs, collected debts owed to the crown, executed the judgments of higher courts, arrested accused persons and empanelled juries. Twice a year the sheriff would come on his 'tourn', to preside over sessions of the hundred courts and inquire into breaches of the peace.

The sheriff presided over the county court: he did not take part in giving the judgments – that was the business of the suitors – but was responsible for executing them. Since the early twelfth

[36] See Pollock and Maitland, *History of English Law* i, 136–225; Harding, *Law Courts*; Palmer, *County Courts*.
[37] See below, p. 163.
[38] Warren, *Governance*, 201–4.

century the county court had dealt with land cases between the tenants of different lords, and even after such cases normally went to the royal courts the preliminary stages were still often heard at shire level, as were those of certain criminal pleas. But by the thirteenth century much of the county's business involved pleas of debt and trespass. The suitors to the court – those with a right and duty to attend – were the local landholders down to knightly tenants and substantial freemen, but at the ordinary monthly meetings the business was conducted by a smaller body chosen in various ways whom the sheriff could compel to attend. In practice the county court came to be dominated by legal experts representing the leading landholders.

In addition to shire and hundred there were also borough and honour courts, and a whole separate hierarchy of church courts. The borough courts functioned in effect as separate hundreds, enforcing the customs of the borough, which differed in many ways from those current among the rural and aristocratic population. Some borough courts had extensive powers in disputes affecting the citizens and urban property. Any lord had the right to hold a court for the free tenants of his estates, his 'honour': the greater lords held courts for their tenants in which their disputes were settled and land grants made and witnessed. The church claimed jurisdiction over matters which, broadly speaking, could be described as breaches of moral law; this gave them jurisdiction over marriage and testamentary matters, and they laid claim to deal with clerics who committed crimes and with disputes involving church property, both of which became points at issue between Henry II and archbishop Thomas Becket.

The centre of political power was also the fountainhead of justice. The king too had a court, not unlike that of an honour, to settle disagreements between his leading tenants and to which those wronged in lower courts could appeal. Difficult cases would constantly come up before the king himself. The term *curia regis*, king's court, applied to all the meetings over which the king's judges presided, but Henry II and his successors kept a body of judges with them to solve these cases, leaving only the most important to themselves. This was the court *coram rege*, 'with the king', later known as King's Bench. Other courts, also the king's, developed from Henry II's reign onwards, as we shall see.

An essential duty of any king, and a touchstone of his authority, was to ensure that the peace, 'the king's peace', was kept. The most serious crimes, such as murder, rape, theft of goods above a certain value, housebreaking and arson, were known as 'felonies', and had long been regarded as offences against the king's peace as well as against the victim. Peace-keeping and what we would call policing were incumbent upon the local community, especially upon the hundred, but it was in the last resort up to the king to provide both the organization and, ultimately, the force necessary to ensure compliance. A number of peace-keeping methods had been inherited from the past. On reaching the age of 12 each freeman was expected to swear before the hundred court to keep the king's peace and to help pursue suspected malefactors – to join in the 'hue and cry' when summoned. Discipline was enforced on the lesser freemen and the unfree by *frankpledge*, a system of collective surety: each freeman had to belong to a group which was responsible for its members. It had to produce him in court to face an accusation, or be collectively fined if it failed; and it had to pay fines imposed on members who were themselves unable to pay. Anyone who possessed enough property to be pledged as security was exempt. Ensuring that everyone who should be was in a frankpledge group (a *tithing*) was part of the duty of the sheriff. In the far north and the Welsh borders, where the hundred organization had not developed, a still blunter instrument was used for police functions: 'sergeants of the peace', virtual vigilantes under the authority of local lords.[39]

The Assize of Arms, promulgated in 1181, was aimed at improving military readiness.[40] It classified men by their money income, and laid down the types of arms each income group was required to possess; for example, a freeman with goods or rent worth 16 marks was to have a hauberk, a helmet, a shield and a lance. Everyone who bore arms should swear allegiance to the king; the export of arms, ships and timber was forbidden. The Assize was reissued in 1223 accompanied by an order to administer the 'oath of arms'. A force thus provided could be useful in time of war too, and might on occasion be used against the Welsh.[41] It was available to form the *posse comitatus*, the 'county force' at the sheriff's disposal for use against malefactors.

The traditional method for seeking redress for injuries of all types was for the aggrieved person to make an accusation in a

---

[39] Warren, *Governance*, 62.
[40] See above, n. 8.
[41] Michael Powicke, *Military Obligation in Medieval England*, Oxford 1962, 82–9.

court. By the twelfth century this had come to be supplemented by prosecution by royal officials, but as they often dispensed with supporting testimony the way was wide open to abuse, and Henry II prohibited prosecutions by officials on their word alone. A better solution was finally found to the whole problem, and promulgated in 1166 in the Assize of Clarendon.[42] This employed the 'jury of presentment' (because it 'presented' suspects for trial), later called the 'grand jury'. It consisted of 12 reputable men of the hundred and four from each vill who declared on oath whether there was anyone in their area suspected of a serious crime, or of harbouring suspects. This was not yet trial by jury – the jury did not give a verdict, it just accused suspects. The effect of the jury of presentment was to add royal power to the efforts of the local community to coerce its recalcitrant members. Presentments on oath could be made before the justices in eyre, or before the sheriff on his 'tourn'.

A new method of inquiring into violent or suspicious deaths was instituted in 1194 with the appointment of coroners. They were originally deputed to keep the pleas of the crown, but lack of precise definition of these pleas led to their activities being largely restricted to cases of homicide and unnatural death. The coroner kept a record of initial proceedings in felony cases which served as a check on sheriffs and local juries.[43]

The two methods of trial available were battle and the ordeal. Battle was normal in serious cases where there was an accuser; an accused man could only escape battle if he was elderly or had a broken bone or a head injury.[44] Battle in criminal cases was not a formality – the front teeth were recommended as a weapon;[45] those involving an 'approver', a confessed criminal who accused his former accomplices, seem to have been particularly savage. When the accusation came from a presenting jury, or when battle was not appropriate, trial by ordeal was employed. There were two types of ordeal, hot iron and cold water: the former for freemen, the latter for villeins. But a verdict of innocence – the wound from the hot iron healing, the water receiving the sinking accused – was not necessarily final: even those who had been 'cleared by the law' still had to leave the realm if they were of bad report.[46]

[42] EHD ii, 408.
[43] Hunnisett, *Coroner*.
[44] Glanvill, 173.
[45] Bracton ii, 410.
[46] Assize of Clarendon, cl. 14.

Punishments were drastic. Those caught in the act of murder or theft or seized by the hue and cry could be executed on the spot. Felons convicted in court were at the king's mercy, usually the judge sentencing, and could be mutilated – a hand and a foot, or eyes and testicles. Hanging was normal for homicide, and was extended to all felonies in the thirteenth century.[47] But in practice many accused of felony did not stay to face trial, preferring to flee and be outlawed. Outlaws could be killed by anyone with impunity: 5 shillings a head was offered under Richard I.[48] But in practice outlaws often seem to have surrendered and bought pardons.

It does not seem that the ordeal was in decline in the twelfth century: the Assize of Clarendon enjoined it, and new pits for the water were being dug and blessed. But there was a strengthening current of clerical opinion opposed to it, as demanding a miracle of God and as intellectually inadequate as proof, and the Lateran Council of 1215 forbade clerical participation in it.[49] Priests were essential to bless the iron or water; their absence made the ordeal unworkable, and in 1219 it was forbidden in England.[50] This left a considerable hole in judicial procedure. There ensued a period when the justices might take a presenting jury's suspicion as a conviction, or allow the accused to find surety for good behaviour. Later the jury was reinforced with representatives of neighbouring vills to produce a verdict; finally, in a somewhat obscure but very important development, the trial 'petty jury' declared the verdict. Jury trial had emerged, but it gained popularity only slowly.

Henry II's reign saw important developments in the procedure for cases involving land and some other kinds of real property. In the procedure then introduced, a jury assembled before royal justices in response to a standardized writ gave a verdict based on local knowledge which it was then up to the sheriff to enforce. The two advantages, a jury verdict and royal power to secure its enforcement, made the new system immensely popular with litigants and drew a lot of cases into the royal courts, in the process reducing the business of the honorial courts and limiting the county courts to the early stages of a suit. The writ was a flexible instrument capable of wide extension into other types of case, and standard forms of writ continued to be developed in the thirteenth century.

---

[47] Harding, *Law Courts*, 57.
[48] PR 9 Richard I, 169.
[49] Baldwin, *Masters, Princes and Merchants*, 324–9; Bartlett, *Trial by Fire and Water*.
[50] Cal Pat Rolls 1216–32, 186.

In land cases an essential distinction was made between possession, which could be temporary, and right, which was permanent. There was need for a rapid process to right immediate wrongs, to reverse the effect of a recent act of violence or injustice and put the ejected party into possession without getting bogged down in the more difficult question of who had the better right. This was provided by the possessory or 'petty' assizes. The word *assise* means a sitting of the royal court, of the jury or of the justices, hence the edict made there, hence the form of action needed to bring it about. The writ of *novel disseisin* ordered the sheriff to summon a jury of recognition to say whether or not X had unjustly and without the judgment of a court disseised (dispossessed) Y since a given date. If yes, the sheriff put Y back into possession and saw that he recovered damages and X was amerced. This process would obviously be useful in the early years of Henry II's reign to quieten conflicting claims dating from the time of Stephen, but the earliest evidence for it dates only from 1168. The assize of *mort d'ancestor*, instituted in 1176, aimed to protect the rights of heirs denied their inheritance. The writ ordered the sheriff to summon 12 men of the neighbourhood who would state on oath whether X had died after a certain date in possession of and with a heritable interest in some stated land; and whether Y was his nearest heir. If the answer to both questions was yes, Y was given possession. Two similar assizes concerned the church: *utrum* summoned a jury to declare whether some land which a priest claimed as held by his church in free alms tenure was indeed that, or the defendant's lay fee. *Darrein presentment* concerned the appointment of a parson to a church, a valuable right held by many laymen. The jury had to declare who last presented a parson. The demandant's penalty if he lost was amercement 'for false claim'.

The procedure for deciding who had the right to the possessions in question was slower and more deliberate, as befitted a verdict which would decide the case more permanently. The place to deal with quarrels concerning land held of a lord other than the king was in that lord's court. The court would consist of the lord's tenants, who might well be biased against an outsider claiming land held by one of them; if the defendant already held the land of the lord, and lost, the lord might find he had to compensate the loser. For these reasons and no doubt many others, the king's court proved a popular alternative with demandants, who could buy a *writ of right*. This was an order to the lord to do right to the demandant or else the sheriff would, so that the king should hear no further complaints in the matter. From Henry II's reign onwards there was a legal rule that no one need answer in his lord's court for his land unless faced with the king's writ. The sanction was that the case would be transferred to the county court, where however hearings could easily be delayed if the defendant was unwilling to come: many excuses for non-appearance (*essoins*) were allowed. An alternative to this process was the writ *precipe*, addressed to the sheriff, commanding him to order the current tenant to give the demandant what he asked, failing which the sheriff was to summon the tenant before the king's justices. The effect of this even more peremptory process was to bring the case straight into the king's court.

Trial in cases of right was theoretically by battle. The demandant could not fight his own battle, unlike in criminal cases: he had to be represented by someone supposedly a witness to the basis of his claim. The defendant could have a champion; professional champions were disapproved of in the twelfth century but were common in the thirteenth, when a monastery, for instance, might retain its own champion. Battles in land cases were not pursued quite as far as in criminal cases: one side could surrender by 'crying craven', and in effect compromises before battle was joined were common. Clerical disapproval of trial by ordeal extended to the judicial duel as well, but failed to stop the practice: priestly ritual was not indispensable here, and a miracle was not required for the judgment to be credible. The demandant always had to be prepared for trial by battle, but from 1179 the defendant had the option of a jury trial. He could buy a writ which ordered the sheriff to empanel a jury of 12 knights, the 'grand assize', before the royal justices. This could also lead to endless delays, but was nevertheless popular.

Thus the writs were the basis of a system which welded existing methods into a new unity. The formulae used in the writs developed out of those employed earlier in the twelfth century, but the essential new feature was that the writs had to be returned to the justices endorsed with a note of the action taken. They were called 'original' writs because they originated a legal process which could be followed through by the justices; the effect, if not the intention, was to bring cases into the king's courts.

Writs continued to develop in the later twelfth and thirteenth centuries, with *precipe* covering cases of dowry and debt and *novel disseisin* developing variants to cover all kinds of property.

But the greatest change came with the proliferation under John and early in Henry III's reign of *writs of entry*.[51] These took the form of a claim by the demandant that the tenant had 'entry' into a property by an invalid, or no longer valid, title – by an illegal grant, or by staying on after a lease had expired, for instance. Tending to break down the distinction between possession and right, they eventually ousted the actions of right. Another major breakthrough began in the 1220s with the gradual development of *writs of trespass*, which eventually brought civil injuries such as assault, negligence and breach of contract before the royal courts as a 'trespass' against the king's peace. To obtain one it was necessary to allege that 'force and arms' had been used. The allegation of force, necessary to get the case into the royal courts, soon became something of a legal fiction.

The rise of legal fiction alerts us to the presence of lawyers. The rapid development of law from Henry II's reign onwards meant that a menu of writs was available for intending litigants. The law was increasingly a world where professional advice was necessary. Lawsuits were not simply a crude matter of fighting battles: it was always necessary to state your case in formal language, which gave rise to formal arguments in which expertise had an advantage. Pleading a case became a game with strict rules refereed by the judges; clever pleading could win a case without it ever going to battle or a jury. Professional pleaders are found at the royal courts in the early thirteenth century, and the number grew as the century went on.[52] The growth of specialization among pleaders in turn gave opportunities to attorneys who would manage a case – buying the writ, hiring and briefing the pleader: the modern roles of solicitor and barrister were already prefigured in the thirteenth century. Judges too were increasingly professional.

The rise of the legal profession went along with the growth of a legal education and a literature, the earliest written intellectual culture in England in which laymen played an important part. Education must have been gained by experience in court and discussion in households, but in the thirteenth century the law courts also spawned specialist written treatises, such as *Brevia Placitata* ('how to plead on writs'), *Novae Narrationes* ('new pleas'), and *Placita Corone* ('pleas of the crown'), a manual to

[51] Harding, *Law Courts*, 70.
[52] Palmer, *County Courts*, 90–7; Turner, *English Judiciary*, 152–4; Paul Brand, 'The origins of the English legal profession', in his *The Making of the Common Law*, 1–20.

help felons avoid conviction. It also produced an early attempt at a systematic treatise, called *Glanvill* after Henry II's chief justiciar. Dating from the last years of Henry II's reign, this work is all about procedure based on writs, and shows how English law had already become a 'law of writs'.[53] The intellectual activity of lawyers in the early thirteenth century in discussing and elaborating their subject can be seen in a yet more ambitious treatise, almost a *summa* of the common law, traditionally named *Bracton* after a prominent lawyer, in fact probably the work of several hands over a period. These two treatises provide essential bodies of information about the state of the law in their period and give coherence to the mass of evidence about individual cases.

These great changes in the mechanics of the law implied changes in administration. In 1166, the year that the Assize of Clarendon was promulgated, high-level commissioners were sent out to travel round the country and, in effect, to check that the Assize was being enforced. Their inquiries revealed shortcomings, and led to the institution of regular visits to the counties by panels of commissioners. The visitations began in 1168 and the arrangements became more elaborate and regular in the following years. The country was divided into a number of circuits, and a commission of itinerant justices sent to each.[54] The journey they undertook was called an 'eyre', and the judges 'justices in eyre'. At first sight similar to the travelling judges of Henry I's reign, who may only have presided over courts and not given the judgments themselves, now they made the judgments; from 1176 their circuits covered the whole country systematically; and their powers and responsibilities were defined in advance by a set of instructions almost like a questionnaire, known as the 'articles of the eyre'. Their main business was to hear pleas of the crown and try those indicted by juries of presentment, in which matters they soon acquired a monopoly; but all kinds of miscellaneous inquiries, political and financial as well as judicial, could be loaded on to them. Eyres soon became cumbersome and lengthy: the one beginning in 1252 took six years to cover the country, and the eyres eventually collapsed under their own weight.

The clogging was relieved by special commissions sent out to hear particular types of case at more frequent intervals than the general eyre – for example, in 1206 commissions went to clear

---

[53] Palmer, *County Courts*, 174.
[54] Warren, *Governance*, 110–11, 136–40.

the backlog of petty assizes and to 'deliver' the gaols by trying those indicted by juries of presentment and imprisoned until the next eyre. Magna Carta demanded that petty assizes should be heard only in the county in which the plea originated and that justices, accompanied by local knights, be sent to try them. This instituted the county 'assizes', whose series of assize rolls begins in 1248. Other commissions were sent out to 'hear and determine' (*oyer* and *terminer*) a specified offence or offences. Since such commissions had to include a number of local knights, they tended to fall into the hands of the local gentry.

The court of the king himself was always the highest and final source of judgment, and king John, who seems to have had a taste for administration and lawsuits, judged a lot of cases himself in his own, necessarily travelling, court. But this way of doing business must have been inconvenient to litigants.[55] Magna Carta insisted that the central court, which had sat at Westminster since Henry II's time but which had closed in John's later years, should be permanent. When Henry III had come of age and began to judge cases himself, in 1234, there were in effect two central courts: 'common pleas' at Westminster took ordinary pleas between subjects, mostly land cases and torts, while 'king's bench', which continued to travel with the king, dealt with any case of whatever kind in which royal interests were involved and reviewed the decisions of lower courts. Pleas of the crown were largely dealt with on eyre, and all the while the exchequer continued to sit judging royal financial cases and even some between subjects.

As the courts became more institutionalized they began to make and preserve records. There was a practical purpose in this, as written methods must have been necessary to keep track of pleading which could drag on for years with procedural ploys and adjournments. The earliest surviving evidence of records of pleading in the royal courts comes from late in Henry II's reign;[56] rolls of pleas become voluminous under John, and very voluminous under Henry III. They often do not record a judgment at the end of the case. But many pleas did not go as far as a judgment, being settled by compromise. A standard form of document, known as a fine, was used to record such compromises. Some survive from Henry II's reign, but in 1195 a system was introduced

[55] D. M. Stenton, 'King John and the courts of justice', in her *English Justice*, 88–114.
[56] Paul Brand, 'Multis vigiliis excogitatam et inventam: Henry II and the creation of the English common law', in his *The Making of the Common Law*, 77–102.

whereby the text of the agreement was written out in triplicate on a single piece of parchment which was then sealed and cut so that the parties should each have a copy sealed by the other side, the third copy, at the foot of the parchment, remaining in the royal treasury for consultation if necessary. These 'feet of fines' have survived in large numbers.

The salient feature of the Angevin period in the history of English law is the rise of a legal system, in which litigation could be drawn or pushed by writs from one court to another, standard forms of initiating cases were available for purchase, and predictable methods of trial, including juries, were employed. The system grew in an unplanned way by accumulating solutions to problems as they arose. The 'common law', the law common to all who used the royal courts, was thus a collection of procedures justified by precedent. Many essential decisions on practice were made by judges, whose role was to declare the law in doubtful cases, to check the correctness of facts alleged in the writ, and otherwise to act as chairmen of a debate designed to narrow down the issue to a question of fact which could be put to a jury. The function of English judges began to diverge from that of many of their continental colleagues, who sifted evidence using inquisitorial methods derived from Roman law. But the common law was not only judge-made: many edicts and decrees were enacted on royal authority of which only the results survive.[57] They would need to be discussed in large gatherings of notables, if only to ensure publicity. In the thirteenth century, with a more articulate legal culture and a developed documentary habit, the results of such consultations were written down as statutes. All these developments brought increasing power to the royal government by enabling it to sort out disputes at a local level. This was the essence of the political power hitherto exercised by the great lords whose courts were consequently reduced in effectiveness, with profound implications for their relations with the monarchy. The common law was a nationwide set of customs interpreted, enforced and partly created by a king's court which worked almost uninterruptedly and over an increasing number and range of cases from Henry II's reign onwards.

Courts in which the suitors gave the judgments must often have been open to the play of local politics, giving scope for

[57] See e.g. Mary Cheney, 'A decree of Henry II on defect of justice', in Diana Greenway, Christopher Holdsworth and Jane Sayers, *Tradition and Change: Essays in Honour of Marjorie Chibnall*, Cambridge 1985, 183–93.

rivalries, old hatreds and vendettas to influence the judgment. The appointment by the king of a core of professional judges who gave judgment supposedly in accordance with rules which applied over the whole country critically altered the balance of power in court. The judges must have had, and may have taken, the opportunity to be tyrants themselves, but there was less room for local factors to prejudice the judgment. Perhaps this was a factor in the popularity of the royal courts. Nevertheless, the legal system undeniably had its imperfections. The great procedural problems were getting the defendant into court and the need to seek the king in person: it was partly these problems that the possessory assizes were designed to solve, by providing a quick, readily available remedy for disseisin. But decisions on questions of right could still be endlessly delayed by unco-operative defendants, and the need to find the king became an issue again under John. Jury trial was not a panacea: the jurors might not know the answers to the questions asked them; they could be bribed, or the jury packed with supporters of one side. They could also blackmail the litigants. There was still plenty of opportunity for self-help, and the law favoured those in posses-sion. The price of both winning and losing could be high. But despite their shortcomings the procedures of the royal courts were immensely popular. The vast quantity of litigation pre-served on the plea rolls is evidence of this. The popularity of the eyres was not anticipated – they consistently failed to keep to their announced timetables because of the press of business, and in the end were swamped by work. Henry II's reign was a crucial moment, when legal institutions were resuscitated and combined with brilliant innovations to set English law on a course of development which it pursued at a great pace right through the thirteenth century.

Machinery

To raise armies, supply the king's needs and run the legal sys-tem required institutional machinery and a supply of willing men to do the work. The central bureaucracy itself comprised two elements, one which travelled with the king and one which remained stationary, generally at Westminster. The heart of the travelling component was the household, which organized the king's daily needs. Its structure was that of many lesser aristo-cratic households, but of course it was larger and its functions more complex as the power of its master was greater. It had to maintain contact with local officials scattered all over England, Wales, Ireland and northern and western France. Its methods seem to have been generally effective, though on one occasion in 1204 John's court ran out of money at Dorchester and had to send urgently to the sheriff of Kent to supply more cash.[58]

The king's butler ran a large administration linking the ports where wine came into England with the moving household; he also supplied the garrisons of royal castles, and when necessary even an army. The larderer was responsible for supplies of meat, taking game from the royal forests, salting and storing it at the various residences. Various constables had responsibility for specific castles, but king John seems to have dispensed with a household constable altogether, the household knights being under the control of the steward. The duties of the stewards or seneschals – Henry II sometimes had two at once – were to oversee provisioning, but they gradually extended their authority until under John they were effectively the head of the royal household. Their financial powers, however, remained subject to the control of the chamber, which emerged during the twelfth century as the household's financial centre.

The king's chamber had long been the place to keep such treasures in money and valuable objects as he carried around with him, and it supplied the luxuries that the king and his retinue used or gave away. It received deliveries of cash from the stationary treasuries and from local sources wherever the household happened to be, without always waiting for it to be channelled through the exchequer. By the middle of Henry II's reign whole sources of revenue, such as vacant abbeys, were being assigned direct to the chamber. The stress of growing financial urgency under Richard and John led to an ever-increasing use of the chamber for organizing the king's income. Gradually under John the keeping and transport of the physical objects began to separate itself from the chamber, and a new office was slowly formed: the wardrobe. Under the child king Henry III the words chamber and wardrobe were used interchangeably.

A governmental machine of such complexity could hardly function without a central writing office accompanying the king on his travels. This was the chancery, presided over by the chancellor who was responsible for the royal seal, the essential

[58] Jolliffe, *Angevin Kingship*, 247, 261.

means of authenticating documents.[59] Between the mid-twelfth and the mid-thirteenth centuries the work of the chancery increased beyond recognition in bulk and complexity, soon outgrowing the king's travelling chapel in which it originated. The huge increase in judicial writs following Henry II's legal reforms, the growth in other types of written instruction, and the practice of enrolling outgoing letters introduced systematically in the first few years of John's reign, led to increasing numbers of scribes and the growth of specialization. In the thirteenth century there was a staff of senior clerks who checked documents before passing them for sealing, and a body of 'cursitors' to perform the menial task of writing out writs in standard form. King John had a small or 'privy' seal which he could use to authenticate written orders, thus bypassing the chancery, part of which was probably now settled permanently at Westminster. The beneficiary had to pay for charters and writs; the chancellor had ample opportunity to feather his nest. The office was always as much political as administrative – Thomas Becket did far more than seal Henry's writs – the routine work being left to someone deputed to bear the seal.

The essential channel of communication between the king in his travelling household and the meetings of the courts which represented the political and legal life of the localities was the sheriff. Each county was assigned to a sheriff and some sheriffs had several counties – neighbouring counties were often paired. To the county he was the representative of royal authority and the agent of its demands, who sat at the centre of both the fiscal and the judicial machinery. To the king and his servants at the centre he was responsible for the delivery of every penny they assessed as owing and the execution of every order. His functions fell into three general areas: collecting royal dues, enforcing the king's peace and administering justice, and acting as the local dogsbody in carrying out a great variety of specific royal orders. He accounted for the revenues and was also the principal collector of debts and taxes. We have already seen some of his judicial responsibilities, and these became more onerous as the legal system grew. The miscellaneous functions were many and various: paying soldiers, summoning those who owed military service, repairing and garrisoning castles, transporting treasure,

---

[59] See T. A. M. Bishop, *Scriptores Reigs*, Oxford 1961; R. Mortimer, 'The charters of Henry II: what are the criteria for authenticity?', in *Anglo-Norman Studies* xii (1989), 119–34.

wine and food, buying cloth, horses and jewellery for the king
or his friends and relatives – whatever was needed the sheriff
was a universal provider. He obviously required a large staff of
helpers, and he had deputy sheriffs, summoners, clerks, sergeants
and 'ministers' as well as bailiffs, who might be renting part of
the royal lands from the sheriff and looking after a hundred
too. The sheriffs thus had immense power, and means were
developed to control them. One method, an inquiry into their
conduct, was adopted in the Inquest of Sheriffs of 1170, as a
result of which 22 out of 29 sheriffs lost office. The power of
Henry II's government is nowhere more clearly seen than in the
measures it took against its own members; but the inquest was
not repeated.

A more regular method of controlling the sheriff had been
devised early in Henry I's reign: he presented his accounts annually to an authoritative and imposing committee, known from
the checked cloth covering the table around which they met as
the 'exchequer'. The way in which the sheriff was held to account is known to us in detail, thanks to the survival of a
remarkable set of documents, the pipe rolls, and a contemporary
account of the workings of the administration that produced
them, the *Dialogue of the Exchequer*.[60] The pipe rolls have
survived in a continuous series from 1155, apart from a brief
period at the end of John's reign when the exchequer broke down.
The name is presumably derived from their pipe-like appearance
when rolled up. The survival of a single roll from 1130 permits
the comparison of Henry II's administration with that of his
grandfather; none have survived from king Stephen's reign. The
Dialogue of the Exchequer was written in or shortly before 1179
and is probably the work of Richard fitz Nigel, who was treasurer
for nearly all of Henry II's reign and most of Richard's as well.
His book lays down in great detail the procedure to be followed,
and we can see from the pipe rolls that it was carried out much
as he describes.

The exchequer was convened twice a year, at Easter and Michaelmas. The Easter meeting was a preliminary session at which
the sheriff had to pay in half the annual farm of his county and
half of any other debts. In return he received as receipt a 'tally',
a wooden stick on which sums of money were represented by
differently shaped notches and grooves cut into it. The stick was
split down the middle so that the incisions remained on both

[60] See Dialogue; Poole, *Exchequer in the Twelfth Century*; Pipe Rolls.

sides, one half being given to the sheriff and the exchequer keeping the other. The main annual session took place at Michaelmas when the sheriff paid the money he had brought into the treasury, where it was counted and placed in sealed sacks and he was given inscribed tallies as his receipt. The coins were then checked in one of two ways, by weighing them against a pound weight or by melting down a sample to examine the silver content, a process known as the 'assay'.

Richard fitz Nigel gives us an elaborate description of the scene at the sessions of the upper exchequer, which was still more an occasion than an institution, and whose science consisted 'not in calculations, but in judgements of all kinds'.[61] The chief justiciar presided when he attended, the treasurer dictated what was to be written on the 'great roll' known to us as the pipe roll, his clerk doing the actual writing. The chancellor's scribe wrote a duplicate of the pipe roll for the use of the chancellor. The chancellor's clerk deputized for his master, keeping the duplicate of the king's seal used for exchequer business. As the post of justiciar fell into abeyance this figure rose to great importance, acquiring in the thirteenth century the title of chancellor of the exchequer. The calculations were performed by using the columns of the checked cloth to represent pence, shillings, pounds and so on; little heaps of coins representing the sum due were piled on one row of squares, and others representing sums actually paid put in the row below. The sum paid was subtracted from the sum due by removing counters alternately from corresponding heaps. This means of calculation had the advantage of easing the problem of doing elementary arithmetic in roman numerals, by introducing what amounted to a zero – when there were no shillings to be counted, for instance, the shilling column was left empty.

The solemn procedure, which Richard fitz Nigel likens to a game of chess, of the 'course of the exchequer' proceeded and during it the pipe roll was compiled. It began by stating how much had been paid into the treasury and then listed various kinds of authorized payment made out of the revenue and various deductions. Income from various sources was then enumerated. The chancellor's clerk questioned the sheriff about revenues arising from legal proceedings in the sheriff's county. These sections could be very long, as it often took years to clear the debts due from court sentences, and each annual roll thus contained a lot of old debts. Then came sums collected or still due in

---

[61] Dialogue, 15.

respect of various taxes. When the accounting had finished and been enrolled, the calculation was made. The farm due was laid out on the table; the adjusted amount paid in was laid out on a lower line and deducted from the farm; the same then happened with the allowed expenses. If nothing was left the sheriff was quit; anything remaining was entered at the head of the roll as still owing, to be accounted for in the following year. If he had been ordered to spend more than he owed his 'surplus' was entered, to be allowed him in the next year.

All this revenue was in the form of the only coinage current in England, the silver penny. Its quality was therefore a matter of lively concern to the king. Henry II inherited what was essentially still the Anglo-Saxon system in which provincial moneyers struck coins using dies issued centrally, and every few years old coins had to be exchanged against those produced from a new die of different design. The moneyers paid heavily for the dies and kept the profits of changing the coins. In 1157 Henry had the coinage overhauled and a new uniform type, the 'cross-and-crosslets', introduced for the whole realm. In 1180 the system was drastically reformed: manufacture of coins was delegated to contracting craftsmen and royal officials appointed to supervise the exchange of old coins for new, taking the profit for the king. The new coins contained slightly more silver in the alloy and were of a new design, the 'short cross' type. By the 1240s the coinage had again become so bad that the king of France forbade its circulation in his realm.[62] Henry III needed the profits of a recoinage but lacked the ready capital to undertake one, and so went halves with his brother Richard of Cornwall, who lent him 10,000 marks. Dies were cast in London and sent to mint towns all over the country, the warden of the London exchange ensuring uniformity. The new coinage bore a cross extending right to the rim with three pellets in each angle, a design which lasted until the sixteenth century.

Henry II's success in acquiring his grandfather's English throne had re-established the cross-Channel state and, like his grandfather, Henry chose, or was compelled, to spend much of his time on the continent, as did his sons Richard and John until the latter was expelled from most of his French lands. Prolonged royal absence from England pushed the kings towards appointing deputies to head the administration, deputies who then came to be valuable even when the king was in England. On occasion

<hr />

[62] Powicke, *Henry III and the Lord Edward*, 316–22; Warren, *Governance*, 96–8.

a member of the royal family was left as regent: in Henry II's early years queen Eleanor, and between 1170 and 1172 his son Henry 'the young king'. The powers of the regent were largely nominal. The king himself handled important matters and the regent functioned as an intermediary. Queen Eleanor was not even in England during some periods of her regencies – the government could function without a royal regent. After the rebellion of 1173–4 Henry gave up the practice. Apart from a brief period in Richard's reign when queen Eleanor was in a position of power, the next regency by members of the king's family was that of queen Eleanor of Provence and Richard earl of Cornwall during Henry III's absence in 1253–4.

The unprecedented size of Henry II's dominions imposed some form of delegation for each of his provinces: methods of administration had to be developed which did not require the king's presence or even his knowledge. A great increase in the use of written instructions to supplement the incessant royal journeyings was one result; a certain distance between the king and his local agents was another. The official who was left in charge in England came to be known as the chief justiciar.[63] He was simultaneously the leading judge, the chief financial agent and chief executive officer of the king. The Angevin period saw the heyday of this office, shaped not only by the need for a reliable lieutenant to keep England quiet during royal absences, but also by the increasing sophistication of administrative and legal business which required someone versed in its ways: those promoted to the head of it had generally worked their way up inside it.

In the early years of Henry II's reign Robert earl of Leicester was at the head of affairs.[64] As a leading magnate with political experience and memories of the court of Henry I, he was useful in lending authority to the reviving royal administration. He was assisted and eventually succeeded by Richard de Lucy, whose background was in the class of tenants by knight service, as was that of his own successor, Rannulf de Glanville.[65] As justiciar, Glanville was particularly active on judicial business: his period of office was a vital stage in the evolution of the legal system, and it is not surprising that the first systematic treatise on the common law was named after him. It was almost certainly written in his circle, if not actually by him. But Glanville was

[63] West, *Justiciarship*.
[64] Crouch, *Beaumont Twins*, esp. 79–96.
[65] R. Mortimer, 'The family of Rannulf de Glanville', *Bulletin of the Institute of Historical Research* 54 (1981), 1–16.

deposed soon after king Richard's accession, and the king made a series of short-lived arrangements for the government of England during his absence on the crusade, including the appointment of William de Longchamps, his chancellor in Aquitaine, who soon fell foul of political intrigue led by the king's brother, John.

Richard chose next as justiciar a man whose talents had impressed him on the crusade. Hubert Walter already had experience in administration and was to prove the most innovative royal servant of the period.[66] Richard had him made archbishop of Canterbury in May 1193, and by the end of that year he was justiciar. From 1195 he was also papal legate for England, thus holding in his hands a remarkable concentration of power in church and state. His legation lapsed in 1198 and later that year he resigned the justiciarship, but king John on his coronation day appointed Hubert chancellor, a post he retained until his death in 1205. The man chosen to succeed him as justiciar was Geoffrey fitz Peter, a layman, who had been working closely with Hubert Walter and who ran the machinery efficiently, though the presence of the king in England after 1204 and John's suspicious nature inevitably meant a curtailment of the justiciar's influence. Geoffrey died in 1213 as the political storm was about to break; John's chosen right-hand man was Peter des Roches, a household clerk from Touraine whose loyalty to his master seems to have been absolute. He was later to show considerable talents, but he had not grown up in the world of the exchequer and the English law. He was not *persona grata* with the king's opponents, and at Runnymede in June 1215 the last of the great justiciars, Hubert de Burgh, was appointed. Of relatively humble Norfolk origins, Hubert had been John's chamberlain before he became king, and had distinguished himself defending John's French territories in 1204. In the circumstances of the civil war and the French invasion his job was again principally military and he withstood a long siege in Dover castle in 1216–17. During Henry III's minority Hubert was responsible for reestablishing and running the administration, but from the time of the king's majority in 1227 it was likely that Henry would eventually want to take control of his government himself. The moment came in 1232; Hubert was deposed, a leading part in the drama being played by the man he had replaced in 1214, Peter des Roches.

---

[66] Cheney, *Hubert Walter*, 90–103.

Medieval English government was a massive enterprise. Its extensive records comprise one of our main sources of information on the period. A large staff was necessary to carry on the routine business. A great deal of the work could be done by the local inhabitants, who served as coroners, jurors, foresters and even justices, but there was a permanent need for staff at the exchequer, the treasury and the law courts, while sheriffs and their assistants were always needed. How were these people recruited and how were they rewarded?

A few offices were in effect hereditary by 1154. Certain sheriffs, though their tenure did not last long into the reign, and a number of officers in the royal household succeeded their fathers. The hereditary tendency could be convenient, and need not be threatening. A spectacular instance from the heart of royal finance is provided by the descendants of Roger, bishop of Salisbury, who organized the exchequer under Henry I: his nephew Nigel, bishop of Ely, was called in by Henry II at the start of his reign to reconstruct the exchequer, and in 1158 Nigel bought the office of treasurer for his son Richard, who became bishop of London and remained treasurer until his death in 1198. He was succeeded by William of Ely, probably his son, who retained the office until 1215. More frequently sons followed fathers and nephews uncles, not into the same post but into other niches, a tendency which gave rise to ramifying administrative dynasties. It was not only relatives who were 'placed' in this way: there was a whole world of patrons and clients revolving round the centres of power. Men found to be useful, competent and perhaps ruthless were taken into the household of a rising star, to the benefit of both. Thus Geoffrey fitz Peter brought in Geoffrey and Simon of Pattishall, whom he probably met when sheriff of Northamptonshire in 1194; they were used as judges, a field in which they excelled.[67] The justiciars' households were particularly important centres of the family and patronage network. In fact, much of the government must have consisted of the households of its leading members. Another source of recruits to royal government was the households of the kings before they came to the throne: William Longchamps had worked for Richard before 1189, for instance, and Hubert de Burgh had been John's chamberlain when his master was still count of Mortain; Henry III was at a disadvantage in this respect, having had no household of his own in which to try men out and sharpen his own skills

---

[67] Turner, *English Judiciary*, 105–6.

before coming to the throne. How clients and patrons made contact is seldom easy to trace: sometimes through feudal ties or attendance at local or royal courts, but often through chance personal meetings or introductions which must always remain unknown to us.

Rewards came from a variety of sources. Direct permanent grants of land by the king were uncommon. A certain amount of land was let to royal servants, often supplemented under Henry III by various gifts in kind – wine, venison or timber from the royal forests. Political patronage also rewarded them: the king's servants married the heiresses, they won their lawsuits, their sins were forgiven and their fines pardoned.[68] These were only minor sources of reward: in fact it was not at the king's expense that his servants were chiefly rewarded, but at the expense of those they were administering. Rannulf de Glanville when deposed as sheriff of Yorkshire after the Inquest of 1170 was held to account for over £1570 in cash plus a quantity of jewels, horses, falcons and other goods which he had taken and over £70 and goods taken by his servants.[69] This is the known result of seven years as a sheriff and does not represent the opportunities open to him as justiciar when he was far more powerful. A further source of profit for many senior royal officials was custody of escheats, of lands of minors in royal wardship, and vacant abbeys and bishoprics. Here the crucial figure is the difference between the sum that could be squeezed out of the lands and the sum that had to be paid to the king for the opportunity. In principle, 'farming' a county was no different: a fixed sum was due to the king, and anything above that was the sheriff's profit.

This means that a good deal of what passes for administration, or 'governance', was actually speculation conducted for the profit of the administrators, with the king taking a large share. For the king the system had many advantages: his profit was almost risk-free, while that of the custodian could be adjusted since it depended on the bargain struck with the king; officials could be encouraged to bid against each other; the custodian could always be removed if necessary or his term would eventually expire, while any odium incurred would attach to the custodian rather than to the king. Any number of ways, more or less crude, could be found in order to increase the farmer's or sheriff's profit, and an end would be called only when the king accepted another

[68] Holt, *Northerners*, 229–37.
[69] Mortimer, 'Family of Glanville', 15.

bid for the office, or as a result of rare general purges such as the Inquest of Sheriffs.

This system of reward lies behind the co-option of relatives and friends to help in the process, behind the complaints of extortion by officials, and behind the anxiety of communities to have a sheriff of their own choice. It is not surprising to find that prominent officials had large cash resources with which to speculate in various ways; even an obscure royal clerk like Henry of Whiston was able to lend money.[70] The problem for such men was how to invest their gains to ensure the future prosperity of their family – how to found a dynasty. Here the key move was to secure good marriages for themselves and their children. Geoffrey fitz Peter, the justiciar, was the son of a forester who managed to force his way into the aristocracy by marrying a co-heiress who also had a disputable claim to the earldom of Essex. Geoffrey's money and influence ensured that the claims of his wife's uncle and sister were passed over, and Geoffrey emerged as earl of Essex.[71] Once started, a family could be raised by hard work and some ruthlessness, but perpetuating it depended on a large measure of luck.

Beginning in the later years of Henry II's reign, a gradually increasing tendency to specialization among some types of royal servant becomes visible. It was the judges who seem to have specialized first, and during the 1190s they coalesced into a fairly stable group at the core of judicial administration. Despite the fact that many judges continued to perform other administrative tasks as well, by about 1200 it is clear that a professional judiciary had emerged. In the 1220s and 1230s the central court at Westminster was run by judges with few or no other administrative duties; in the same period there was in effect a 'school' of legal studies at Westminster, with specialists who set about refining and extending their subject. While there were always complaints about the rapacity of royal officials, there were hardly any about their level of skill. It also seems to be the judges who first received what looks like an official salary, in the 1220s.[72] This was eventually the way out of a system of government which rewarded its officials chiefly by allowing them to reward themselves, but as a general practice it lay far in the future in the thirteenth century.

The social origin of many of the men who worked in the royal administration lay at the level of feudal sub-tenants. It was these

[70] Turner, *English Judiciary*, 179–80.
[71] Turner, *Men Raised from the Dust*, 55–8, 67–9.
[72] Ibid., 245; Brand, 'Origins'.

people who formed the backbone of both the honorial and the county courts; their experience in the secular law made them good candidates for all sorts of governmental jobs. Their knowledge was practical rather than academic, but they must have had some degree of literacy: it is simply not credible that the chief justiciars could have done the work they did without at least being able to understand the basic Latin used in writs and charters. They need not have been skilled at writing, since there were others to do that. A number of clerics in government posts were called 'Master', which implies proficiency in the learning of the schools, but to what real level is never likely to be known. We cannot assume that all laymen were illiterate or that all clerics were learned.

Clerics as royal administrators had both advantages and disadvantages from the king's point of view. A great advantage was that they could be handsomely rewarded at the church's expense, by being put in as rector of a parish or given some higher preferment – even, for the top flight, a bishopric. Not all the parish churches given were in the king's gift: compliant abbots, bishops or lay patrons could be persuaded to appoint a royal clerk to a benefice. The clerk would then pay a lesser cleric to do the work of the parish while drawing the church's revenue himself. Individuals could assemble formidable totals of church benefices in this way. The disadvantage of clerical servants from the royal viewpoint was that churchmen were subject to pressures other than the king's, deriving from their loyalty to the clerical order and especially to the pope. Under normal circumstances this could be ignored, but in times of crisis it was apt to cause problems. There was a current of moral disapproval of churchmen acting as administrators for princes; the Lateran Council of 1179 forbade clerks to act as lawyers in cases before secular judges, or to accept the office of steward or judge from lay rulers. Other legislation discouraged them from participating in criminal trials which might involve the shedding of blood. They were prohibited from bearing arms. In practice these orders were only obeyed in part; about half the royal judges were clerics, but few sheriffs or stewards were. The greatest crisis came with king John's quarrel with the papacy and his excommunication: it is not surprising to find that his judges were a more lay body than their predecessors.[73]

---

[73] Turner, *English Judiciary*, 149, 291; Cheney, *Hubert Walter*, 5–6; Baldwin, *Masters, Princes and Merchants*, 177–9.

The clerics in royal administration were the sons and brothers of laymen who were often administrators themselves; they were not in any way a caste apart. Working for the king was a way of rising in the social hierarchy; administrative families did not belong to the existing aristocracy, though some married their way into it. This might appear to imply that the king was raising 'new men' to curb the power of the baronage, but in fact evidence for conscious social engineering of this kind is not to be had, and reality was never so schematic. There was work to be done, due to the popularity of the royal courts as well as to the king's increasing need for money, and certain groups in society were best able to supply the workers. Not all aristocrats were denied royal favours; no king could ever afford to be hostile on principle to all the major landowners, and it is unlikely that the idea ever occurred to them. The political fault line at the end of John's reign left some barons and some administrators on each side.

Thus a governmental machine of great power and sophistication had been built, largely the creation of the Angevin kings. They had adjusted the military service dues to create a smaller and more useful force and had experimented with scutage and fines to pay for it. The royal forests and their administration had been considerably extended by Henry II, and the Jews made more profitable to the king. They had experimented with custodians accounting directly for all profits, at first from escheats and wardships but eventually from the demesnes too. They had also experimented with taxation, revising the land tax and introducing revenue taxes and customs. The feudal sources of income – reliefs, fines, and proffers of all kinds – had been made to yield large sums, and the resulting indebtedness was exploited as a threat to control baronial behaviour. The administration of law had been overhauled, many types of dispute being reduced to routine matters and kept under central supervision. The machinery had evolved over the whole period, but there seem to have been three particularly creative periods: the 1170s after the suppression of the revolt of 1173–4; the period of Hubert Walter's justiciarship in the second half of Richard's reign; and the reign of John after the loss of Normandy in 1204. The effect was cumulative: the strain increased with each turn of the screw.

The machine did not work without friction. There survives a chorus of complaint about its oppressiveness, from almost anyone whose opinions have survived. The government's few defenders were royal servants, notably the author of the *Dialogue of the*

Exchequer: even he admitted that the wealth of kings 'proceeds sometimes from their mere arbitrary power', though subjects 'have no right to question or condemn their actions'.[74] The more a subject had to do with the government, the more money he was likely to owe it. Tenants-in-chief, especially the great magnates, who could not avoid encounters with the king at crucial moments of their lives, were both the likeliest victims and the best placed to protest. Though the legal system was led by demand from litigants, the financial apparatus was driven by a king desperate for money to pay for increasingly hopeless wars. Once the machine had been built it ran with a momentum of its own, and politics became largely a struggle for control of it.

[74] Dialogue, 1.

3

The King and the Aristocracy

Relations between the king and the magnates lie at the heart of politics in the medieval period. There were three major crises in this relationship: the rebellion of 1173–4, the wars at the end of John's reign continuing into the minority of Henry III, and the troubles of 1258 leading into the 'barons' wars' which themselves lie outside the scope of this volume. There were also lesser crises in Henry III's reign, but on the whole relations were quiet. It was never a question of general hostility between the king and all the barons: royal and baronial power were not antipathetic. Why then did the crises occur? What did the barons concerned hope to achieve? The answers to these questions are bound up with the nature of baronial power and the changes that had been taking place below the surface of events.

The greatest aristocrats of Angevin England were the earls. There were 25 earldoms held at some time in the century 1150–1250, after Henry had deposed 'certain imaginary pseudo-counts' who had been recognized by Stephen.[1] Five of the 25 – Derby, Devon, Hertford, Norfolk and Oxford – descended in the unbroken male line. A further five continued throughout but were transferred to another lineage via female inheritance: the opportunity which thereby sometimes arose for the king to manipulate the descent of great estates was a significant political factor. The honour of the Warenne earls of Surrey went to Henry II's illegitimate half-brother Hamelin and his descendants, who adopted the name Warenne. The granddaughter of earl Robert of Leicester, the justiciar, took the earldom to the de Montfort family, and her son Simon became the best known in England of all his kin. The earldom of Lincoln came to the Lacy family from the defunct Chester complex, and the earldoms of Aumale (actually

[1] Torigni iv, 183.

a Norman county with English land) and Warwick also passed to new dynasties in this way. In each case the king was able to reward, promote or satisfy his men.

In three instances earldoms continued via the female line, but with a definite hint of sharp practice and political expediency: Isabel, the youngest daughter and co-heiress of the earl of Gloucester, was married to the young John who divorced her as soon as he became king. The earldom passed according to the political needs of the moment to Isabel's and her eldest sister's subsequent husbands before passing finally to the son of Amice, the middle sister: this was Gilbert de Clare, earl of Hertford, who thus combined two earldoms. The earldom of Richmond had always been an appendage of the ducal house of Brittany, thus coming with the duchess Constance to Henry II's son Geoffrey and so to his ill-fated grandson Arthur, before descending via Constance's daughter Alice to Peter Mauclerc, duke of Brittany. The last Mandeville earl of Essex died in 1189, and one of his female relatives was married to the justiciar, Geoffrey fitz Peter, who offered the king 3000 marks for the earldom, which he accepted. Geoffrey was embroiled in lawsuits with other claimants, but his position made him secure and he passed the earldom on to his son, who took the name Mandeville.

Five earldoms died out completely: Cornwall and Salisbury on the deaths of illegitimate sons of Henry I and Henry II, Northampton on the death of Simon de St Liz III in 1184, and Huntingdon, which had descended to David, the younger brother of kings Malcolm IV and William I of Scots, on the death of David's son John in 1237. King Stephen's son William count of Boulogne was an immensely wealthy English landowner, with the honours of Boulogne and Warenne and other lands stipulated in the treaty between Stephen and Henry II, and it was Henry's good fortune that William died heirless in 1159. The earldom of Chester was probably the greatest in the land, its vigorous earls having strengthened their powers over Cheshire, excluding the royal administration, and extending the tentacles of their influence across the Midlands to Lincoln and down to Coventry. It was therefore a political event of the first importance when Earl Rannulf died childless in 1232; his estates were divided between his four sisters and the earldom passed to his nephew John 'the Scot' who himself died five years later.

Two earldoms, Arundel and Pembroke, were divided between co-heiresses and their husbands or sons. The posterity of the great William Marshal, earl of Pembroke, was singularly unfortunate: his five sons succeeded each other in turn, all dying childless, and the estates were divided between the lines of his five daughters. Three earldoms were created, two of them by king John. Hereford was re-created for Henry de Bohun, great-grandson of Miles of Gloucester who held it in Stephen's reign, and Winchester for Saer de Quincy. Hubert de Burgh, the justiciar, was created earl of Kent in 1227 but he failed to found a dynasty.

So of 25 earldoms five continued in the male line, eight were transferred through female inheritance to a new dynasty, two were divided between heiresses, seven died out and three new ones were created. At the highest level this was a very fluid society, with a continuous turnover of the leading families. Of the great earls of the mid-thirteenth century only the Clares of Gloucester and Hertford descended directly from ancestors important in Normandy before 1066. But this did not prevent the aristocracy from holding a strong sense of dynasty, expressed for example in the growing cult of heraldry and the adoption of the mother's surname where that was of higher lineage.

Below the earls there stretched a spectrum of landowners, to the greatest of whom the term 'baron' was coming to be applied. This word had a variety of contemporary meanings, but was increasingly restricted to the greater tenants in chief who were not earls. This was the sense used in Magna Carta, which fixed the relief due to the king from the successor to a barony at £100, the same as for an earldom. Barons such as the Mowbrays of Thirsk and Kirkby Malzeard in Yorkshire, Burton-in-Lonsdale in Lancashire, Axholm in Lincolnshire and Melton Mowbray in Leicestershire were not inferior to an earl. Important barons were to be found all over England, from the Cardinans of Restormel in Cornwall to the de Vescis of Alnwick in Northumberland. Their castles were as strong as any earl's, and their estates were often scattered as widely: Eustace de Vesci was also lord of Malton in Yorkshire and Sprouston in Roxburghshire, Scotland.[2]

Aristocratic incomes were derived from a variety of sources, and though the proportion supplied by each would vary from one estate to another, the sources were much the same. The lands of the Lacy family, constables of Chester, outside Cheshire, when in royal custody in 1211–12 were worth a total of £1258.[3]

[2] Holt, *Northerners*, 19–21, 23 n3.
[3] PR 14 John, 3; cf. Miller and Hatcher, *Medieval England*, 179–80.

Of this the largest item was rent (£408). A tallage yielded the
large sum of £336, no doubt severe because the king took the
opportunity to soak the tenants. Sale of produce was also higher
than it would otherwise have been (£248) because when there
was a resident lord his household would probably take provisions. Courts and related sources produced £187 and the mills
yielded £79. Earls were entitled to the 'third penny' of court
profits in their shire: in fact they were paid a regular annual
sum which was never very large, for instance the earls of Essex
received £40 10s 10d annually under Henry II.[4] Some fortunate
lords also owned towns – Leicester belonged to its earl – and
fairs, of which the most important were Winchester, which
belonged to its bishop, and Boston in which the earl of Richmond had a large share. Under the impact of inflation in the
decades around 1200 most great landowners changed from letting
out their manors to direct farming, which put up their profits,
but rents continued to be important.[5] Barons were sometimes
keen businessmen, founding towns and markets and furthering
industry and trade. A number of local lords had an interest in the
iron works of Cleveland, and Eustace de Vesci tried to develop
Alnmouth as a port.[6]

Attempts to arrive at a league table of the greatest lords are
fraught with difficulties. The number of tenants owing military
service does not necessarily represent the extent of the lord's
power. All sources of monetary income were liable to fluctuate
from year to year; a lord could raise a lot of money quickly by
selling stock or felling timber to an extent that impoverished him
or his successors for the future, and what the king's custodians
extracted from an estate in custody, for which accounts are
more likely to survive, might be more than the owner would
ordinarily derive from it. Inflation and managerial changes make
comparisons over time invalid. Nevertheless, we have a good
deal of financial information, and it can be illuminating if used
cautiously.

In Henry II's reign few lords had an income of £500. A number
of honours were in royal hands in 1184–5 and appear on the
pipe roll for that year.[7] The earldom of Gloucester lands were
worth £590, Arundel £390, Cornwall £210. The escheated honours of Eye (£340) and Rayleigh (£250) were worth more than

[4] E.g. PR 21 Henry II, 71.
[5] See below, pp. 168–9.
[6] Holt, *Northerners*, 33.
[7] PR 31 Henry II, brought together in Stringer, *Earl David*, 111.

some earldoms. An indication of the value of such sums is given by the king's expenditure in building a major new castle, at Orford, which cost him £660 in the first year, averaging about £175 a year over eight years.[8] Figures would tend to be higher in John's reign because of inflation. William de Stuteville, the lord of Knaresborough in Yorkshire, drew some £500 at his death in 1203. By the mid-thirteenth century sums were very much higher. The honour of Richmond was now worth between £1500 and £1700. The Marshal estates in 1245 produced an income of £3350, over half from the Irish lands. The bishop of Winchester, one of the wealthiest lords in England if not in Europe, received £6100 in 1258, a year of exceptionally high prices for agricultural produce: in a less-favourable year the income could go down to below £4000.[9]

Some lords, including many religious institutions, held private hundreds. They differed from those managed by the sheriff mainly in the destination of the profits. The king's law applied to both. Even one of the greatest of these private 'franchises', that of the abbey of Bury St Edmunds which extended over all of west Suffolk, had points of contact with outside jurisdiction. In the town of Bury the abbot was the ruler. In the eight-and-a-half hundreds the abbot collected the royal dues and kept them. He or his official held the hundred courts and a kind of shire court for the tenants of other lords as well as his own. But the royal justices came to hear pleas of the crown, the hundreds sent representatives to the shire court, and some of the proceeds had to be divided with the sheriff.[10] The earl of Chester in Cheshire and the bishop of Durham in his county were the largest franchise-holders in the land, and their privileges grew in scope and precision as the royal administration developed more routines for them to be free from. The earl of Chester's justice presided over the county court, writs of assize were issued by the earl's chancery; the earl even issued his own version of Magna Carta to his men.

Landed power often did not correspond to position in the tenurial hierarchy. The top layer in the hierarchy, the tenants-in-chief who held directly of the king, were anything but equals – they ranged from the mightiest of earls to quite insignificant holders of one manor or less. The greatest earls had beneath

---

[8] Brown, Colvin and Taylor, *History of the King's Works* ii, 769–71.
[9] Painter, *Studies*, 174; Miller and Hatcher, *Medieval England*, 179–80, 201.
[10] Warren, *Governance*, 49–50.

them important sub-tenants holding wide lands who were better endowed than many a tenant-in-chief. Men had held of more than one lord since the time of the Norman conquest, and before long important barons might come to hold some land of other, even lesser, barons. Wealth, landed influence and military power did not correspond to the feudal hierarchy, and had never done so.

The estates of aristocratic families were not static. Great estates had been confiscated after rebellions, some had been kept in hand by the king and others granted out again, not always unchanged. Families had died out, and division among co-heiresses, or rather between their husbands and descendants, had brought further changes. Those high in royal favour had obtained more land from the king. But the number of really significant lords was always fairly small – probably never more than 200 at any one time.

The knights were not a society of equals, either. From the start there had been wide variations in the quantity of land given to the sub-tenants, not corresponding with the knight service demanded of them. Land was held and military service owed for it, but that is not to say that the land was given to secure military service alone. It was not necessarily those knights best able to fight who were given land: being granted a fee might be a form of pensioning off, while the younger and fitter knights were kept in the lord's household and given rewards other than land; there were other ways of rewarding knights than endowing them with land. The lords did not recruit their following only from their tenants, but as far as we can tell from a variety of sources including some tenants and younger sons, neighbours and distant relatives. There was a gradual evolution from an earlier world in which a lord appears surrounded by his tenants, and his household officers hold land of him, though not always much land, to the thirteenth-century magnate household which appears much more professionalized with little overlap with tenant families on the estate. But this evolution was gradual, and ties between tenants and lords long remained strong: most knightly tenants appear to have followed their lords in the war of 1215, or at least their main lord, though ties of neighbourhood were important as well.[11] It would be a foolish knight who acted differently from his neighbours in such circumstances, and the lead was given by the dominant local lord.

---

[11] Holt, *Northerners*, 35–7.

English honours were geographically fragmented, largely as a result of the way land had been distributed by the Conqueror to his followers after 1066. The earls of Surrey, for instance, actually held little land in Surrey, their chief centres being Lewes in Sussex, Castle Acre in Norfolk and Conisbrough in Yorkshire, while the Clares added Glamorgan and lands in Gloucestershire and right across the south of England to their original holdings round Tonbridge (Kent) and Clare (Suffolk). Many important English barons also held in Normandy. The earls of Chester and Leicester were among the greatest lords of Normandy; the Braose and Mowbray barons still held their places of origin at Briouze and Montbrai and a number of other families did likewise. Baronial interests also spread into Wales, Ireland and Scotland. Their horizons were wide; just after he had been given Meath in Ireland, Hugh de Lacy was serving Henry II in Normandy where he acquired the honour of Le Pin from its owner. His tenants' estates also took no notice of borders.[12]

This fragmentation had important consequences. It meant that very few magnates were able to dominate an area to the exclusion of all other powers. Except in Cheshire and Durham the king and his sheriff were ever-present. This facilitated the development of nationwide systems of government and law rather than, say, the provincial customs and parliaments that developed in France. Aristocratic independence from royal government was not even an aspiration in England: politics therefore evolved not as a struggle to exclude the machinery of government, but to control it and modify its functioning. The scattered nature of the honour was accompanied by a confusion in the tenurial hierarchy, in which great magnates might hold of much lesser men. There was thus no prospect of a horizontal stratum of noblesse developing with higher legal privileges: there was no legal grade higher than freeman.

The heart of the honour was its court. Despite its importance this institution remains obscure to us: no court records as such have survived until a later period when its character had changed, and all we have with which to reconstruct its activities are the lords' charters which we can only assume to be connected with it. They show the court attended by a nucleus of household officers, of whom the steward is the commonest – by the thirteenth century the steward regularly held the court himself. But attendance was not limited to knights or tenants by military

[12] Robin Frame in Davies, *British Isles*, 143; see below, pp. 140–1, 144, 146–7.

service: the court was far more broadly based, attended by tenants of every status down to freemen smallholders. It must have been more like a public meeting than a modern law court, and the better attended it was, the better it expressed the grandeur of its lord. The law it enforced was not enacted or written but customary, emerging from the collective memory of the tenants even though it might be affected by the example of the king's court. Its primary business was to regulate the transfer of property at the two principal moments when it passed from hand to hand: inheritance and marriage. But there was also other business arising from tenure, such as military service, scutage and wardship. Lords with powers of various kinds did not hold several kinds of court but did all the business in the one court, which might combine 'franchisal' with 'feudal' business. There was no real distinction between law and government: the honour court enabled the lord to control his fee. For this he needed the assent of the tenants, who remembered the custom and witnessed the transactions. A large and scattered estate, like that of the Mowbrays, would have several courts arranged geographically for greater convenience, and would thus seem more like a series of different honours.[13]

In the later twelfth century a number of factors were working to undermine the coherence of the honour, and eventually they wrought great changes in the relations between the magnates and their tenants, in turn affecting the nature of aristocratic power and furthering the emergence of a class of virtually independent small landowners. First, there were always relations between the tenants and outside powers, especially the king. At least since the Salisbury Oath of 1087 there had been a feeling that a man's first duty was to the king, and under the Angevins the growth of jury work and governmental activities of all kinds had brought many lesser tenants into direct contact with royal power, opportunities in royal service opening up for those able to seize them. Many tenants, especially but not only the more important, held of several lords. It is clear that many honours had never been self-contained societies. Then many an honour had seen changes of lineage at the top. When that happened the sitting tenants would owe nothing to the new lord; several such changes would produce layers of tenant families introduced by successive lords. Even in honours with stable families of lords the inheritance of land by tenants would inevitably increase their

[13] Greenway, *Charters of the Honour of Mowbray*, lvi.

distance from the lord, slowly replacing personal bonds by tenurial ones. The sheer geographical fragmentation of many honours added to the difficulties of control.

As well as these structural weaknesses in the coherence of the honour, specific legal developments occurred which worked in the same direction.[14] Eleventh- and early twelfth-century sources reveal a world in which the lord had wide powers to rearrange tenancies and choose his tenants, though to some extent circumscribed by custom and not entirely without royal intervention. Land passed because the lord passed it; the lord's recognition was both necessary and sufficient for succession to land. Nevertheless, there was a strong presumption of inheritance. It was usually clear who was the heir.[15] It was normally the custom to accept a tenant's heir on his death. This was convenient for the lords as it provided for a known successor with a minimum of disruption, and it is likely that the tenants expected it as well. But the course of the history of lordships seldom ran smooth. With the cumulative effect of the actions of lords, forfeitures and expropriations by the kings, and especially the civil wars of Stephen's reign, two tenants had sometimes been accepted for one holding, whether by two different lords or by the same lord at different times. It was to sort out rival claims to land that the writ of right and the assizes were developed in Henry II's reign. But these legal processes meant in practice that a tenant the lord had recognized could be put out by judgment of a royal court. The effect was to undermine the conclusiveness of the lord's decision. Even if the intention of the legal changes was to make the lords' courts work more effectively and abide by their own rules, the result was to strip them of their power of final decision. The effect on inheritance was also drastic: criteria for the lord's choice of tenant were transformed into an abstract right of inheritance, a hereditary claim enforceable by a royal court. The end result of these developments was to turn a personal relationship between lord and man into a tenurial relationship between landlord and tenant. The powers which once enabled the lord to control his fee became a mere right to hold a court, perhaps a profitable item of property. Tenants obtained royal protection for their seisin, slipped out of their lord's control and rooted themselves in their lands.

[14] Milsom, *Legal Framework*; Brand, 'The origins of English land law: Milsom and after', in *The Making of the Common Law*, 203–25.
[15] Holt, *Feudal Society and the Family*, ii, 193–220.

The problems that might beset a small and incautiously managed barony are illustrated by the Kentwell fee in East Anglia.[16] In 1166 Roger of Kentwell owed the king the service of ten knights; five had been enfeoffed on his lands. By 1231 the Kentwells had enfeoffed a further five knights, as well as giving some land to the Hospitallers, and had run up a considerable debt to the crown in unpaid scutage. William of Kentwell, the lord, was unable to collect the service owed by seven of the tenants – in fact, he did not even know who some of them were. How this could happen is shown by a court case in 1214: one of the fees was held by William of Wicheton of William of Hastings who held it of Aubrey de Vere, earl of Oxford, who held it of Gilbert of Kentwell.[17] An inquest in 1242 listed only the three fees he could still trace – the other seven had effectively escaped from the barony. When William of Kentwell died in 1244 the only demesne land he held was two carucates in the manor of Kentwell: his heirs sold the manor to the king for £50. This small barony disintegrated between 1166 and 1244, largely as a result of granting out land to tenants by knight service, failing to keep track of property transactions and leaving insufficient demesne. The future of a landholding family lay with the demesne. A lord's power came to depend not on his loyal tenants, but on the financial resources of his demesne manors. Nevertheless, the honour was long in dying; these changes worked quite slowly, and at no time in the twelfth century was the honour a decayed or anachronistic institution.

The rebellion of 1173–4

The first major crisis was the rebellion of 1173–4.[18] The initial centre of the revolt was Normandy; the local magnates who rebelled there were joined by the leading English rebels, some of whom held Norman lands. In the summer of 1173 invasions of the duchy aimed towards Rouen were mounted from the south by king Louis of France and the young Henry, and from the north east by count Philip of Flanders and his brother and heir Matthew of Boulogne. A summer of fast movements aided by luck resulted in brilliant success for the elder king: Matthew of

---

[16] Painter, *Studies*, 181–2.
[17] CRR vii, 184.
[18] Warren, *Henry II*, 117–36; Gesta i, 41–79; Howden ii, 41–69; Gervase i, 242–50; Newburgh i, 169–98; Torigni, 255–65; Diceto i, 353–87.

MAP 3.1   Places involved in the wars of 1173–4 and 1215–17

Boulogne was killed in the fighting and Philip called off the invasion. King Louis and young Henry were expelled from the duchy with apparent ease, whereupon Henry trapped the leading Breton rebels in the castle of Dol, which surrendered at the end of August. The elder Henry's victory was convincing enough for talks to be started with Louis and the rebels, but they foundered on the elder Henry's unwillingness to give up his powers of government and justice.

Robert earl of Leicester, the young son of the great justiciar, was among the irreconcilables: at the negotiations he had even drawn his sword and threatened Henry. When the meeting broke up he hurried to Flanders, collected a band of mercenaries and invaded England, landing in Suffolk and joining up with another prominent rebel, Hugh Bigod, earl of Norfolk. The centre of rebellion in England was the Midlands, where the earls of Chester, Derby and Huntingdon were in revolt as well as Leicester: the town of Leicester had been taken by royal forces in July 1173 but the earl's men still held out in the castle (see map 3.1). The king of Scots had been raiding as far south as Yorkshire, but a royal army under the justiciar, Richard de Lucy, and the constable, Humphrey de Bohun, had driven the Scots back across the border. On hearing of Leicester's landing at the end of September the royal leaders made a truce and hurried southwards. Earl Robert meanwhile had begun to move to the relief of Leicester, but royal forces under the constable and the earls of Cornwall, Gloucester and Arundel intercepted him. In a battle at Fornham St Genevieve near Bury St Edmunds his mercenaries were routed and the earl himself captured along with his wife who had accompanied him throughout. The whole invasion was over 'in the wink of an eye'.[19] The victory in England was not followed up. A truce was made with Hugh Bigod and that with the Scottish king prolonged until the following spring.

When fighting resumed in 1174 it was more general than in the previous year, with the royalists besieging rebel castles at Tutbury, Axholme and Huntingdon, and the rebels attacking Nottingham and Norwich. King William of Scots invaded, capturing castles this time and blockading Carlisle. It was in the north that the decisive blow was struck. A royalist force from Yorkshire under the sheriff, Robert de Stuteville, marched to the relief of Alnwick castle which king William was besieging. Arriving under cover of mist, they found most of the Scottish army dispersed on foraging and plundering expeditions, and the king near the castle accompanied only by a small force of knights. The English seized their chance: after a brief, desperate fight the Scots were either killed or captured. Among the captives was king William. News of the unexpected triumph came to Henry at Canterbury where he had just done public penance for his part in the death of Becket. Of course, it seemed like a benediction by St Thomas, and the chroniclers made much of the king's dramatic reconciliation with the dead saint. The cult of St Thomas could no longer be seen as hostile to the king.[20] The rebellion in England collapsed in barely a fortnight, and Henry returned to the continent.

[19] Gesta i, 62.
[20] E.g., Battle Chronicle, 274–7.

Normandy in 1174 had been largely quiet, and Henry had spent the spring and early summer before his crossing to England suppressing rebels in the south and west of his continental domains. It was a threatened invasion of England by the young king and the count of Flanders that had taken him to Canterbury in July. The end of the rebellion in England now compelled the young Henry, count Philip and king Louis to stake everything on a last attempt to take Rouen. They began to invest the city, but Henry arrived on 11 August and quickly broke up the siege. He then turned south to deal with Richard, who was fighting Henry's supporters in Poitou. Before the end of September Richard had surrendered and been forgiven.

Ralph Diceto, dean of St Paul's, had no doubt about what impelled some of the baronage to cast in their lot with young Henry: discontent at the elder Henry's government. He had disinherited them for just and reasonable causes, he had trampled on the necks of the proud and exalted, he had overthrown or brought into his own power castles suspected of hostility, he had punished traitors with exile and fined oppressors of the poor.[21] And indeed the revolt came within a few years of the Assize of Clarendon, the inquiries into the behaviour of baronial officers associated with the Inquest of Sheriffs, and the arguments about knight service which arose from the *Cartae Baronum.*[22]

Nevertheless, these alleged general causes did not deter the earls of Essex, Arundel, Gloucester and Cornwall, and many lesser barons, from being active on the elder king's side. Henry II needed baronial support – as did any medieval king – and had not been pursuing an anti-baronial policy. It is not difficult to find possible grievances for most of the major rebels, some of which could be construed as disherison. The Mowbray family had a long-standing conflict with the Stutevilles, who were the original possessors of the Mowbray lands but who had been expelled from them by Henry I; the Stutevilles had not given up their claims and under Stephen had been reinstated in some of the lands. The Stuteville brothers, Robert and Roger, were among Henry II's leading lieutenants in the north, and Mowbray accordingly was to be found in opposition. Hugh Bigod of Norfolk, a veteran of Stephen's reign, had unsatisfied claims: Henry II had never trusted him, had confiscated his castles and

---

[21] Diceto i, 371.
[22] Warren, *Henry II*, 124; Keefe, *Feudal Assessments*, 116–41.

charged him £1000 to have them back in 1165. Earl Hugh of Chester had come of age in 1168 but had not been given some of the lands which his father earl Rannulf had held: in the 1150s Henry II had had to treat earl Rannulf very carefully, and had made him generous promises which had not been fulfilled, adding to the sense of dynastic grievance. The hostility of the king of Scots, based on a claim to the border counties, was of long standing and sufficiently accounts for the rebellion of his younger brother David, earl of Huntingdon. Old rivalries and specific discontents thus account for many of the participants, though not obviously for earl Robert of Leicester's actions: he seems to have had a particular personal dislike of Henry II. This takes us into a world of personal relations which will always remain closed to us. Except for Mowbray and Bigod, the leading rebels were all young men, who may have sympathized with or been charmed by the young king, or have looked to the future and sided with the heir apparent. It is quite possible, as a contemporary suggests, that many more wavered than actually joined the revolt;[23] but if they did not stand up to be counted in the rebellion we need not count them either.

The war of 1215–17

The disasters which engulfed king John at the end of his reign began in earnest in 1212. From this year on, all his troubles seemed to come together. He had kept up his quarrel with the pope over the appointment of Stephen Langton as archbishop of Canterbury for seven years, he had been personally excommunicated and England had been laid under an interdict.[24] He had never resigned himself to the loss of most of his French lands, conquered by Philip Augustus in 1202–4, and in the summer of 1212 he was once again planning a great French expedition. The need to raise huge sums to finance reconquest led him deeper into extortion and blackmail, incurring the growing hostility of his subjects. In 1212 he launched a forest eyre and an inquest into lands held by knight service, the one proceeding to raise a fortune, the other threatening to do so if and when its purpose was revealed. But the expedition did not sail, a Welsh rising in the summer causing the muster for Poitou to be transferred to

---

[23] Newburgh i, 181.
[24] See below, pp. 120–2.

Chester to cope with this new emergency. In the event the army did not invade Wales either, for a plot was uncovered to murder the king or abandon him to the Welsh who would do the conspirators' job for them. John was obviously shaken: he ordered the army to disperse and brought in mercenaries, he took hostages from suspects, and he strengthened the northern royal castles. Two barons, Robert fitz Walter and Eustace de Vesci, fled the country; but they were not so much the leaders, more the ones who were found out. And John tried to reduce the number of his enemies by opening negotiations with the pope.

A French invasion loomed all through the winter and the spring of 1213. John was busy organizing resistance, wooing some of his subjects by relaxing some of his demands and granting calculated concessions, while simultaneously negotiating with the pope. In May 1213 John's army, comprising an unusual number of English barons, was assembled in Kent ready to repel the expected invasion, when the destruction of the French fleet in the harbour at Damme relieved the immediate pressure from that direction. The army nevertheless witnessed the king's humiliating surrender of the kingdom to the pope, and the promises of reform and good government which accompanied his absolution. When John attempted to follow up the naval victory with a campaign on the continent, a group of recalcitrant barons denied that the terms of their tenure obliged them to serve abroad. John was again forced to abandon the expedition, but set about isolating his main opponents, who soon came to be referred to as the 'northerners' as most of their estates were in Yorkshire and the border counties.

The long-awaited French campaign finally took place in 1214. Most of the English baronage co-operated with it, but a hard core of northerners still refused and the king left a discontented country behind him when he sailed. Especially unpopular was the scutage, taken at 3 marks to the knight's fee, the heaviest ever levied, intended to finance the enterprise. The situation deteriorated even further when the campaign turned out to be a complete and humiliating failure. John fled from western France while his German and Flemish allies were dealt a defeat of historic proportions at Bouvines in July 1214. The scutage fell due at the end of September, and many refused to pay. John returned in mid-October and was confronted with demands for reform based on Henry I's coronation charter. His opponents were an increasingly organized body bound together by oath, and had progressed from crude regicide to a more political, even

constitutional approach. From autumn 1214 until the spring of
1215 John and his opponents negotiated and wrangled, while
John hired mercenaries and fortified castles. Some of the barons
mustered in arms at Stamford in Easter week 1215 and went to
Northampton for a meeting with John, who did not arrive. At
one point the negotiations must have looked like being successful, as John sent home some Poitevin soldiers he had summoned.
From this period dates the so-called 'unknown' charter of liberties, an expanded version of Henry I's charter which represents
a stage in the negotiations. But it came to nothing, and on 5 May
a group of rebel barons meeting at Brackley, between Oxford
and Northampton, renounced their homage to John, in effect
declaring war. On 12 May John ordered their estates to be
seized.[25]

Though the initial moves of the baronial army were unim-
pressive, failing to take Northampton and moving on to Bedford, they pulled off a great coup when some of their partisans
let them into London on 17 May. Possession of the most important city in the kingdom greatly strengthened their hand and
encouraged others to join them. Negotiations continued, coming
to a head on and after 10 June, when John met the rebels at
Runnymede on the Thames near Staines. Terms were gradually
hammered out, the 'articles of the barons', a sealed draft agreement of uncertain date, being superseded by Magna Carta itself,
which was dated 15 June but not issued until the 19th. John did
not of course 'sign' Magna Carta, but neither did he seal it – that
job belonged to a functionary; it became law when he and his
opponents swore to observe it. The rebels now renewed their
oaths of allegiance.

John was certainly not acting in good faith, and very soon set
about obtaining papal condemnation of the agreement so that he
could ignore it with every appearance of righteousness. On the
rebel side some never accepted the terms, holding out for something more radical, and John was soon able to accuse his opponents – they had never ceased to be that – of not keeping their side
of the bargain. Some of John's men would no longer obey him,
some barons refused to surrender London. Each side waited for
the other to carry out its part of the ageement, and neither did.
Soon papal fulminations began to arrive: the pope quashed
Magna Carta and suspended archbishop Langton, whose attempts at mediation looked suspiciously like sympathy with the

[25] Holt, *Magna Carta*, 232–5.

rebels. Genuine negotiations with John had proved impossible: the more-determined rebel barons now had no alternative to electing a new king. Some time in the autumn they offered the crown to Louis, son of Philip Augustus of France.

The country slid inexorably into civil war. Rochester castle was handed over to the London rebels, and John moved up to besiege it. The castle fell on 30 November, and John immediately set out on a long march north which took him up to the Scottish border by January. Perhaps if he had captured London at this point he would have won the war at a stroke, but John always seemed to prefer the indirect, devious approach. He had good reasons for going to the north: it was alive with rebels who were backed by Alexander II of Scotland, he had had little contact with his lieutenants there, and a landslide of the as yet uncommitted into the rebel camp was imminent. Though he took many castles others were left untaken, the rebels retreated before him and reappeared when he left. By March 1216 John was in East Anglia, the other main centre of the rebellion, and in April he moved down to Kent to await another expected invasion under prince Louis. His six-month campaign had been indecisive.

In May John's fleet was scattered in a gale, and Louis landed. This was just the lift the rebels needed, and caused a rush to join them. Louis was recognized as king, and the rebel barons and the king of Scots did homage to him. John retreated before his advancing forces, first to Winchester, then to Worcester as Louis took over the south. In September John crossed the Midlands to relieve Lincoln, and in early October he was struck down by dysentery at Lynn. Moving back westwards, he lost his baggage train somewhere in the Fens between Wisbech and Swineshead. He arrived exhausted at Newark, where on 18 October 1216 he died.

On 28 October John's nine year-old son Henry was crowned at Gloucester by the bishop of Winchester, under the direction of the papal legate.[26] William Marshal, earl of Pembroke, accepted the regency of the kingdom, which meant the leadership of Henry's party. Among his first acts was to reissue a modified version of Magna Carta, which thus made the transition from a standard of revolt to a royal guarantee of rights. Despite disagreements in Louis's camp between his French and English supporters, and the Marshal's efforts to win over waverers, it was not until the spring of 1217 that there were serious defections

[26] Carpenter, *Minority*, 13–49.

back to Henry's side, and then mainly because of a great victory won by the Marshal and his allies at Lincoln. Some of Louis's supporters were besieging the castle, held by its castellan Nicola de la Haye, when William Marshal and the main royalist force appeared and defeated them in a battle in the streets of the city. Louis meanwhile was finding it impossible to capture Dover castle, where a garrison held out under Hubert de Burgh. In August 1217 the resurgent royalist forces defeated a fleet carrying French reinforcements in a battle off Sandwich, some English ships getting to windward of the French and blinding them with clouds of pulverized lime. Louis cut his losses, and by a treaty agreed in September 1217 he was given easy terms. His supporters were to retain their lands, prisoners were to be released, and in addition he received a payment of 10,000 marks for damages against a vague promise to try to persuade his father to return the lost French provinces or else to do so himself when he became king. The Marshal had retained his Norman lands throughout John's reign, holding them of Philip of France; he was later blamed for allowing Louis such generous terms. Once peace was agreed, the regent's government set about securing it with a reissue of Magna Carta and an entirely new charter, the Charter of the Forest.

There seems little doubt about the nature and substance of baronial grievances. Financial pressure had risen inexorably throughout John's reign, pumped up by inflation and the desire to reconquer Normandy. The incidence of taxation increased, sheriffs faced a surcharge on their farms, and the king exploited his rights to charge fines and reliefs from tenants-in-chief. Alongside these went judicial amercements and fines to regain the king's goodwill. An extreme example is the fine of 10,000 marks demanded of Nicholas de Stuteville for succession to his lands, from which he never recovered. He had to surrender Knaresborough and Boroughbridge to John as a guarantee of payment. He had to lease and sell his estates, and borrow from Jewish moneylenders.[27] William de Mowbray attempted to regain lost lands by offering John 2000 marks for a judgment; when the decision leant in his opponent's favour, Mowbray still owed the money. Other barons were led on by a taste for speculation. 'It was a rebellion of the king's debtors.'[28] When a baron offered the king a large sum he was seldom able to pay at once: he had to

---

[27] Holt, *Northerners*, 27, 173.
[28] Ibid., 34.

call on friends and allies to pledge security for eventual payment. In this way each large debt came to involve or threaten a wider group of lords than just the debtor's family. Since John had lost most of the French provinces in 1204 the pressure had increased. The 'safety valves' which worked before, such as the sale of office, land and privilege on easy terms, had been blocked: there was a new stringency in royal debt collection from 1207 onwards.[29] The financial methods John used to enforce political subordination produced a widespread sense of grievance. It was not that John had broken the law, rather that he had failed to be a good lord. He had treated so many barons so badly that individual discontent was converted into widespread revolt.

The most drastic maltreatment was meted out to William de Braose and his family. An important baron of Sussex and the Welsh border and a former intimate of John, William fell behind with instalments of some large proffers he had made for lands in Ireland and castles in the Marches. In 1209 he was compelled by a royal show of force to surrender his castles, pledge his lands and give hostages for repayment. He was unique in attempting to resist this treatment by force, starting a war against the king in which he had sympathizers but no allies. Possibly he was the guardian of guilty secrets about the fate of John's nephew Arthur, and John was determined to destroy him. John certainly pursued him through Ireland; his wife and young son were said to have been starved to death in Windsor castle.[30] The fate of the Braoses was an awful warning but occasioned no widespread conflict. John's increasing intrusion into the north, on the other hand, his installation of outsiders in key posts and failure to smooth the feathers thus ruffled all produced one of the main groups of rebels, the discontented 'northerners'.

Discontent was based on personal experiences, but underneath it lay widely held assumptions about collective rights and a feeling that these had been infringed. Discontent crystallized into specific proposals for reform, and the process of negotiating on them with the king and his advisers can be followed through the series of documents which represent each stage: the 'unknown charter', the articles of the barons, and the Magna Carta of 1215. After John's death the charter was taken over by his erstwhile supporters, and the reissues of 1216 and 1217 show by omissions and alterations what they found distasteful or

---

[29] Ibid., 147–74.
[30] Ibid., 184–6; Painter, *Reign of John*, 242–50.

impracticable in the document of 1215. The charter received the final form in which it remained law for centuries, as do a few parts today, at the reissue of 1225.

The barons' response to the intolerable burdens of John's government was to appeal to custom, envisaged as routine procedure. They sought a predictable basis for relations with the king, and in doing so they selected precedents to suit themselves. The king also appealed to custom; but was custom what the king's predecessors had done, or what they ought to have done? Custom was variable and partly a product of royal will; there was no firm historical datum line when practice had been specific and regular. Writing down selected routine procedures, enshrining them in 'the first English statute',[31] transformed them into rights which could then be pressed against future kings. In seeking the king's agreement to their propositions the rebels had to compel him to limit his powers voluntarily. This contradictory aim was unobtainable from an adult king: it was only the minority of Henry III that established the charters.

The charter brought regularity into the king's tenurial relations with his tenants-in-chief. It fixed the relief for earldoms and baronies at £100, where John had charged varying but large sums. Minors were no longer to pay reliefs; the crown's rights of wardship were limited (cl. 37) and the rights of widows better defined (cls 7–8). The heart of baronial grievance was that while their own tenants had access to predictable legal routine in the form of the petty assizes and the writ of right, the magnates were immediately subject to the arbitrary will of the king.[32] The law provided routine and thus acceptable ways of settling disputes, but those between magnates about land were used by John to raise huge sums of money and exert discipline of an overtly political nature. Clause 61 of the charter of 1215 had set up an elected commission of 25 barons to enforce its terms, and this group settled a large number of outstanding disputes very quickly, using routine processes with the king's will not intervening. This drastic clause, setting up a committee to supervise the king, was dropped from the reissues, but in Henry III's minority the justices continued in the same way, and by his majority in 1227 these procedures were entrenched. Even a case concerning the succession to an earldom could now be heard in court without automatic reference to the king.[33]

[31] Holt, *Magna Carta*, 15.
[32] Ibid., 123–87.
[33] Ibid., 172.

The judicial provisions on the whole perpetuated the existing system, largely Henry II's, and laid down general principles: justice was not to be sold, delayed or denied (cl. 40), and the king promised that 'no free man shall be taken or imprisoned or disseised or outlawed or exiled or in any way ruined . . . except by the lawful judgement of his peers or by the law of the land' (cl. 39). This famous clause was less specific than it seems, leaving open the form of judgment – John was quite capable of persecuting individuals using legal forms – and begged the question of what constituted the law of the land, but it stated a vague generality flexible enough to be reinterpretable in many future situations. It is a particular feature of Magna Carta that it shows concern not just for the magnates but for the whole class of 'free men', and even specifies that the liberties granted to tenants-in-chief should be granted by them to their own men (cl. 60). While some clauses applied to specific groups, such as the Londoners, or holders by certain tenures, others could only be held by the kingdom as a whole. It thus presupposed the existence of the realm as a corporate body.

At the 1217 reissue the royal forest was the subject of a separate Charter of the Forest, which became the fundamental forest law for the rest of the century. As elsewhere, the barons did not wish to abolish the king's rights, but to moderate the exercise of them. The charter sought to take out of the royal forests whatever lands Henry II had included in them, and provided amongst other things that no man should lose life or limb for taking deer but only be fined, and that free men could arrange the exploitation of their own woods as long as their neighbours' rights were not damaged.[34] Conflict soon arose over whether the charter meant returning to the boundaries of 1154 or 1135, Henry's recovery of king Stephen's losses not counting as Henry's additions. Boundary surveys, called 'perambulations', were made in 1219 and again in 1225: arguments continued as juries contradicted each other and the legal status of changes to royal rights during the king's minority was called in question. In 1227 Henry III declared himself of age. The boundary question was reopened for some forests, and many found it prudent to secure individual charters granting disafforestation of their lands.[35]

In other areas the charters were less successful. For example, it was the clauses on the restitution of unjust disseisins (cls 52,

[34] Carpenter, *Minority*, 61–3, 89–92.
[35] Young, *Royal Forests*, 71–2.

55–6, 59) which more than anything reopened the war in 1215. Then clause 16, that no one should be distrained to do more service from a tenement than was owed for it, was obviously vague. Military service, especially on the continent, had been a major issue, and it was not resolved in the barons' favour: Henry III and Edward I continued to require and receive service in Gascony. The definition of the three occasions on which aids could be taken (cl. 12) was dropped in 1217, as was the quite unprecedented requirement that scutage could only be taken with consent. The 1215 charter was itself in some ways a watered-down version of baronial demands as represented by the 'unknown charter', which for example sought to limit overseas service to Normandy and Brittany, to disafforest areas brought within the forest since 1154, and place close restrictions on scutage (cls 7–9). There was a general tendency towards dilution of the original demands, yet clause 12 of 1215 had its effect in the long run: the taxes on moveables counted as aids, so the effect was 'to transfer these matters to debate in great councils'.[36] The composition of such councils was addressed in clause 14: greater barons were to be summoned individually, other tenants-in-chief through the sheriffs; and 'the business shall go forward on the day arranged . . . even if not all those summoned have come'. This practical provision for the representation of the absent by those present cannot yet have been generally acceptable, and the clause was dropped from the reissues. But the charter laid a new ground-plan for relations between the king and his tenants-in-chief, though it remained in some ways more an ideal to which the barons would revert than a code establishing common practice. In Henry III's reign relations between king and magnates centred on periodic meetings, and issued in baronial attempts to control the king by influencing membership of his council.

The reign of Henry III

The royalist and rebel camps soon dissolved after the death of John, but before long factions reformed on different lines. At the centre the Marshal presided until his death in May 1219, with the papal legates, first Guala and then Pandulf, adding stability and legitimacy to the new régime. Afterwards Peter des Roches,

---

[36] Holt, *Magna Carta*, 322.

bishop of Winchester and guardian of the young king, and Hubert de Burgh, the justiciar, struggled with each other and with the warlords into whose hands local power had largely fallen, some of them, such as Fawkes de Bréauté or Philip Mark, former agents of John, some of them magnates with great regional power, such as the earl of Chester. With the aid of archbishop Langton and a group of earls including the young William Marshal, Hubert gradually edged out Peter des Roches and prized loose the grip of the locally powerful on the royal castles and demesne lands. The king was the keystone of the political system and he would not be able to safeguard the rights of others if his own were not respected.[37] Yet the minority also put in place the charters which sought to control that power, as well as the practice of holding large councils to discuss important decisions. This situation did not suddenly end at Henry III's majority, as his majority was not sudden – he came of age gradually from 1220 to 1227, gaining increasing powers at each step.[38]

In 1232 Henry withdrew his support from Hubert de Burgh and recalled Peter des Roches. it was the temporary victory of a faction, largely of Poitevin origin. Richard Marshal, son of the former regent, irked by the power of the court clique over wardships and patronage, now rebelled and was murdered in Ireland in 1234. Henry put the blame on Peter des Roches and, yielding to the insistence of the bishops led by archbishop Edmund of Abingdon, dismissed des Roches. From now on Henry was more directly in control, his council dominated by the archbishop and Henry's brother Richard, earl of Cornwall. Richard himself rebelled briefly in 1238, joined by Gilbert, the new earl marshal, apparently in disgust at the marriage of the king's sister Eleanor to Simon de Montfort. The reconciliation which ensued left Richard even stronger.

It was Henry's marriage to Eleanor of Provence in 1236 that began the influx of newcomers whose non-English origins attracted and crystallized the hostility of those less favoured by the king. Eleanor's relatives of the house of Savoy and their dependants included Boniface, made archbishop of Canterbury, and William and Peter; the latter was granted the Richmond lands. The Savoyards were useful allies: Thomas of Savoy was count of Flanders (1237–44), and the family ramified over the Alpine lands controlling access to Italy from France. In 1247 Henry

[37] Carpenter, *Minority*, 160, 213, 237.
[38] Stacey, *Politics, Policy and Finance*, 35.

took in his Lusignan half-brothers, the sons of his mother Isabella's second marriage. This Poitevin contingent included Aymer de Valence, bishop-elect of Winchester, and William de Valence, lord of Pembroke and Wexford. There were thus two distinct groups of French incomers, whose behaviour was not identical: in fact, they were generally hostile to each other, though the native English barons and chroniclers did not bother to distinguish between them.[39] They were Henry's relatives and he found them useful; in patronizing and rewarding them he was not behaving in an outrageous or even exceptional fashion.

Nevertheless, their influence over the king was sufficient to cause resentment, especially when added to royal financial demands. Such a request for funds in 1244 brought magnate anger to a head, accompanied by episcopal anger at the manipulation of elections. In October 1244 a large baronial gathering elected a committee to oversee the expenditure of any money granted, and demands were heard for the appointment of a justiciar and chancellor. These offices, which would function as a permanent check on the king and a channel of communication with those outside his circle, had been vacant or inoperative for ten and six years respectively. The demands were written down in the so-called 'paper constitution' of 1244, which proposed that four men chosen by common consent were to sit on the king's council with supervisory powers and control of some appointments.[40] But the king refused even token concessions.

From the late 1240s the expenses of Henry's kingship rose inexorably. He was involved in war in Gascony, and the sums lavished on the reconstruction and decoration of Westminster abbey were vast. In 1250 he took the cross, and began to tax the clergy with the pope's help, thus raising clerical discontent another notch. But it was Henry's ambitions for his younger son Edmund which finally brought his financial affairs to chaos. Pope Innocent IV was keen to find a champion to rid him of the Hohenstaufen dynasty, emperors in Germany and kings in Sicily and southern Italy. He offered the crown of Sicily to various potentates, who to take possession would have to expel Conrad IV, the son of the emperor Frederick II, and Frederick's bastard son Manfred, the effective power in the kingdom. Richard of Cornwall refused the offer, as on this occasion did Charles of

[39] Huw Ridgeway, 'King Henry III and the "Aliens", 1236–72', in Coss and Lloyd, *Thirteenth Century England* ii, 81–92.
[40] D. A. Carpenter, 'Chancellor Ralph de Neville and plans of political reform 1215–1258', in ibid., 69–80.

Anjou, Louis IX's brother. In March 1254 Henry accepted the kingdom of Sicily for Edmund. In May 1255 the pope commuted his crusading vow to the conquest of Sicily, securing in return for this favour Henry's promise to pay the pope's debts, amounting to about £90,000, by Michaelmas 1256. Henry was plunged into a complicated financial nightmare and had to ask the pope to moderate his terms: he was given an extension until 1258. In April of that year Henry finally turned to the magnates for help.

It was unfortunate for Henry that discontent in several areas came together, and coincided with a rupture between the Poitevin contingent at Henry's court and their opponents which divided Henry's friends. In April 1258 a body of earls, barons and knights appeared armed at Westminster and presented Henry with an ultimatum: they would do their best to obtain an aid from the realm if the pope would further moderate his terms and Henry would agree to reform the state of the kingdom. The king had to agree, and reform was undertaken by a body consisting of 12 men from Henry's council and 12 magnates. In June a 'parliament' at Oxford elected a justiciar, Hugh Bigod, and deputed a permanent council to oversee escheats and wardships. The 'Provisions of Oxford', which emanated from this meeting, consisted of 'a bundle of lists, notes of administrative changes and of regulations for future guidance'.[41] Many castles received new castellans, and later in the year the sheriffs were changed. The council of 24 ordered the resumption of alienated royal demesne and attempted to exact an oath of loyalty. In the autumn a systematic, minute investigation of grievances was set on foot. Some of the reformers' supporters were angered by this, others did not like the tutelage imposed on the king. The solidarity of the baronial reformers began to crumble, and the way opened to the next stage in the complex relations between the king and the magnates.

At no point, then, did the entire baronage rebel against the king. Describing such revolts as occurred as 'baronial' risks being misleading, given the number of barons who supported the king on each occasion; 'factional' might often be more accurate. Many of the rebels of 1215 were related by blood or marriage, but such ties are never a sufficient explanation of political alliance. Where an alliance existed a marriage might strengthen it, but members of the upper level of society had numerous points of mutual contact and interaction, and their motives cannot be

---

[41] Powicke, *Henry III and the Lord Edward*, 395.

assumed to be simple. Rebellious barons tended to have specific grievances to add to those which applied more generally. Revolt was brought about by a combination of the specific and the general: individual circumstances – the level of grievance, plus the susceptibility to drastic or emotional behaviour of the person concerned – and generally, the degree to which the king had violated expected norms of behaviour. On each occasion, as in 1173–4, there may have been many whose sympathies were with the rebels but who did not dare to join them: the alacrity with which the regency government of William Marshal took over much of Magna Carta makes clear the appeal of the reformers' programme to many who had opposed them. Trouble came to both John and Henry III at times when personal relations with a large proportion of the baronage had broken down. This was still an age of personal kingship and personal lordship, and the cumulative impact of personalities was an underlying factor in both the occurrence and the timing of political crises.

The crises of John's later reign and of the 1250s happened when desperate external circumstances brought the king to his knees, and opened up an opportunity for the discontented to force the king to make, or appear to make, concessions. For John the defeat of Bouvines was the fatal moment; for Henry III it was the financial collapse of his government. The lack of any rebel programme in 1173 other than a redistribution of lands and castles draws attention to a novel feature of the war of 1215–17; it was fought for a written agreement, almost a manifesto, which contained general statements of principle. This was not because the baronial class had just discovered principles: they had long wanted and expected to be treated in certain ways. In the political culture of 1215 the way to achieve that aim appeared to be to codify their desires in writing; 1215 was the first occasion in English history when an attempt at resolving a political crisis took the form of written concessions from the crown. The types of concessions demanded provide the best evidence of the grievances that lay behind them.

In 1215 the demand was for regular procedure and an end to extortion. It was not the rebels' wish to strip the king of his powers, but rather to make him observe the kinds of rules in his treatment of the magnates that the kings had made the magnates observe to their own men. They did not seek to dismantle the legal and governmental machinery: they accepted it and attempted to regulate and control it. They were given increased leverage over the monarchy by developments in taxation. The vast yield of the new proportional taxes, the thirteenths and tenths, made them irresistibly attractive to the king. They both aroused opposition and provided a means of controlling the king, for as 'aids' they could only be taken with consent. In 1258 the demand was for control of the king's expenditure and of the sources of patronage, access to the king and influence on his decisions. Government was politics and politics government.

Government by consent had always been the ideal, implicit in the mutual relations of lordship, emerging from the reality of the household and its expectations. It was part of the mental equipment of the kings too, and even John had asked for, and claimed to be acting with, the compliance of his subjects in some form. Historians have made much of the evolution of means for obtaining consent, seeing in it the origin of parliamentary democracy. But in the thirteenth century no new institution suddenly appeared. Existing methods of consultation gradually grew firmer, rules were clarified, the imprecise became more precise – change of this kind is a feature of the age in many areas of life, and English politics followed suit. The term 'parliament' was used for some royal councils from the 1230s, but it was not exclusive to these, and they could be given other names too. It was John who first summoned knights from the shires, in 1212, to hear his commands; they were summoned again in 1227, and representatives of the county communities gathered in 1254. But the common council of the realm was not a well-defined body.

The appearance of lesser men in the councils of the great is perhaps less of an innovation than it seems: wise magnates had always listened to their followers, and wise kings had taken their servants and advisers from quite far down the social scale. The rebels of Magna Carta were concerned with the interests of their tenants too – if they were good lords, they would have to be. But the evolution of local society had created a group of middling landholders relatively independent of the magnates, and their interests and concerns began to be of some weight. The political nation slowly expanded to include them. This did not represent a growing political consciousness so much as the growth of new forms to accomodate new social relations. The stalwarts of the honorial and county courts of the twelfth century needed no political lessons from their grandchildren.

Magna Carta spoke of the 'commune of the whole land';[42] the Provisions of Oxford set out an oath to be sworn by the

[42] Clause 61, *communa totius terre.*

commune. The idea behind these words is perhaps more likely to have been the sworn confederacy such as the 'communes' of city government, often found on the continent and in the 1190s in London, than a developed idea of 'the community of the realm'. The ideas, language and political forms of a kingdom-wide community were developing slowly in the first half of the thirteenth century, but on a firm basis. The Articles of the Barons stated that the king conceded liberties to 'the kingdom' (cl. 48). There existed an idea of the realm as a unit to which the king could make concessions.

There was conflict between the monarchy and the magnates, but it was not built into the political or social structure. If the magnates had limited the power of the monarchy by imposing Magna Carta, the monarchy had imposed strict limits on the powers of the great lords to run their fees. A process of accommodation had been taking place, the kings and their greater tenants finding new ways of rubbing along together as circumstances required; and rubbing produces friction.

4

The King and the Church

Clergy and laity

The medieval church was a hierarchical system of authority
fully integrated into the social order. It had its own law, its
own intellectual and artistic culture, its own common language
and a head who was an independent potentate. It demanded, and
received, loyalty from both its priests and the laity. It possessed
vast estates given by past generations of laymen. Its leaders held
baronies, owed service to the king, and governed wide areas of
countryside. Even its village priests were landholders, though
they also derived income directly from their parishioners in the
form of tithes. Yet it was a very diverse organization, embracing
so many conflicting interests that it seldom or never spoke with
one voice. Entangled with the laity at every level, the clerical
hierarchy paralleled that of the laity. Parish priests might be of
low social origin and be little, if any, more learned than their
parishioners, while some bishops were the sons and brothers of
earls. The church and the lay society from which it drew its
support and its personnel were interdependent. Churchmen
needed the lay power for protection and the enforcement of their
demands; the church provided society with its ideals and its
justification.

Yet for a century before 1150 a strong current of reform had
been flowing which sought to raise the status of the clergy above
the laity and disentangle the church from lay control – thus, in
the reformers' view, making it better able to fulfil its spiritual
aims. A desire for reform could be said to be characteristic of
most ages of church history, but the period from 1150 to 1250
must count among the most active in defining clerical objec-
tives and even in carrying them through. The law of the church,
canon law, was being elaborated with increasing subtlety and

definition in the twelfth and thirteenth centuries by successive
generations of lawyers, usually working privately and making
their own collections of papal decisions on specific questions ('decretals'). This process culminated in 1234 with pope Gregory IX's
issue of an official textbook, the *Liber Extra*. Formal legislation took place at the great councils of the western church, of
which three were called in this period: Alexander III's Third
Lateran Council of 1179, Innocent III's Fourth Lateran of 1215,
and the Council of Lyons, summoned by Innocent IV in 1245.
Canon law came to set out very far-reaching claims for the whole
clerical order. Churchmen were not to be tried for criminal
offences in lay courts and were not to be punished or imprisoned
without the approval of the church authorities, whose communication with the pope was not to be restricted. The clergy could
not be taxed, and the laity were not to exert influence over
appointments to church posts. As well as benefiting from privileges, the clergy had to show proper discipline: they should be
strictly celibate, not indulge in worldly amusements or renounce
their clerical status, should not hold several posts at once in
order to enjoy the revenues, and should not offer bribes for
advancement.

Canon law was one intellectual centre of reforming ideas:
theology was another. The schools, especially those of Paris,
concerned themselves amongst other things with pastoral theology, doctrines of confession, penance and the sacraments. A
reform programme had been largely worked out by about 1170,
and thereafter the priority was to take it to the people. Both the
legal and pastoral approaches thus attempted to impose an ideo-
logical programme from above, first requiring the capture of key
positions in the church. The reformers immediately encountered
both overt resistance and the reluctance of inertia from two
sources: the unreformed clergy, especially the parish priests, and
the laity, principally lords whose control of 'their' clergy was
threatened. One of the main themes in the history of this period
is the often painful process of adjustment of clerical claims to the
realities of lay power. Most of the time the process went on
quietly, almost unnoticed. But it also produced two exceptional
crises: the conflict between Henry II and Thomas Becket, and the
struggle between John and pope Innocent III.

The structure of the church was well defined. England was
organized into two provinces, Canterbury and York, with an
archbishop at the head of each. The two archbishops were more
often rivals than friends. The clamorous disputes of the early

part of the twelfth century had subsided, leaving a residue of sullen suspicion which might at any moment break out into conflict. Neither had any powers in the other's province, unless he was a papal legate. Within his province the archbishop was empowered to examine, confirm and, with other bishops, consecrate each new bishop, who promised obedience to him. In practice this gave little power. The archbishop's position as the direct subordinate of the pope meant that his powers were especially subject to erosion from above: the greatest lawsuits usually went to Rome. Nevertheless, the archbishop of Canterbury did retain and develop certain legal powers, and he was always regarded as the leader and mouthpiece of the English clergy.

Below the archbishops were the bishops, each with responsibility for a diocese and based at a cathedral, a church containing the bishop's throne or *cathedra*. Each diocese then had territorial subdivisions within which archdeacons, and below them rural deans, supervised the clergy and people. The whole country was divided into parishes, each with a church and one or more responsible priests. The English dioceses had had a long history by the twelfth century, and they varied greatly in size and their bishops in wealth. The presence of the bishop of the diocese was not actually essential for church government. He had an 'official' who could institute rectors and vicars and hear lawsuits; the archdeacon supervised the parishes; and even for those things that only a bishop could do – ordaining to the priesthood, confirming children, consecrating churches, dedicating altars, and blessing the new head of a monastery – other bishops could be found. Many bishops of this period led busy lives in the royal administration, though there were others who lived and worked in their dioceses.

Parish churches had landed endowments and a tithe income – one-tenth of the annual harvest and of the increase of livestock in the parish. This made churches a form of property. Only a priest could serve a parish church, but the right to present the priest, the 'advowson', was held in the great majority of cases by laymen, a situation of which many in the church disapproved. There was a tendency, gathering speed in the twelfth century, for laymen to grant this right to monasteries – sometimes their own foundations. Generally the monks were unable or unwilling to serve the churches themselves, and therefore paid a priest to do so. The more important non-monastic, 'secular' churchmen might also make use of this way of drawing the revenue of the church without having to live in the parish and do the priest's work. Thus 'rectors', who 'ruled' the churches, employed 'vicars' (from the Latin *vicarius*, a substitute), who might have a proportion of the tithes or a fixed cash income, paying the rest to the rector. In the twelfth century, if not later, laymen had the right to grant two-thirds of their demesne tithes to monasteries, a practice which produced many complicated situations ripe for litigation. A parish church would often be at the centre of a web of interlocking rights and payments. The effect on the religious life of the parish was often felt to be harmful.

Such was the structure through which the reformers had to work if they were to impose their ideals on the church. Reform generally meant that some of the higher clergy sought ways of persuading or compelling reluctant subordinates to accept ways of life that had not hitherto been customary. One channel of communication between upper and lower clergy was provided by the diocesan synods. Very little legislation is left from these in the twelfth century – it seems they were more concerned with litigation than law-making. The emphasis changed after 1215, when a number of reforming bishops began to issue 'constitutions' for their dioceses, taking from the decrees of the Lateran and other councils what they felt to be most useful for local conditions. The most influential constitutions were those of Richard Poore, bishop of Salisbury, which were reissued after he moved to Durham in 1228. Even before 1215 the archbishops of Canterbury had occasionally held councils for the southern province, issuing decrees in which the shortcomings of the parish clergy figured prominently.[1] Much of this repeats the decrees of earlier councils, proving both the good record-keeping of the church and the ineffectiveness of its legislation.

There was little direct supervision of the parishes by the bishops before the later thirteenth century: systematic visitation of the diocese was carried out, if at all, by the archdeacons who, to judge from the volume of complaints at their activities, often used the opportunity to make unauthorized exactions. Archdeacons also held their own synods or 'chapters'. Church government was rapidly becoming more bureaucratic and legal, and the administrative framework for the enforcement of canon law was tightened to the point where churchmen could no longer ignore it. Lawsuits, for example the enormous quantity concerning tithes, were by the thirteenth century often decided by bishops

---

[1] Councils and Synods i, part ii, 965–93, 1055–74.

sitting 'in consistory', surrounded by their expert legal advisers. The church was leading the way in the use of writing for every day purposes. The skilled lawyers and administrators produced by the schools found posts in bishops' households. A growing professionalism is visible everywhere; the documents produced by the bishops in their everyday routine increased in number and became more businesslike. Growing sophistication is as characteristic of ecclesiastical as it is of royal government; in fact, it was often carried out by the same people, with similar results – 'the reign of law was never established. What prevailed was the reign of lawyers.'[2]

In their attempt to control the clergy the hierarchy had the greatest difficulty in enforcing celibacy. Though the demand for clerical celibacy was nearly as old as clerical marriage, it did not reach the top of the agenda until the eleventh century. The reformers made little headway against an entrenched married clergy at parish level. There was even a current of opinion among some theologians that the celibacy requirements should be reduced,[3] but the 1215 Lateran Council renewed the full demands with stronger penalties for non-compliance. Conscientious bishops, such as Robert Grosseteste of Lincoln (1235–53), led constant campaigns to enforce celibacy. Married clergy were by no means necessarily scandalous, and their sons included some of the most distinguished churchmen of the period. They were familiar with their parishioners' concerns, having wives and children of their own. The problem arose with the children, especially if the sons succeeded to the job. A hereditary parish clergy blocked the attempts of both the church hierarchy and the lay aristocracy to control appointments. The bishop, where he could exert his influence, could refuse to admit the son of a priest; another solution came when lay patrons granted their parish churches to monasteries, though some monasteries condoned hereditary succession in benefices. Grants of churches were a popular way of endowing new monasteries, costing the patrons comparatively little and getting off their hands a form of property which it was less and less respectable to hold. As a result of continual pressure the incidence of openly married clergy probably declined without being completely eliminated.

[2] Cheney, *Becket to Langton*, 75.
[3] Baldwin, *Masters, Princes and Merchants*, 337–40.

With the endowments of many parishes in the hands of monasteries or absentee secular rectors, it was important for bishops
to do all they could to ensure a decent minimum income and a
basic level of competence for the vicars who undertook the work
of the parishes. When sanctioning the gift of an advowson to a
monastery or the succession of an absentee rector they would
'institute' a vicarage with a specified income sufficient to maintain the vicar. Candidates for ordination were examined, usually
by the archdeacon, though rejection was apparently unusual.
Very little was done to improve opportunities for clerical education until later in the middle ages.

The religious orders presented reformers with a special problem. The Cluniac, Cistercian and Premonstratensian orders were
all exempt from the control of the local bishop, the two latter
having their own highly articulated internal system of visitation.
The Augustinian order was not a centralized institution, consisting of many small houses with a variety of customs, and they
were normally subject to the bishop. Both the Augustinians and
the Benedictines were instructed by pope Innocent III to hold
provincial chapters – and they did, from time to time, though
attendance was patchy and the practical results were small. The
Benedictine houses, many of them ancient, wealthy and influential, guarded their autonomy with passionate jealousy. Attempts
by bishops to assert their right to visit these monasteries, and
thus interfere in their internal affairs, resulted in some of the
most clamorous and lengthy disputes of the period – that between the bishop of Chichester and Battle abbey, for instance, or
between the bishop of Worcester and Evesham abbey. Canon
law was on the bishops' side, but by appealing to Rome and
citing earlier privileges many of the greater monasteries managed
to secure exemption. The price was direct subordination to the
papacy, a privilege which could turn out to be expensive as each
new abbot had to go to Rome, bearing gifts, to secure confirmation of his election. Particularly bitter were the disputes between
bishops and the monastic chapters of some cathedrals, and even
here the bishop could not be sure of winning. Monks, as members of an undying institution with interests that stayed the same
for generations, always had a tactical advantage over bishops
who were mortal and whose successors might not wish to continue the fight.

The reform of the clergy was only the first stage of a greater
design: evangelizing the laity. The 1215 Lateran Council set out
a minimum of observance: annual confession and at least one

communion, at Easter. This made compulsory what had previously been spontaneous, if it had happened at all. It was the
practical outcome of twelfth-century theologians' intensive analysis of the sacraments, and the desire to make them the centre
of the devotional life of the laity. With this was associated an
attempt to increase the distance between the clergy, as per-
formers of the sacramental mysteries, and the laity, both literally
and metaphorically. The laity were excluded from the sanctuary
of the church, and told to bow to the altar and kneel at appropriate moments. Confession was usually only to be made to a
priest, and marriage was to take place on church ground (*in facie
ecclesie*).[4] Confession and marriage were on their way to being
'sacramentalized'. The programme was energetically introduced
by archbishop Stephen Langton, a former theologian of the Paris
schools, especially in the legislation of his provincial council held
at Oxford in 1222. This meeting also had the dubious distinction
of witnessing the first judicial execution for apostasy in English
history, that of a deacon who was burnt for being circumcised.
An old woman was walled up for thinking she was the Virgin
Mary, and a young man for claiming to be Christ.[5]

The church's claims to jurisdiction were becoming better
defined. Archbishop Thomas Becket's claim to try criminous
clerks in church courts was one of the causes of his conflict
with Henry II. In Henry's time jurisdiction over wills went to
church courts, as did decisions on whether a marriage had taken
place or not.[6] On one point, though, the laity stuck to their old
position. Despite a campaign by some bishops to enforce the
canonical view that children were legitimatized by the subsequent
marriage of their parents, the lay magnates assembled at Merton
in 1236 refused 'to change the laws of England': in English law,
once a bastard, always a bastard.

Perhaps it is a reflection of the state of the parish clergy that
there is very little sign of regular preaching to the mass of the
population despite legislation ordering priests to instruct their
parishioners. Abbot Samson of Bury St Edmunds used to preach
to the people in his native Norfolk dialect,[7] while abbot Eustace
of the French monastery of St-Germer de Flay caused a considerable stir by a preaching campaign in England against working on
Sundays, but both these preaching abbots were exceptional. The

---

[4] Councils and Synods i, part ii, 1067, canon 11.
[5] Coggeshall, 190–1.
[6] Glanvill, 81, 87.
[7] Jocelin, 40, 128.

gap was filled by the friars, especially the Dominicans. The second general chapter of the Dominican order, held at Bologna in 1221, sent a mission to England which arrived later that year under the wing of Peter des Roches, bishop of Winchester. The leader of the group preached a sermon before archbishop Stephen Langton, no mean judge, who was impressed. The group went straight to Oxford, as their twin purposes were preaching and study. They were immensely successful, founding the London house and rapidly colonizing all the major towns. They benefited greatly from the support of reforming bishops such as Robert Grosseteste, and soon became popular among the aristocracy as private confessors.

In September 1224 Brother Agnellus of Pisa and eight companions landed at Dover to found the English province of the Franciscan order. They went immediately to Canterbury, London and Oxford, where they were sheltered at first by the Dominicans. Their success was rapid, too, and by 1256 there were 1242 Franciscans in England and houses in every town of importance. St Francis's original vision was of poverty, humility and service to the poor, but the order's success among the clergy soon brought in recruits who valued learning, and it gradually turned into a preaching and studying order parallel to and in rivalry with the Dominicans, though some groups always held fast to the original concept. A similar tension was felt in the much smaller order of Carmelite friars, originally a group of hermits on Mount Carmel in the Holy Land which transferred itself to western Europe after 1240. The first general of the order was Simon, an Englishman, and the English province long remained important. As well as centres at Oxford and Cambridge, the Carmelites also maintained more hermitage-like establishments in the depths of the countryside.

King, pope and church

The most noticeable part of the history of the church in this period was the triangular relationship between king, pope and church. Lying behind this is the rise of the papacy to what has been called a 'bureaucratic superpower'.[8] Both canon law and theology increasingly emphasized the supremacy of the pope, who alone could definitively reconcile conflicting authorities and

---

[8] Barlow, *Thomas Becket*, 69.

whose every pronouncement was potentially law. The bureaucracy was expanding rapidly, but it would not have done so if it had not rested on a foundation of acceptance of the claims made by and on behalf of the papacy. It was moral authority that made the pope a 'superpower'. The bureaucracy was at the service of that moral authority, and had not yet begun to bring it into serious disrepute. Apart from 'providing' its members with benefices, papal officialdom had no income except what it could charge those making use of its services, and although many were keen to enlist its judgments they were less willing to pay for them. There was an eternal chorus of complaint about the corruptibility of the court of Rome, pointing to the gap between pretensions and reality, becoming louder but as yet still in the background.

But the exercise of papal power faced serious practical limitations. One, of a very basic nature, was the distance between England and Rome. It took a month to get to Rome from southern England if circumstances were favourable, and even lesser distances could cause practical difficulties: king Richard died in central France on 6 April 1199, but the papal chancery was still addressing letters to him on 28 April.[9] Papal letters were often out of date on arrival, and could only be ignored. It seems to have been a common practice in political affairs to obtain a batch of papal letters saying different things for use as circumstances dictated – in which event there was bound to be doubt about whether the pope would really stand behind them. Nor were the popes particularly well informed about England. Adrian IV (1154-9) was the only Englishman ever to become pope, but even he had made his career on the continent; no pope ever came to England, and though some had crossed the Channel as legate or nuncio before their elevation, generally all they knew about the country was what they were told by people with axes to grind. Another factor constraining the exercise of the pope's authority was the political situation in Italy, especially his relations with the emperor; as this fluctuated, so would the pope's ability to take a strong line with kings he might need as allies. The popes were generally in alliance with the kings of France, on the basis of mutual hostility to the emperor in Germany and northern Italy, though that did not always prevent conflict between them. Alexander III, threatened by Frederick Barbarossa, and Innocent IV by Frederick II, took refuge under the wing of the king of France.

[9] Cheney, *Innocent III and England*, 9.

There was also a more corrosive force at work, eating away at the 'superpower's' foundations. Moral authority has to be exercised with great delicacy and depends on the consent of others. The clergy paid lip-service to papal claims, which may imply intellectual consent, but they did not always follow it up with obedience. There is a strong suspicion that the clergy were happiest with papal power when they could enlist it on their side in their quarrels with the laity or each other. Relations between pope Innocent III and the English church have been characterized as 'unstable and unsympathetic'.[10] The attitudes of the laity in general are harder to ascertain as they were much less given to expressing their opinions in writing, but there is little sign of interest, let alone enthusiasm. In the vernacular poem *L'Histoire de Guillaume le Maréchal* the only reference to Rome is a denunciation of its avarice.[11] The general interdict which Innocent III launched against England in 1208 to undermine king John in the eyes of his subjects may have damaged the pope more. A contemporary wrote that all the laity and most of the clergy sided with the king.[12] The pope's moral authority seems to have rested more on silent acquiescence than on enthusiastic consent. There was as yet no competing theory of the secular state which could confer independent legitimacy on lay power. The only legitimacy Henry II could allege for his demands in his conflict with archbishop Thomas Becket was that conferred by the custom of the realm, and to this Thomas's answer came readily: 'Christ did not say "I am custom", but "I am truth".'[13]

For both the laity and churchmen the king was a much nearer and more dangerous power than the pope. His interest in the English church was proprietary, a traditional attitude shared by laymen at all levels down to the patrons of parish churches. The ancestors of laymen had endowed the church, which held land in return for service: knight service in the case of the older churches, and in all cases prayers for the souls of benefactors. The king also took the view that the first loyalty of Englishmen was to himself: he was responsible for the kingdom and that included the church within it. He wanted to put his own loyal servants into his bishoprics, so as to reward them at no expense to himself while ensuring that wealthy and influential positions were held by men he could trust. His success in this meant that in conflicts

---

[10] Cheney, *Innocent III and England*, 50–1.
[11] Marshal, ll. 11360–72.
[12] Margam annals in Ann Mon i, 28.
[13] Fitz Stephen in Mats Becket iii, 47–8, quoting John xiv, 6.

the church was never united – some, even most, bishops would always side with the king. A complaisant episcopate then enabled him to place his lesser clerks in lower benefices, while they would often respond helpfully when he turned to them for financial assistance. The royal clerks who were thus rewarded saw their labours crowned with wealth and dignity usually far beyond anything to which their birth would have entitled them.

The working out of this three-sided relationship produced its first great crisis following the appointment as archbishop of Canterbury in 1162 of Thomas Becket (the form 'à Becket' is an invention of seventeenth-century antiquaries and should be avoided). The famous story of the brilliant chancellor whom king Henry II made archbishop, the turning of their friendship into bitter enmity, the king's hounding of the archbishop, his exile, return and murder, together with the swirling sub-plots involving the pope, the king of France, the English bishops and a host of minor characters, has often been told. It is not the events which continue to cause discussion but the rights and wrongs of the case and the characters of the protagonists. The issues of principle, as so often, were entwined in a personal quarrel. Effective settlement of the issues had to await the bloody solution to the quarrel.

Trouble was foreshadowed soon after Thomas's consecration when he resigned his chancellorship, which vexed Henry, but it began in earnest in the summer of 1163. The conflict arose through Thomas's treatment of his tenants and royal officials in lawsuits deriving from the archbishop's claims to property in Kent, and to the advowson of all churches on lands held of him. He excommunicated a tenant of his who was also a tenant-in-chief of the king without previously notifying the king. Thomas then opposed Henry's plan to collect a due known as sheriff's aid and pay it into the royal treasury. Then there was the notorious matter of the criminous clerks: Henry wanted the royal courts to decide if a clerk should be tried by royal or church courts and, if subsequently found guilty, he demanded that the church should not protect the clerk. The effect would be to incorporate the church courts into the royal judicial machine and bring the clergy under royal control. Penalties were far more severe in the royal courts, despite a clumsy attempt by Thomas to punish a clerk by branding and exile, which only further annoyed the king. The demands of canon law in the matter were not clear, but there was a suspicion among the laity that clerical privileges were being used to protect the undeserving. There was an underlying conflict about serious jurisdictional matters, but these disagreements would not have caused such a clamorous and embittered quarrel had they not been bound up with Henry's more emotional complaints against Thomas – ingratitude and treachery.

The issues crystallized at a council held at Woodstock in October 1163. Henry demanded that Thomas respect the customs of the realm as observed in the time of his grandfather, Henry I. Thomas would only agree 'saving his order'. The outcome was deadlock until the famous council at Clarendon in January 1164. Here, after three days of wrangling, Thomas agreed to swear to observe the customs of the realm, whereupon Henry ordered a commission of barons to produce a list of the customs – the 'Constitutions of Clarendon'. To these Thomas could not agree. During the summer further lawsuits were brought by his enemies, who scented his weak position. He was cited to a further council at Northampton in October, where argument turned into outright persecution. Henry demanded accounts from Thomas's period as chancellor although he had been declared quit, and refused all offers of compromise. The bishops implored Thomas to surrender to Henry's mercy, but he appealed to Rome and left the council before judgment could be passed on him. He then fled in disguise by secret ways to France, to king Louis, and to pope Alexander who was then in France. He eventually took up residence at the Cistercian monastery of Pontigny.

There then ensued six years of diplomatic activity. Thomas received support from the pope which fluctuated according to the demands of international politics and the military situation in Italy, and from Louis which varied with the state of his relations with king Henry. Most of the English bishops sided with the king under the leadership of Gilbert Foliot, bishop of London. By 1169 serious attempts were being made to bring the two principals together, though Henry's denial of the kiss of peace, which would have signified that their quarrel was really at an end, led many to doubt his good faith. It was the coronation of Henry's son, the young Henry, by the archbishop of York in the face of papal prohibition in June 1170 that ushered in the final scenes of the drama. In a series of meetings Henry and Thomas agreed on restoring the status quo before their disagreement, amnesty for Thomas's supporters and absolution for those who had been excommunicated. Henry still studiously avoided giving Thomas the kiss of peace. Ignoring warnings from his friends, the archbishop returned to Canterbury, to great popular enthusiasm but hostility from some bishops, barons and local enemies. The actions of the latter caused a new series of archiepiscopal excommunications on Christmas Day; on 29 December 1170 the archbishop was murdered in his cathedral by four knights who had arrived from king Henry's court in Normandy.

While pope Alexander laid an interdict on Henry's continental lands and excommunicated the murderers and their helpers, Henry set sail for Ireland, ordering the ports to be closed behind him. Once there, he was cut off by contrary winds for five months. It was not until May 1172, at Avranches in Normandy, that Henry formally made his peace with the church. The effect of this agreement overall was to revert to the situation before the quarrel, but with the stage now cleared for the real conflict. The substantive points at issue were gradually sorted out by negotiation over the next ten years, and Henry's strong position was hardly undermined at all by Becket's death. The issues had widened and become more fundamental during the dispute. The initial disagreements were about the rights of the archbishop in his estates and his relations with royal officials. A conflict about jurisdiction over criminous clerks came next, while the Constitutions of Clarendon raised fundamental issues of principle, especially the jurisdiction of church courts in lay matters, and access to Rome. Finally, the conflict became one between the claims of Caesar and those of God, at least in the minds of Becket's supporters.

Although the conflicts between the archbishop and some of his tenants were quickly subsumed in the wider issues, these disagreements caused some of the most bitter enmities and ultimately facilitated the archbishop's murder. It was another of the rights claimed by the archbishop, that of crowning the king, that precipitated the final act of the drama. Historically Becket's claim was not strong – two of the five coronations since William the Conqueror had not been performed by the archbishop of Canterbury – but Thomas had been in archbishop Theobald's household during the crucial years when the archbishop's refusal to crown Stephen's son Eustace had delivered the throne to Henry.[14] He had witnessed the immense leverage that this right gave the church at a vital moment and was not going to abandon it. In fact, the re-crowning of the young Henry in 1172 was performed, eccentrically enough, by the archbishop of Rouen in

---

[14] Gervase i, 150.

Winchester cathedral (the see of Canterbury was still vacant at the time), but subsequently Canterbury lengthened its lead until archiepiscopal coronation became normal if not actually requisite.

Contact with Rome was the only major issue on which pope Alexander insisted that Henry give way in the compromise of Avranches, though even here the king retained the right to take security from suspect persons. This paved the road to Rome for a great increase in the legal cases taken there, usually on appeal. Standard practice was for the pope to delegate hearing, and usually judging, the case to local 'judges-delegate' who had readier access to necessary information. Though the system was popular with litigants it had its drawbacks: it increased the expense of litigation, frivolous appeals could be used as a delaying tactic, and judge-delegate work itself was laborious and unpaid. The years after Becket's murder witnessed the growth of what has been called 'a pervasive papalism'[15] in the English church, seen in appointments ('provisions') to even minor benefices, indulgences, dispensations, and the visits of a series of legates *a latere* (literally, from the pope's side). In 1199 the pope for the first time imposed a direct tax on the English church, which was becoming part of a Europe-wide administrative organism in a way it had not been before. Papal government itself was becoming more elaborate and immediate, and England was not sheltered from it.

On the issue of the powers of church courts Henry gave away less. In negotiations with cardinal Hugh Pierleoni in 1176 he conceded that accused clerks were to be handed over to the bishop and not to be brought before secular judges except for forest offences, and were not to undergo trial by battle. In the end the effect of this concession was less than it may have seemed at the time: when jury trial came in for criminal offences in the thirteenth century the court proceeded to a verdict before the clerk was handed over to the bishop, and he lost his chattels if found guilty. Legitimacy and marriage cases were heard by church courts, but from 1178 Henry insisted that their verdicts could not affect lay fee. Cases concerning advowsons were causing considerable difficulty. The old lay attitude that the grant of a church to a monastery was valid only for the donor's lifetime was widespread. The right to present a parson could only be effective on the death of the sitting incumbent; now if the donor

---

[15] Cheney, *Becket to Langton*, 75.

died first, his heir might claim back the right – the monastery would never have had 'seisin' of the right to present. By the assize of *darrein presentment*, introduced in 1179 or 1180, the right would return to the heir if the monastery had not yet presented. Henry had claimed such cases for the royal courts, and they continued to be heard there. The decision as to whether a tenement was held in free alms or for feudal service was also decided in the royal court by process of assize *utrum*; the answer might effectively decide who should hold the tenement, as only a clergyman could hold in free alms. If the church courts attempted to try any of these matters they could be prevented from doing so by a 'writ of prohibition'.

It appears that Henry recovered brilliantly from the tactical disaster of the archbishop's murder and surrendered little of substance. This is certainly the case concerning the competition for jurisdiction; the king remained paramount in his kingdom. But more areas of church life now escaped his control: England was open to the workings of the 'bureaucratic superpower' in a way the Constitutions of Clarendon would have made impossible, yet it was not aggression or interference from Rome that brought ordinary cases before papal judges, but the willingness of English litigants to seek papal intervention and the desire of some of the clergy for direction.

The extent to which Becket's actions were justified will always be debatable. His stridency and obstinacy have always attracted condemnation and may have been due to the underlying psychological weakness of his position arising from his former worldly life and his friendship with Henry. Many would find his sudden conversion to an extreme exponent of the rights of the church irritating and unconvincing, while his own awareness of his lack of prior qualifications for leadership of the church would drive him to try to 'out-bishop the rest'.[16] On the other side, to reduce the customs of the realm to writing in order to confront the archbishop with them was a tactical error, smacking of a chicanery visible in other instances of Henry's behaviour, while the king's very vengefulness may have denied him total victory at Northampton. Becket's ultimate legacy was more important than the individual causes he fought for. He bequeathed two kinds of cult: his own, and that of the liberty of the church. The rapidly developing cult of St Thomas of Canterbury welled up from below despite some initial discouragement from the authorities.

[16] Barlow, *Thomas Becket*, 89.

Thomas was a popular hero on his return and a popular saint thereafter because of his opposition to the mighty of the earth; it was the coruscation of miracles among the poor and sick that made the fame of his shrine. But his cult was not overtly anti-royal – Henry enlisted his late enemy's aid with spectacular success in the rebellion in 1173–4. The apotheosis of Becket raised his cause above worldly wranglings and made him a talisman even for his old opponents. As the chronicler of Battle abbey, writing in the 1190s, put it, he died 'in the church, for the church, as the shepherd of the church'.[17] Two of his achievements are undeniable: he inhabited medieval England's most famous shrine, and he bequeathed a splendid example of consecrated awkwardness for all his successors to use or be shamed by.

One area over which Henry II retained close control was appointments to bishoprics, often persuading the chapter to elect one of two or three royal nominees. The appointments to vacant bishoprics in 1174 underlined Henry's continued power over the English church in symbolic fashion by rewarding Becket's worst ecclesiastical enemies – at least, those who were not bishops already – with the richest posts. Henry was said to be proud of never giving bishoprics for money; his appointments were generally respectable, and in his last years he advanced some men of outstanding personal holiness, but Richard and John again preferred trusty royal clerks. Such men were seldom actively scandalous; in fact, their background often made them good bishops in the bureaucratic fashion that the office increasingly demanded. It could be said that the canonical ideal of free election rested on naive expectations of the members of cathedral chapters, a good many of whom in secular cathedrals were themselves royal clerks, while chapters of monks were keen to elect a monk who might well be insufficiently skilled in legal and administrative work.

It was an appointment which, after 30 years of generally good relations, brought about the next crisis in relations between king and church. The problem was to find a successor to archbishop Hubert Walter, who died on 13 July 1205. There ensued a three-cornered fight between the king, the bishops of the province and the monks of Canterbury cathedral as to their respective rights in the election. The monks elected their subprior, the bishops appealed to the pope, king John forced both bishops and monks to request the translation of his confidant John de Grey from Norwich; this the pope refused, summoning all parties to Rome and finding for the monks as legal electors. The monks now split, some for their subprior and some for John de Grey. Pope Innocent cut the Gordian knot by persuading the monks to elect a distinguished English cardinal, Stephen Langton, a former master of the Paris schools and a noted theologian and preacher.

The only remaining difficulty was to persuade king John to accept Stephen as archbishop. The pope asked politely for the king's consent, which was refused. The pope consecrated Langton archbishop at Viterbo on 17 June 1207. The quarrel was not of the pope's choosing. In canon law and in his own high view of his office Innocent had acted quite properly. King John had accepted an unwelcome archbishop of Armagh in 1206 after much protest, a precedent Innocent must have found encouraging; but for a pope to force an archbishop of Canterbury on an unwilling king of England was unheard-of and, coming so soon after John's loss of most of his continental possessions, must have seemed the final humiliation. King and pope dug in their heels. John took his revenge on the monks of Canterbury by expelling them from his dominions. Innocent commissioned some bishops to try to persuade John, and when they failed launched an interdict on England on 23 March 1208. This amounted to a clerical lock-out, the services of the church being forbidden to all but certain privileged communities of monks. It did not appear to shake the king, who confiscated the property of those who observed the interdict or went abroad. John's personal excommunication followed in November 1209, which was more threatening to him as a possible pretext for rebellion. Nevertheless, both sides were reluctant to go to extremes: Innocent did not depose John or release his subjects from their oaths of fealty, while John extended his protection to individual clergy, threatening to have anyone who harmed them hanged from the nearest oak. Much of church life continued as normal but without public masses.

It was John's increasingly desperate political and military difficulties, not the pressure of papal censures, that finally ended the stalemate. With discontent rife among the baronage and the French king threatening to invade England, John took the drastic step of surrendering to the pope in order to enlist his aid against the king's other foes. The ploy worked – Innocent was completely won over, especially as John not only accepted Langton, renounced the rights he claimed in elections and promised to make amends for his confiscations, but in May 1213 he also surrendered the kingdom itself to the pope, receiving it back to hold as a fief paying the pope 1000 marks a year. It is not certain whose idea this was, and opinions on its wisdom varied at the time: one chronicler thought it was the only way out of such an accumulation of difficulties, while a Yorkshire Cistercian, Matthew of Rievaulx, declared that death was better than servitude and urged England to throw off the burden without delay.[18] The annual tribute was regularly paid by Henry III, less so by Edward I and Edward II. It was last paid in 1333, and repudiated entirely in 1366.

John's surrender and the papal overlordship ushered in a new period in relations between king, pope and local church, bringing the papacy much closer. John remained as slippery as ever, obtaining very lenient terms on compensating the clergy and fanning the disagreements which soon arose as the English church discovered that its interests were not the same as the pope's. But Innocent was now solidly behind John; his authority was always available to support the monarchy, to the extent of quashing Magna Carta in 1215. To circumvent distrust and hostility from the English hierarchy he sent a legate *a latere* whose authority overrode Langton's. Papal support, expressed through a series of legates, was crucial in securing the succession for the young Henry III.

Most tension in subsequent years occurred in two areas of conflict: appointments and taxation. Royal servants, mostly from the king's household and the chancery, continued to be rewarded with bishoprics under Henry III, but papal and legatine pressure secured the appointment of a group of learned and virtuous secular clerks, often academics, small in numbers but disproportionately influential. Papal influence was still generally beneficial, the worst threat being Henry III himself, whose attempts to put his relatives into the wealthiest bishoprics produced some long and bitter wrangles. This was the ecclesiastical equivalent of the favour shown to his lay relatives; he succeeded in putting Boniface of Savoy, the queen's uncle, into Canterbury and Aymer de Valence into Winchester, but he did not always get what he wanted. The abbots of the large and wealthy monasteries generally exerted little influence beyond their immediate surroundings; here king John's concession of free elections by a charter given in 1214 was put into practice and the great abbeys were allowed to do what they wanted, which was usually to elect one of their own number as abbot.

One group with surprisingly little influence in higher church appointments was the lay magnates, which accounts for the lack of their relatives among the bishops. This contrasts with the situation elsewhere in Europe, where the episcopate was much more aristocratic. Where the magnates, and laymen generally, did possess patronage was at parish level, and here immense anger was caused by the growing practice of papal 'provision', whereby the pope simply appointed the priest or reserved the income of a parish for one of his clerks, usually an Italian. The rage was out of all proportion to the scale of the problem, which was quite small, but it was a symptom of a growing feeling of nationality in England and of the Italianization of the papacy as the Roman bureaucracy developed. The Italian clerks were blamed for not residing, but were unpopular if they did. King, laymen and the English church all protested to the pope, and in 1246 Innocent IV went some way to mitigating the practice of 'expectative' appointments, whereby Italian simply succeeded Italian in English benefices.

Both king and pope wished to tax the English church. With the king the clergy could negotiate, and generally preferred to give a lump sum rather than be assessed for scutage, as in 1229 and 1242. Up to a point royal help could be enlisted to resist papal taxation, though Henry III supported Gregory IX's demand for a clerical tax in 1239. It was Henry's own financial straits and his hopes of taxing his subjects that led him to join them in opposing Innocent IV's demand for 10,000 marks in 1244. Loud protests made at the Council of Lyons in 1245 were supported by Henry who forbade collection of the money, but the king eventually backed down when the pope threatened a general interdict. The situation changed when Henry took the cross in 1250. As a crusader the English church actually offered him a tenth of their income for three years; when Henry's vow was commuted to the undertaking to conquer Sicily and pay the pope's debts, king and pope found they could combine to wring money from a more reluctant church. Loud were the protests against this 'alliance of shepherd and wolf', as Matthew Paris called it,[19] and the church responded by summoning a meeting attended by representatives of the monasteries, the cathedrals and the lower clergy, an important step in the development of

---

[19] Chron Maj v, 532.

the later Convocation of Canterbury. It met in August 1257 and drew up a list of grievances which it wanted attended to if it were to produce an offer of money. These involved clerical subjection to the common law, and the effects of the activities of royal administrators on church estates – factors which underlie much of clerical discontent throughout the period from Thomas Becket to Robert Grosseteste, and suggest that less had changed in that time than it might have seemed.

As a member of the western church, England was part of a much larger whole. The centre of power in the western church, Rome, was growing stronger all the time. Its links with England, its control over aspects of English church life, increased somewhat in consequence of the Becket controversy, and strengthened again as a result of developing routine. There was also the natural demand of petitioners and litigants to seek out the centre of power and authority for pronouncements of all kinds, an advantage papal justice shared with its competitor royal justice. Papal authority in England took a huge stride with John's surrender and Henry III's dependence on legates, though it met with resistance both from less-impressionable laymen, among whom nationalistic feelings can be observed, and from a local church which, when it could, took what it wanted from the papal legal and administrative menu and left the rest.

5
England and its Neighbours

The continent

The dominant feature of England's political relations with its continental neighbours was that it was part of a larger group of lands whose lord was in constant conflict with the king of France (see map 1.1). This was a long-term smouldering affair apt to burst into flame periodically; conflict was perhaps inevitable, given that the kings of France could hardly avoid feeling threatened and belittled by a vassal whose lands in France alone were so much more extensive than those under their own direct control. Henry II had all the advantage on his side, Richard I had to give a little ground though he kept the French at bay by strenuous fighting, but in 1202–4 John was dealt a disastrous defeat and lost a crucial part of the French lands of his house. Henry III's attempts at recovery met with no lasting success, until in 1259 he secured generous terms in a treaty with Louis IX. The result of the loss of so much French land was a complete change in the part of France with which England had most contact. At the beginning, relations with Normandy were much the closest, the result of nearly a century of joint development. At the end, the Norman connection had been severed and relations with Gascony had developed: these were to last over 200 years, much longer than those with Normandy had done.

The French kings ultimately turned the tables on their Angevin rivals. The rise of the French monarchy was both the cause and the result of its success in this crucial conflict. The French monarchy has been the dominant political feature of long stretches of European history since the thirteenth century. Though its rise began slowly in the twelfth century, and much remained to be added later in the thirteenth, the crucial period was that of the reigns of Louis VII (1137–80) and especially his son Philip

(1180–1223), whom contemporary eulogists, recognizing the magnitude of his achievements, called 'Augustus' after the first great Roman emperor. The growth of royal power was founded on the success of Louis VII's father, Louis VI 'the Fat', and his adviser, abbot Suger, in gaining control of the core of the royal demesne lands around Paris. Once the grip of the local baronial families had been prised loose the growing wealth of the area, increasingly an exporter of wine and grain to Flanders and northern France, enriched the royal coffers. The other essential precondition was the careful cultivation of the image of the royal family, called Capetian after its first king, Hugh Capet. For the rise of the French monarchy was also a great propaganda triumph, an example of the corrosive and constructive power of ideas and feelings. Pious, holy, just, preservers of the kingdom, defenders of the church, the natural leaders of the crusades, the Capetians enjoyed an air of moral superiority untainted even by political success.

The technique employed in extending their influence beyond the royal demesne was to stress the jurisdictional superiority inherent in their royal and feudal pre-eminence, attracting powers of arbitration and judgment to their court, extending protection to bishops and lordless men, reclaiming lapsed public obligations. To make these methods effective required a good deal of opportunism and flexibility, only pushing hard at open doors, and the resilience to absorb defeats knowing that they could always try again later. For once a royal presence in an area was established it attracted influence and lands to itself, undermining rival powers and jurisdictions in a manner which one historian has compared to the onset of tooth decay.[1] Whatever the previous position had been, there was no doubt that Louis VII was Henry II's lord for all his French possessions. Technically the conquest of the Angevin lands in 1202–4 was the execution of a judicial sentence passed in the court of Philip II. In the end it depended on military power, of course, but the king of France was a difficult enemy to fight; for him a defeat was never final, but victory usually was.

There were other methods of expansion, too, the common aristocratic tools of inheritance and marriage. Philip Augustus acquired very valuable lands in Artois and Vermandois by these means before the war with John. Economic development no doubt also contributed to the 70 per cent rise in Capetian income

---

[1] Dunbabin, *France in the Making*, 266.

between 1180 and 1203. Quantifying medieval finance and armies is notoriously difficult, but the result may well have been that Philip Augustus was able to bring to bear resources superior to John's at the point where the conflict took place.[2] This alone would not necessarily be decisive, but it would certainly give Philip an added advantage.

It was obviously the Norman conquest of England that had brought about the close relationship between England and Normandy. The enrichment of the Conqueror's followers in England had created a strong interest group of cross-Channel landholders which, despite the breakup of the spectacular agglomerations of the Conqueror's half-brothers and many other forfeitures and redistributions, still survived into the thirteenth century.[3] It was to the advantage of the barons who held land on both sides of the Channel to hold them of one lord, in order to avoid agonizing choices. Normandy was marked off from other French provinces by the exceptional strength of its duke, whose close control of his aristocracy and thorough exploitation of his sources of income had led to a precocious development of bureaucratic government. The Norman duke also controlled the local church, its estates and personnel, in a way unique in France but similar to the situation in England. There were some ways in which Normandy resembled England more than the other lands within the kingdom of France. Like England, Normandy had itinerant justices, juries of presentment, possessory assizes, exchequer rolls, forests with forest courts and forest offences. William the Conqueror and his sons had refused to do homage to the king of France for the duchy. Geoffrey of Anjou was the first ruler to do homage for Normandy.

Yet there were signs of divergence between England and Normandy by 1200. The Norman French of England was becoming noticeably different from that spoken in Normandy. The cultural pull exerted by Paris was causing some Norman churchmen to look there for architectural models.[4] There were estates which straddled the Norman–French border too, and some Norman lords were in direct relations with the king of France. It is significant how much John relied on Anglo-Normans to man the defences of the duchy against the French: Robert fitz Walter and Saer de Quency at Vaudreuil, the earl of Salisbury at Pontorson, Roger de Lacy at Château Gaillard, though Englishmen were

[2] Baldwin, *The Government of Philip Augustus*; and see above, p. 51 n. 31.
[3] Powicke, *Loss of Normandy*, 482–520.
[4] L. Grant in Coss and Lloyd, *Thirteenth Century England*, IV, 1991.

prominent there in Henry II's reign too, when William fitz Ralph was seneschal and Richard of Ilchester ran the exchequer. It was not so much that the king-duke was an absentee as that he was more and more peripheral to the life of the province, which was run by a bureaucracy.

Something similar happened in Anjou. The first half of the twelfth century was a period of outstanding success for the counts of Anjou. Fulk V (count 1109–29) and Geoffrey (1129–51) had more than recovered the losses of Fulk le Réchin (d.1109), restoring internal peace, asserting control over the local barons, recovering Maine, checking Henry I of England, and finally even conquering Normandy. Fulk V was a figure of European importance, becoming king of Jerusalem which he ruled until his death in 1142. The inevitable prolonged absences of the counts led to government at a distance with increased powers for the seneschal who now ruled the county. This did much to disrupt the community of interest between the local lords and their supposed leader. The seneschals were well chosen, proving loyal and efficient, and even in 1173 there was little discontent. But local aristocratic society drifted slowly away from the king-counts whom it rarely saw. When in 1203 the seneschal William des Roches went over to Philip Augustus he took the whole county with him.

Normandy and Anjou are good examples of the type of principality centred on its duke or count which had grown up across northern France from the tenth century, and of which the Capetian royal demesne can be seen as another instance. But Celtic Brittany was culturally, linguistically and politically quite different, as different from France as Wales was from England. Ducal authority was small, the machinery for enforcing it simple, and the ducal family bedevilled by succession disputes. Some dukes had recognized the Norman claim to suzerainty. Count Alan, a cadet of the ducal house, had participated in the conquest of England and been rewarded with extensive lands centred on Richmond in Yorkshire. English kings used these lands to exert influence over the rulers of Brittany, granting them to favoured candidates or withholding them entirely. In 1166 Constance, daughter and heiress of Conan IV, was betrothed to Henry II's third surviving son, Geoffrey, and Conan was gradually persuaded to relinquish control of the duchy before his death in 1171. From then until 1181, when Geoffrey came of age and married Constance, Henry ruled Brittany, and thereafter Geoffrey was its duke until his death in 1185. In these years a strong administration was created, controlling and supported by an expanded ducal demesne. A number of rebellions by local magnates were easily crushed. After 1186 Constance ruled the duchy pending the succession of her son Arthur.

Normandy and Anjou, already centralized principalities intended as the endowment for the eldest son of the Angevin house in Henry II's scheme, stayed together under Richard and John and were taken over together by Philip Augustus. In Brittany, originally intended for a younger son, a strong principality was created by the Angevins which avoided incorporation in the Capetian monarchy and instead survived to trouble Philip Augustus's successors. The destiny of the great province of Aquitaine, nearly as large as lowland England and much less united, was different again. The centres of ducal control under William IX (1086–1126) were Poitiers, Saintes near the coast and Bordeaux, but elsewhere the dukes presided over a loose confederation of powerful semi-independent lords rather than a principality like Anjou or Normandy. Such lords might always feel the temptation to enter into direct relations with the king of France. The acquisition of Gascony in the eleventh century had overextended the counts of Poitou, who were increasingly drawn towards Spain and Toulouse to the neglect of their interests elsewhere. William IX allowed control of the castellans of Poitou to slacken, and the counts of Angoulême and La Marche went their own way. The rule of William X did nothing to strengthen the duke's position, and his solution for the future was to marry his elder daughter, Eleanor, to king Louis VII in the hope that he would make good her rights. But Louis paid little attention to his wife's lands, and the aristocracy of the area became used to an absentee duke. From 1152, when Henry II took over the duchy in right of Eleanor whom he married after her divorce from Louis, to 1173 they certainly saw more of their duchess than they had done previously. Henry's intention for Aquitaine was as an endowment for his second surviving son, Richard, who took it over in 1174. Richard attempted a greater degree of control than had been applied before, and was met with more concerted resistance. He defeated a general rising in 1176 and won a number of more restricted wars in subsequent years, but the house of Lusignan and the counts of Angoulême were still powerful and independent, perhaps even more so, when Richard died. He claimed the right of wardship of minors and asserted control over fortifications, but his power to enforce such active lordship depended to a great extent on his presence in the area, which became very intermittent after 1189.

Other kinds of change made more difference in the long run. The ducal town of La Rochelle had been founded in 1130 and rapidly became a boom town, joining Saintes, Bordeaux and Bayonne in an expanding trade with England. It was now that the English began to develop their taste for Bordeaux wines, sending cloth, grain and silver in return. The tolls on trade enriched the duke. The desire of the townsmen to have the same political authority at both ends of the trade route became very clear in the thirteenth century. While the maritime towns were gravitating towards England and Richard checked the influence of Aragon in southern Gascony, Poitou was strengthening its links with northern France in legal custom and language: the border between the lands of customary law and those of written law, and between the *langue d'oil* of the north and the *langue d'oc* of the south came to sever Poitou from Gascony. The two regions had never sat comfortably together, and the French conquest of Poitou but not Gascony recognized an old difference that was gaining new vigour.

It will be clear from this rapid glance that even the French provinces of the 'Angevin Empire' were quite disparate, their overlord being their only common feature. They had been brought together by conquest and marriage, not by accident – in fact, quite deliberately and with some effort – but without any intention of founding a unified or permanent 'state'. We have already seen how Henry intended to divide them among his sons. His plans were frustrated by the accidents of mortality – these really were accidents – and it was conquest that eventually decided their fate.

During Richard's captivity on the return journey from his crusade, Philip Augustus had taken the Vexin, a strategically vital region on the border between Rouen and Paris. Some important border fortresses had also fallen, and Richard was unable to regain them all in subsequent fighting. On Richard's death John, who ironically was staying with his nephew Arthur of Brittany and Constance his mother, quickly seized the treasury at Chinon and then rode to Rouen where he was acclaimed as duke. Meanwhile an assembly of barons from Anjou, Maine and Touraine had declared for Arthur, who was sure of Brittany in any case and of the support of Philip Augustus. After a brief visit to England for his coronation John returned to the attack in Anjou. On his approach William des Roches, the seneschal, went over to John's side to save his own position, and helped John come to an agreement with the Bretons. The aged Eleanor made over her inheritance to John at the same time. Deserted by his allies, Philip also made peace with John. By the treaty of Le Goulet of 22 May 1200, John was recognized as Richard's heir for all his continental fiefs and Arthur was to hold Brittany of him. But what appeared to be victory for John was undermined by the terms of the treaty in two important respects: he agreed to pay an enormous sum, 20,000 marks, as relief to Philip for recognition, something none of his predecessors had ever done, and he accepted Philip's demand to receive back some Aquitainian rebels and to renounce his alliance with the count of Flanders, who was Philip's vassal. The treaty thus recognized Philip's feudal superiority and gave practical effect to it in an unprecedented and prophetic fashion.

It was an appeal to Philip's court from Aquitainian rebels that began the chain of events which ended in John's defeat. On a rapid tour of the south in the summer of 1200 John quite suddenly married Isabella, daughter and heiress of the count of Angoulême. In some ways this was a sensible move, bringing John allies and the prospect of important lands in an area where they would be very useful, but unfortunately Isabella had been engaged to Hugh, lord of Lusignan, and before long John heard rumours of forthcoming trouble from the widespread and powerful Lusignan kin. He ordered his officials to harry their lands. Their response was to appeal to Philip, who went so far as to invite John to Paris to discuss the affair. John agreed to try the Lusignans in his court and, if this was satisfactory, Philip would not press the matter. But the trial was a farce: John charged the Lusignans with treason and offered them trial by battle against professional duellists. Unsurprisingly, they again appealed to Philip, and John, after further prevarication, was cited to appear before Philip's court in Paris. John neither went nor sent an excuse. The court judged him contumacious and sentenced him to forfeiture.

The story is interesting as an illustration of the difference in political style between John and Philip. John was chronically suspicious, high-handed in his treatment of men whose loyalty would be a great advantage, arrogant when he thought he was winning. Philip covered himself: it was impossible to accuse him of being unreasonable, impossible to think of John's behaviour as anything else. Philip clothed his wiliness in dignity and respect for legal processes. John's deviousness earned him contempt. As the sequel showed, John's fear of disloyalty was justified, but he had only himself to blame for bringing it about.

While Philip besieged the frontier fortresses of Normandy in July 1202 Arthur attacked up the Loire valley, turning aside to besiege Eleanor at Mirebeau in Poitou. John now, for once in his life, emulated his father and brother and suddenly turned up with an army where he was not expected. He rescued Eleanor, and in the process captured Arthur and all the leading rebels of Poitou. The prisoners were taken to Normandy and England. Arthur now disappears from view. What happened to him is not known: one chronicler says John murdered him one day after dinner in a drunken rage, another that John stabbed him in a boat on the Seine. Whatever happened, John was blamed for it, though pope Innocent III later took the view that a better fate was not to be expected for a young man who had broken oaths of fealty to rebel against his uncle and been caught besieging his aged grandmother.[5] Arthur does not seem to have been popular, except with the Bretons, who were entranced by the magic of his name. Rumours of his death soon began to circulate and Philip made the most of them. William des Roches again changed sides and took the Loire provinces with him, while John misguidedly released Hugh de Lusignan who immediately went into rebellion. In Normandy once the frontier fortresses had fallen there was a general slide into Philip's camp by such of the Norman barons as dared; by this time most of John's men were mercenaries, Gerard d'Athée and his band in the Loire valley, and Louvrecaire in Normandy. It was not long before John lost his nerve, and on 5 December 1203 he fled to England. On 6 March 1204 Château Gaillard was taken by storm. Louvrecaire surrendered Falaise and went over to Philip. Caen surrendered without a fight, but not before John's clerks had removed the Norman archives to England. Finally, on 24 June 1204 Rouen, isolated and without hope of assistance from John, gave itself up to Philip. Of the duchy of Normandy only the Channel Islands remained to the English crown. The last strongholds of the Angevin empire to surrender were Chinon, held by Hubert de Burgh, at Easter 1205 and Loches, held by Gerard d'Athée, in June. John paid the commanders' ransoms and brought them to England.

John did not resign himself to his losses. He took a small force to Gascony and Poitou in 1206 which helped to stabilize the

---

[5] M. Dominica Legge, 'William the Marshal and Arthur of Brittany', *BIHR* 55 (1982), 18–24; Flores Hist ii, 186.

situation there, but he spent much of his reign planning French expeditions which never sailed. It was not until 1214 that he again set foot on the continent. This expedition was part of a wide and ambitious scheme of European diplomacy, involving John's nephew Otto of Brunswick, who had been crowned emperor but excommunicated by the pope, and a coalition of princes along the northern border of France including the duke of Brabant and the count of Flanders. Meanwhile, Philip Augustus planned an invasion of England, but his fleet was destroyed at Damme, the port of Bruges, in April 1213. The way was clear for a two-pronged invasion of France. John struck north-east from Poitou, and Philip detached a force under his son Louis to deal with the threat. Louis caught up with John at La Roche-aux-Moines; the Poitevins refused to fight, and the deserted John was compelled to flee to La Rochelle. The more serious invasion, from the east, Philip met himself at Bouvines. There a rare decisive battle was fought on 27 July 1214. Philip was nearly killed, but the French victory was complete; Otto abandoned the field, and some of John's allies were captured. The battle locked Philip's achievements in place, and gave the French monarchy a European dominance it retained until the Hundred Years' War.

The defeat of Bouvines spelt disaster for John's plans, even though he was not directly involved there, and ushered in a period in which English governments, both that of the minority and Henry III, seemed powerless to do anything but hold the line in Gascony – and that at great cost. In 1224 Louis VIII overran Poitou but failed to penetrate Gascony. He died two years later, and the regency for his young son Louis IX was assumed by his widow Blanche of Castile, in political skills the most impressive of Henry II's grandchildren. She held together French royal power and frustrated Henry III's attempts to assert himself on the continent. In 1230 Henry sailed with a fleet to Brittany, encouraged by the count, Peter Mauclerc, who had married Alice of Thouars, the daughter and recognized heiress of Constance of Brittany. Henry paraded through Poitou down to Bordeaux dispensing money; the local lords submitted to him as he passed but went back to their French allegiance as soon as he left. Significantly, there was no attempt, in 1230 or later, to recapture Normandy: the south-west was Henry's priority, and the English lords who still harboured memories of Norman lands now recognized the hopelessness of regaining them by coming to a series of family arrangements rationalizing the remaining cross-Channel claims.[6] English support for Henry's continental ambitions dried up.

It was 1242 before Henry mounted another expedition, prompted by the installation of Louis IX's brother Alphonse as count of Poitou. Encouraged by his mother Isabella, now married to Hugh de Lusignan, count of La Marche, Henry came with all the forces he could raise in the teeth of opposition at home. The ensuing confrontation with a French army at Taillebourg was less a battle than a precipitate retreat by the English forces. In the 1240s and 1250s the prospects deteriorated further: a French noble had become king of Navarre, and Capetian influence was steadily strengthening throughout the Languedoc and Provence. The conquest of the south of France by the north, beginning with the Albigensian crusades and continuing through the thirteenth century as Capetian princes were placed in Provence, Poitou and Toulouse, altered the political context and left Gascony with its English lord increasingly anomalous. Even though the towns welcomed the English trade and the nobles preferred the weak authority of a distant king, Gascony was riven by noble and urban feuds. The appointment of Simon de Montfort to govern the province with a firm hand ended in bitter recriminations and the trial of Simon in 1242. Henry now made over Gascony to his son Edward, and to bolster his position there arranged an alliance with Alfonso X, king of Castile, and Edward's marriage with Alfonso's half-sister Eleanor.

In the middle 1250s a favourable diplomatic conjuncture led to the peace agreement with the French king, finalized as the Treaty of Paris of 1259. Louis IX was concerned, perhaps unnecessarily, at Henry's alliance with Castile and anyway wished for a stable peace to free his hands for the crusade. Alfonso's aims were similar: he planned an invasion of north Africa for which he hoped to enlist Henry's help. Pope Alexander IV (1254–61) wished to arrange peace in France so that Henry could concentrate on the Sicilian venture. The English barons had no further interest in expensive conflicts with the French kings, while Henry's influential Savoyard relatives also wished him to concentrate on Sicily. Finally, Henry himself wanted security in Gascony for his son, and was now prepared to buy it by surrendering his other claims. Henry was now Louis's brother-in-law, and enjoyed his extended family; he had gone to a Christmas

---

[6] Stacey, *Politics, Policy and Finance*, 173.

party in Paris in 1254 and taken the opportunity to see the sights. The peace, and to some extent the wrangles which ultimately followed from it, were a family affair. The treaty was concluded on 28 May 1258, but ratification was delayed until December 1259 by arguments about the dowry of Henry's sister Eleanor, married to Simon de Montfort. Under the treaty Henry renounced his claims to Normandy, Maine, Anjou and Poitou, receiving in return a Gascony extended eastwards to include the three dioceses of Limoges, Périgueux and Cahors. Henry performed liege homage to Louis, who agreed to help Henry with his Sicilian commitments. The agreement was widely unpopular in France, especially in the three dioceses where ill-defined rights gave rise to much future conflict. Louis was blamed at the time for excessive generosity, but replied that Henry was now his man, which he had not been previously. Louis was right in the sense that the English kings were once again bound into a subordinate relationship with their relatives of France. The Angevin empire had ceased to be even an aspiration: 'English Gascony' had arrived, and the Hundred Years' War was just over the horizon.

We have seen how John in 1214 and Henry III with the Sicilian affair and the Treaty of Paris were involved in the web of European diplomacy. All the English kings of this period were in diplomatic contact with potentates across the continent, as is clear from the marriages of the royal family (see figure 5.1). The chief organizing principle was hostility to the king of France, with the fluctuations of papal–imperial relations and ecclesiastical quarrels adding complications. The acquisition of Gascony brought the English kings into serious contact with Spain. The result was a series of marriages aimed at securing peace and allies beyond the Pyrenees. The first was that of Henry II's daughter Eleanor to Alfonso VIII of Castile, and then Richard's to Berengaria of Navarre; the young Edward's to Eleanor of Castile kept up the connection. Henry II acted as peacemaker in the south, mediating between Alfonso II of Aragon and Raymond V of Toulouse in 1173, and again between Alfonso VIII of Castile and Sancho 'the Wise' of Navarre in 1176. The marriage of Henry's daughter Joan to William of Sicily was unusually distant; the unique adventure of the crusade brought Richard I into direct contact with Sicilian politics, but the southern kingdom remained generally beyond the reach of English kings, as Henry III's disastrous acceptance of its crown for his younger son Edmund made all too clear.

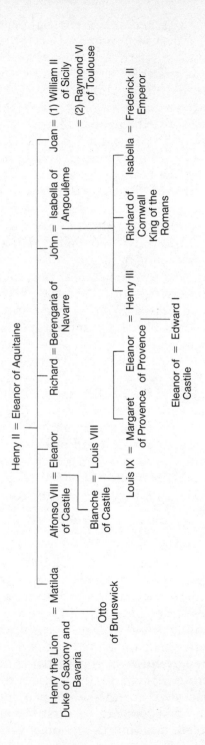

FIGURE 5.1 Selective table to indicate the continental connections of the Angevin family

With Germany and the Low Countries relations were much more continuous. Henry's mother had been married to a German emperor, and in 1165 the emperor Frederick Barbarossa's chancellor, Rainald of Dassel, archbishop of Cologne, arranged a marriage between Henry's daughter Matilda and Henry 'the Lion', duke of Saxony and Bavaria, a member of the Welf family. The Welfs were more often enemies than allies of Barbarossa's dynasty, the Hohenstaufen, and for Henry II and his sons the Welf connection periodically threw them into opposition to the emperors, who in turn were often allied to the Capetians. Richard was captured on his return from the crusade by the duke of Austria, who handed him over to Barbarossa's son Henry VI. Richard had to pay a vast ransom for his release, and on his return journey to England he took the opportunity to construct a coalition of princes, including the archbishops of Cologne and Mainz, the bishop of Liège and the counts of Brabant and Flanders, aimed at Philip of France. This network of alliances lasted until Bouvines in 1214. On Henry VI's death in 1197, Richard supported the candidacy of his nephew Otto of Brunswick for the empire, and he and John supported Otto in his war against the Hohenstaufen candidate backed by Philip Augustus. The 20 years to 1214 saw an unusually coherent Europe-wide conflict, with well-defined groups of protagonists. Henry III's diplomatic manoeuvring was more *ad hoc*, and despite the marriage of his sister Isabella to the emperor Frederick II in 1235 he cut a much less impressive figure than Henry II or Richard I. With the loss of most of the French lands the Plantagenet dynasty had been forced out of the centre of European politics, a situation which they could not begin to repair until the 1259 treaty.

The British Isles

From the Welsh coast near St Davids, and from many places in south-west Scotland, Ireland is clearly visible. Whatever the silent toll in human discomfort – the Irish Sea is infamously rough – the western seas have been a highway since prehistoric times, linking Britain and Ireland in settlement, trade and politics. From the ninth century to the twelfth the organizers of the Irish Sea world were not the Celtic peoples or the English but the Norse, who had founded the first towns in Ireland and established a scattered maritime dominion covering Man and the

Hebrides, owing secular allegiance to the king of Norway and ecclesiastical obedience to the archbishop of Trondheim, when they could enforce it. The century after 1150 saw the rise of English hegemony in the British Isles. The hegemony was political, cultural and economic: the English replaced the Norwegians on the sea, institutions modelled on those of Norman England spread into Celtic regions, and English kings and lords wielded the dominant political power. The crucial event in an evolving situation was the partial conquest of Ireland.

Wales and Ireland in the twelfth century had a great deal in common. Both possessed a high degree of cultural and linguistic unity and distinctiveness, but were riven by political fragmentation and local particularism. The basis of the economy of both countries was pastoral, despite some cereal-growing in favoured lowlands; this made for a much more physically mobile society than was normal in most of western Europe. Moving to the uplands for summer grazing was the normal way of exploiting vital natural resources, and it was this that caused outsiders to think of the Welsh and Irish as pastoral nomads. In Ireland especially, cattle were the form in which wealth was held, despite the presence of Norse trading towns round the coasts.

Kingship in Welsh and Irish society implied little in the way of governmental or legal responsibilities. Administrative machinery stayed rudimentary as, with no native coinage, comparatively little in the way of towns or trade, and taxation taken largely in the form of food renders and hospitality dues, there was little to administer. Though the Hiberno-Norse towns struck coins, Gaelic Irish society was 'essentially coinless'.[7] Law was customary, interpreted by a professional hereditary caste of jurists. The king was primarily the leader of his war-band, and his proper function was raiding. The main booty was cattle, which Irish kings distributed among their subject people or returned in exchange for hostages when hostilities ended. Plundering was a normal feature of life, and was directed at whoever was in reach, Welsh, Irish, English or Norse. 'The glory of the Welsh is in plunder and theft', wrote Walter Map; it was a reproach to die without a wound, so few Welshmen lived to be old.[8] This meant that political activity in both countries was driven by the momentum of the war-band, which required a constant rate of successful aggression to keep up the flow of plunder and main-

---

[7] Michael Dolley in A. Cosgrove, *A New History of Ireland*, 816.
[8] Walter Map, 197.

tain the prestige which kept the war-band large and loyal. Gerald
of Wales remarked on the primitive nature of the Irish soldiery,
armed only with short spears, darts and sling stones, and upro-
tected by armour.[9] Though this may reflect poverty and back-
wardness, such forces were in fact well adapted to raiding,
burning and rustling.

The situation was exacerbated by the rule of partible inheritance among male heirs. Though some princes attempted to pass
on their principalities to a designated heir, the strength of other
claimants plus belief in the legality and justness of partibility
ensured that it was what normally occurred.[10] The group of potential heirs could be scattered widely over collateral branches.
In Ireland the church's most basic teachings on marriage had
made little impact on the behaviour of princes, and the pool of
potential heirs could be very large: 'Irish dynasts married early
and often'.[11] In this situation a number of basic patterns of
events could emerge; the heirs might co-operate, but strife between brothers and cousins was commoner. Sometimes, all the
princes but one died natural or assisted deaths, leaving a single
survivor; sometimes a large principality could fragment to the
point where it virtually ceased to count in national politics – as
happened in Wales to Powys after 1160 and in Ireland repeated-
ly to the O'Neills of Ulster. Sometimes, a successful chief would
outlive all his rivals and for a couple of generations conflicts
would be confined to the relatively small group of his immediate
descendants. Lineage was a prerequisite, but effective succession
took personal military prowess and leadership. And whatever
the outcome, civil war was a near-certainty.

But succession was not the only cause of strife, as would-
be princes did not confine themselves to the lands of their
dynasty. The situation was much more a free-for-all in which
the strongest took whatever he could wherever he found it: the
boundaries of a prince's territories fluctuated according to his
military power and success. In a society made up of a large
number of small chieftainries an aggressive king could by these
means put together a personal empire of subject chiefs, but it
would not survive his death or other misadventure and his
subjects would be looking for the first opportunity to break free.

[9] Gerald of Wales v, 150–1.
[10] Davies, *Conquest, Coexistence and Change*, 267; cf. J. Beverley Smith, 'The succession to Welsh princely inheritance; the evidence reconsidered', in Davies, *The British
Isles*, 64–81.
[11] F. J. Byrne in Cosgrove, *A New History of Ireland*, 41.

He might also have imposed his power on groups of recalcitrant relatives who would be itching to depose him. This provides the background to another of Gerald's strictures, that the Irish were too ready to break their oaths of allegiance – the oaths were extorted by force, and held only so long as that force was superior.[12] A king's principality was his own creation and was likely to die with him. This was both a curse and a blessing: while it fostered internecine strife and divided the Welsh and Irish, it presented the Anglo-Normans with a much harder job of conquest as each fragment had to be conquered separately, a new foe could spring up anywhere, and there was no overall authority with which to make agreements. Though in Ireland a smaller number of kingdoms were gaining greater definition and the power of their kings was growing in the eleventh and twelfth centuries, and they were open to outside influences particularly visible in the reorganization of the Irish church, the contrast with the types of power structure prevalent in England, and much of Europe, remained.

The use of foreign mercenaries appeared to offer a possibility of more lasting domination to those kings who could afford to hire them. An Irish king hired a Scottish-Norse fleet from the Hebrides in 1154, and the western Highlands of Scotland were the source of the heavily armed infantry known as *galloglass* prominent in Ireland from the thirteenth century. But for a brief period in the later twelfth century, with consequences that soon became clear, a number of kings took to hiring Anglo-Norman lords and their forces from Wales.

The political situation in Scotland differed from Wales and Ireland in a crucial respect; here a strong, unitary monarchy had developed in the eleventh and early twelfth century which had long had close ties with England and which aimed to treat with English kings on equal terms. Many of the social and economic institutions of the contemporary European world – towns, coinage, armoured knights, castles, religious orders, parish organization – came into Scotland by royal invitation, and remained under royal control. Themselves major English barons, they or close relatives holding the honour of Huntingdon, the Scottish kings imported Anglo-Norman knights and settled them on fees and in castles, creating an aristocracy owing military service in the Anglo-Norman manner. Wars with England were infrequent in the century after 1154, and the Scottish monarchy took the opportunity of peace in the south gradually to extend its in-

[12] Gerald of Wales v, 165.

fluence outwards from its base in the east and south-east of the
country into Galloway and the western and northern Highlands.
It did so with a minimum of disturbance of the native aristocracy, which was quietly assimilated into the new dispensation.
The result was the bringing together in a single kingdom of
originally quite disparate people; the English of Lothian, the
Gaelic-speakers of the Highlands and the Norse of the Isles. One
component of this variegated world were the Anglo-Norman
newcomers, who were introduced into the towns and the church
as well as the military aristocracy. Those who had landed interests in England did not thereby lose them: a group of barons
came into existence for whom the border had no reality.[13] The
occasional Anglo-Scottish wars made their position difficult but
did not destroy them as a group.

To the Scottish kings, on the other hand, the border was of
more concern. The way in which the kingdom had developed,
with a power based in central Scotland conquering Lothian and
thus dividing the lands of the ancient kingdom of Northumbria,
had left uncertainty about the border line. The situation contrasted with that on England's other land frontier, where Offa's
Dyke had been recognized as a border for centuries even though
Norman conquest had pushed beyond it. At Henry II's accession
Northumberland, Cumberland and Westmorland were in the
hands of the young king of Scots, Malcolm IV (1153–65), having
been taken over by his grandfather, David I, during Stephen's reign.
Despite a promise to David, who had supported the Angevin
cause throughout Stephen's reign and who had knighted Henry,
the English king in 1157 simply demanded the counties back.
Malcolm surrendered them, 'wisely considering that the king of
England had the better of the argument by reason of his greater
power'.[14] In return Malcolm received the Huntingdon lands and
did homage to Henry. Malcolm's successors did not all show his
wisdom, and the northern counties remained a bone of conten-
tion although the Scots never won them back. His brother and
successor William the Lion (1165–1214) joined enthusiastically
in the war of 1173–4 and invaded England, only to suffer the
ignominious fate of capture while his army was dispersed on
foraging expeditions. By the 'treaty of Falaise' he was made
to do liege homage to Henry specifically for Scotland and to
surrender the main royal castles in order to secure his release.

[13] G. G. Simpson in Stringer, *Essays*, 102.
[14] Newburgh i, 105–6.

The subordination of the Scottish kingdom became another issue between the kings. William bought his release from feudal subjection from Richard in 1189, and in 1237 his son Alexander II (1214–49) gave up his claim on the northern counties, receiving in return estates in England to add to the honour of Huntingdon – for which, of course, he had to do homage. Henry III implicitly accepted Scotland as a separate kingdom; its king was in effect subordinate, though precisely in what way and how far did not bear close examination.

MAP 5.1 The British Isles in the early thirteenth century

Henry II's first concern in Wales was re-establishment of the situation of his grandfather's day. The strongest and most resilient of the principalities was Gwynedd, based on the lowlands of Anglesey, which had the strategic advantage of being furthest from the centres of English power (see map 5.1). Powys had lost land to the border lords of Cheshire and Shropshire, while the dynasty of Deheubarth had been restricted to the upland and forest. But Stephen's reign had seen a general revolt of the Welsh under Norman rule and recaptures of territory by the princes. The Norman conquests in Wales are often regarded as private enterprise, but this period of Welsh resurgence shows how dependent they were on the final sanction of a strong king ruling in England. Henry brought the Welsh princes to heel, not without difficulty. It could be that a more precise and demeaning interpretation was placed on their subordinate status than they were prepared to accept: otherwise it is hard to explain the rare unanimity of the Welsh revolt of 1164. Henry's great punitive expedition of 1165 was opposed by all the princes and they dealt him one of his rare defeats, greatly assisted by appalling weather. Henry seems to have learnt a lesson, reconciling himself with the princes and hiring Welsh mercenaries for use in France.

In all these events the linkage between the component parts of the British Isles can be seen working. Henry's allies in putting pressure on king Malcolm included Murrough Mac Lochlan, the Irish high-king (1148–66), and a chieftain from Gaelic Argyll bearing the Norse name Somerled, who disrupted the Norse lordship of Man and the Isles by taking over the Inner Hebrides. In 1165 Henry hired a fleet from Dublin to combine with his land invasion of north Wales. But it was the conquest of much of Ireland by Anglo-Norman lords that ushered in a new stage of British politics, finally shouldering the Norwegians out and binding Ireland much more tightly into a British political system in which the dominant power was England.

Long previously the English pope Adrian IV had given Henry II permission to take over Ireland, allegedly in order to reform the church, but the conquest did not begin under royal auspices and Henry had to act quickly to retain a measure of control. In 1166 Dermot Mac Murrough, king of Leinster, defeated by a powerful combination of Irish chiefs led by the high-king Rory O Connor of Connacht, took the unprecedented step of going into exile to hire Anglo-Norman support. He travelled to the continent to obtain Henry II's permission to recruit, and found soldiers ready to follow him in south Wales. The Bristol merchant and money lender Robert fitz Harding played a shadowy but important role in financing the expedition and in introducing Dermot to Richard de Clare, lord of Chepstow and earl of Pembroke, known to posterity as 'Strongbow'. The first group crossed in May 1169 and helped Dermot re-establish himself. Strongbow followed in August 1170, capturing Waterford and soon afterwards Dublin. He was rewarded with the hand of Dermot's daughter Aife and the succession to Leinster after Dermot's death. The latter grant was invalid in Irish law, and when Dermot died in May 1171 Rory O Connor challenged Strongbow for possession of Dublin. Though the Anglo-Normans won the ensuing battle Richard's position was extremely precarious, especially as Henry had seized his Welsh and English lands. He was forced to surrender the towns to Henry and hold his Irish lands of him. Strongbow, who may never have intended to set himself up as an independent king, remained loyal to Henry and fought for him in Normandy in 1173–4.

Henry II's own expedition to Ireland in the winter of 1171–2 did much to establish the outlines of the later medieval lordship. The royal demesne, consisting of Dublin, Wexford and Waterford and their lands, remained too small to back up real power, especially as Wexford was soon given to Strongbow, while the grant of Meath to Hugh de Lacy to hold for the service of 50 knights established both the feudal subjection of the great Anglo-Norman lords to the English crown and the practice of assigning areas under Irish control to lords to conquer if they could. The Lacys succeeded, but many others in future were to fail. Most of the Irish chiefs submitted to Henry; if they hoped to secure his backing against the invaders their hopes were illusory, as royal interest in Ireland was never more than intermittent and the colonizing lords exerted political influence in England. Ireland was incorporated into Henry's scheme for his dominions when it was assigned to his youngest son, John. By the time of John's first visit in 1185 the east and south coastlands had been conquered, Hugh de Lacy had pushed west to the Shannon and John de Courcy had taken over Ulster in the last of the great Norman private-enterprise conquests. John made expectative grants to his followers, introducing Theobald Walter, ancestor of the Butlers, and William de Burgh, progenitor of the Burkes, who expanded towards Limerick. Anglo-Norman power in Ireland reached its height after 1235 when Richard de Burgh achieved a short-lived conquest of much of Connacht, aided by dissension in the O Connor family.

A dramatic instance of the British political unit being conceived of and treated as such came in 1209–11. John's campaigns then were probably the only time in the middle ages when
an English king set out to impose his will throughout the isles
and succeeded. In August 1209 he intimidated William the Lion
of Scotland into giving hostages and surrendering some border
castles. In October most of the Welsh princes submitted and did
homage, and English free tenants had to do the same. In June
1210 the king crossed to Ireland with a large army. He was
pursuing his vendetta against William de Braose, but he also
wanted and obtained the submission of the magnates and recognition from the Irish. The campaign was a brilliant success and
he was able to leave Ireland in August. The following year he
broke with Llewelyn of Gwynedd and mounted the most effective royal invasion yet seen in Wales, overrunning Gwynedd and
burning Bangor. But the triumph was of short duration: in 1212
Wales was engulfed in revolt, and thereafter John slowly sank
into the sea of his other troubles. The next royal expedition to
Ireland was in 1394.

Much of thirteenth-century Anglo-Welsh politics resolves itself
into relations between the kings of England and the princes of
Gwynedd. When the kings were embroiled in difficulties elsewhere the princes were not slow to seize their opportunity, but
when the king's attention was seriously directed towards Wales
the power and pretensions of the princes were drastically reduced. Llewelyn ap Iorwerth dominated Wales until his death in
1240. The extent and nature of his authority, though 'patri-
archal rather than institutional in character',[15] were more impressive than those of any previous Welsh prince, but he did not
rule over a united principality of Wales and made no attempt to
create one. He tried to hand his authority on to his son Dafydd,
but much of it died with him. Dafydd was hampered by the
claims of his half-brother Gruffudd, but even more by the power
and interest of the English crown. The situation had begun to
change to the king's advantage even before Llewelyn's death, a
crucial factor being the escheat to the crown of the earldom of
Chester in 1237. The young lord Edward was given Wales in
1254 and, although not called prince, the connection between
Wales and the heir to the English crown was established. In the
next year another portentous event occurred: Llewelyn, son of
Dafydd's half-brother, defeated his brothers and emerged as sole

15 Davies, *Conquest, Coexistence and Change*, 245.

ruler in Gwynedd. The two principal actors were in place for the next scene in the drama, the conflict between Llewelyn ap Gruffudd and Edward I.

Ireland and Wales continued to have much in common in the way they were affected by conquest and settlement. By 1170 the initial period of conquest in Wales had ended, and Ireland enjoyed relative peace from the early thirteenth century, although nowhere in Wales was ever free from the threat of raiding, and there were many wars. Both countries moved from a period of conquest to one of consolidation and intensified economic exploitation. In both the newcomers occupied most of the best arable lowland and soon began to organize manors and build mills, while boroughs quickly grew up at the gates of castles, introducing south Wales and much of Ireland to the kind of society and economy common to most of Europe. The native princes were now largely confined to the Welsh uplands and the far west and north of Ireland, harder and less profitable to conquer.

Among the Welsh there was a gradual shift away from raiding towards more systematic economic exploitation, and the political geography was crystallizing, with the three major principalities, Gwynedd, Powys and Deheubarth, becoming more stable. The tendency was increasingly towards armed coexistence with the incomers. There was much mutual hatred and some bitter feuds, but there were also alliances and intermarriage. Wales eventually developed a single dominant principality, Gwynedd, which was left sufficiently alone to benefit from economic changes and an increased princely power which became more noticeable after 1257. In Ireland also 'two nations' began to emerge, the Gaelic-speakers remaining defiantly unaffected by the doings of the incomers while the 'Anglo-Irish' gradually became more Hibernicized and aware of their separateness from the English of England. But Irish kingship languished, pushed to the periphery of the island, its royal claims abandoned by the church, and always endangered by family feuds.

It was in the period after 1170 that the term 'the March of Wales' became current to describe those parts of Wales not under native Welsh rule. The lordships of the March differed from those in England in a number of important ways. They were generally compact, with the lord owning all the land except that belonging to the church, holding it of the king but admitting nothing in the way of royal power except the feudal incidents such as wardship of minors. In the precarious conditions of the Welsh frontier personal military service by vassals remained essential for security, and society long retained a militaristic air. A superstructure of government and exploitation based on English models, such as writs, baronial exchequers and sheriffs, and a hierarchy of manorial, burghal and county courts, developed in the thirteenth century on a basis often distinctively Welsh. The Marchers paid no taxes to the king. The king's writ did not run and there were no royal sheriffs or justices and no final appeal to the king's court. The 'law of the March' was described as the only one applicable to the March in Magna Carta. The larger lordships such as Glamorgan, Pembroke or Brecon were in effect miniature kingdoms whose lords held privileges that those in other lands subject to the king of England did not even dare to claim. This combination of compact, virtually independent lordships and a population inured to warfare provided the major Marcher lords with a power base from which they were sometimes able to exert decisive influence in England.

The Irish situation differed in that the king was always represented by a justiciar who was virtually a viceroy; the common law applied to the settlers, though not to the Irish, and a semblance of royal administration was introduced with an Irish exchequer and chancery. The introduction of counties provides a good indication of the spread of settlement: Dublin before 1200, Cork and Waterford by 1208, Louth and Kerry by 1233, Limerick and Tipperary in the 1230s and Connacht by 1247.[16] The royal interest in Ireland reaped some financial rewards: Henry III was able to draw cash from the Irish exchequer, and supplies in kind were useful when campaigns in Wales were organized. But Ireland also had its great 'liberties', equivalent to the Welsh Marcher lordships, notably Leinster, which descended to the Marshal family, and Meath and Ulster. On the extinction of the Marshals in the male line in 1247 their vast Irish estate was partitioned among numerous husbands and descendants of the six Marshal sisters, who all had more important interests elsewhere.

By 1250 the British Isles were more of a unit than they had been a century earlier. A world of Anglo-Welsh, Anglo-Irish and Anglo-Scottish estates had grown up whose holders looked ultimately to the king of England as their lord. This world was underpinned by similar economic and social developments and

[16] James Lydon in Cosgrove, *A New History of Ireland*, 170–3.

expanded trading links; and tenant families and church connections followed in the wake of the great lords. In Wales and
Ireland this world had largely been created by the lords themselves, with the English kings running to catch up; neither Henry II
nor John tried to conquer Wales or Ireland. From the later
twelfth century marriage and inheritance did more than royal
grants to create strong aristocratic bonds between England and
Scotland. The Marshal family were the most spectacular of the
'international' aristocrats, holding Longueville in Normandy, a
group of English manors, Chepstow, Usk and Pembroke in south
Wales, and Leinster in Ireland, but the Lacys and others were
scattered nearly as widely, while many of the leading families of
Scotland held English land, and there were instances of Scottish-
Irish estates. In all three Celtic countries new settlers had been
introduced, towns and markets founded, and institutions of law
and administration developed on the English model. It is not true
that trade followed the conquerors, since Dublin, and probably
other Norse towns of Ireland, had extensive contacts with England and across northern Europe before 1169, but the relative
peace and order of the thirteenth century in much of Britain
encouraged an agricultural boom which led to large surpluses
available for export, and the direct links with English towns and
lords did much to stimulate trade across the Irish Sea. Irish ports
also traded directly with Gascony. The Norwegians were on the
brink of finally being forced out, and the organizers of the lands
around the western seas were now people who could, with
increasing justification, be called English.

Part II

Society and Culture

6

Rural Society

The landscape

The England of the Angevin kings was a very old country. The landscape had developed through thousands of years of human activity, and traces of its antiquity were to be found everywhere. Much of England had been intensively farmed in Iron Age and Roman times, and it seems likely that in a number of places the estate boundaries, fields and paths laid out then survived into the medieval period and later. Historians no longer believe that the Anglo-Saxons faced a land of extensive virgin forest, in which earlier settlement was confined to the uplands with light soils. The history of the English landscape is, rather, one of an ebb and flow of settlement and agriculture. Parts of the Midland forests, such as Needwood and Wychwood, which were woodland in Domesday Book and royal forest under the Angevin kings, had been quite intensively settled and farmed in prehistoric and Roman times, but later reclaimed by woods.

The forms of settlement had also changed over centuries: the creation of nucleated villages, where all the farms and houses are grouped together surrounded by the fields, is now held to be a development beginning in the later Saxon period and continuing into the twelfth century; it is not a type of settlement that the Anglo-Saxon invaders brought with them from their continental homeland in the fifth and sixth centuries. Villages might grow, move or contract, hamlets grow together to form a village or house sites be abandoned, creating a scatter of habitations. The fields themselves could be reorganized, to include new areas cleared of woodland or to accommodate a change in agricultural practice. The countryside was the scene of continual change. But each change left its mark, resulting in an intricate pattern of new and old.

Angevin England was also a complex country. To some extent this was the inevitable result of a complex geology which produces a variety of land forms in a small area, but it was also brought about by human activity. No county was homogeneous: Kent, for instance, had wooded chalk downland, cleared chalk country, wooded clay lowland, marsh, and fertile, long-cultivated lands and river valleys – all within 60 or 70 miles. North and east Kent had been thickly settled in Roman times and was the heartland of the old Kentish kingdom in the sixth and seventh centuries. The forests of the Weald had long been used as swine pastures, but permanent settlement there was slow to start and much clearing was being done in the twelfth and thirteenth centuries. Types of countryside show some significant similarities wherever they are found: the forest of Arden in Warwickshire, for instance, resembles the Weald of the south-east in its late settlement, its pattern of landholding and its industrial activity. Land use varied widely with geology, climate and settlement history, producing an interlocking pattern of farming regions. The variety of countrysides and the constant gradual change experienced in each of them show clearly the inapplicability of that most misleading generalization, 'traditional society'.

The historian of the rural economy of the century from 1150 to 1250 labours under serious disadvantages compared with those of the periods before and after. There is no nationwide survey of population and resources, which Domesday for all its shortcomings provides for the late eleventh century; while the manorial court and account rolls and royal inquests which give so much detail for the later middle ages do not become common until the 1270s – there is only one series of manorial accounts from the first half of the thirteenth century, those of the bishopric of Winchester. Despite the great increase in written business documents from the late twelfth century onwards, there is hardly ever enough information to make more than a sketchy attempt to fill in the long gap from 1086 to the period around 1300. It is often clear that great changes took place over those centuries, but the mechanisms and driving forces are usually hidden from us.

It is quite clear, for instance, that there was a massive increase in population, but figures are little more than guesswork. Estimates of the population in 1086 range from 1.1 to over 2.25 million, while the maximum reached about 1300 has plausibly been estimated at some 6 million, which would be a level not

reached again until the eighteenth century.[1] Both in 1086 and in
the later middle ages the bulk of the population lived south and
east of a line from the Severn to the Humber, and the situation
is unlikely to be different at dates in between. But there were
probably regional variations in the rate of increase, and they
could have been dramatic: it is likely that the lowlands of Yorkshire saw some of the biggest increase as the area recovered after
the devastations of the eleventh century. The colonizing regions
– the Fens of Lincolnshire, Cambridgeshire and Norfolk, where
drainage was in progress, and the forests of the east Midlands
and the Weald – also show great increases between 1086 and the
fourteenth century. Well-settled lowland areas may have increased correspondingly slowly. There was internal migration as
well as a general rise in the numbers of those remaining in one
place. It seems clear that very local factors could lead to neighbouring villages having different population histories, depending
on the strength of lordship, the tenurial structure, inheritance
customs, the availability of woodland for clearance and so on.
But despite the unquantifiable nature of the increase and the
complexities of its geographical distribution, the fact of a great
and general rise in population underlies all the economic and
social developments of this period.

There is no doubt that the agrarian economy as a whole was
expanding: new areas were being brought into cultivation and
pasture. There could well have been some rise in productivity,
linked to increasingly sophisticated crop rotations while the
rising population made more labour available. Horses were increasingly used for haulage and harrowing, replacing the cheaper
but slower oxen. Horses were beginning to be used for ploughing in this period, mainly in the south and east, and more by
smallholders than on the large demesnes. But the effect of technological change on productivity remains debatable: the modest
increase in the use of horses to work the bishop of Winchester's
demesnes, for instance, did not lead to increases in yield.[2] The
basis of the economy remained subsistence agriculture supplemented by stockraising. Livestock were essential for trac-
tion and their dung was a necessary fertilizer. But no village
was completely self-sufficient, and the need to pay rent and
dues to lords as well as to buy necessities had spread the use

[1] Richard Smith, 'Human resources', in Astill and Grant, *The Countryside of Medieval England*, 190–1.
[2] John Langdon, *Horses, Oxen and Technological Innovation*, Cambridge 1986, 269 n2.

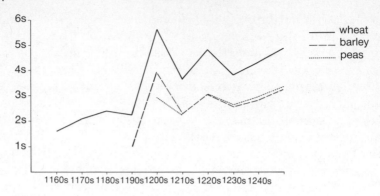

FIGURE 6.1   Wheat, barley and pea prices

of money widely and deeply. The whole of the rest of the economy was expanding too. New towns were being founded and old ones were growing. Commercial opportunities were increasing as markets were founded. There was growing production for the market, both in agricultural produce and in the output of industries. The volume and intensity of exchanges were increasing. It was a money economy, and another basic fact of life was inflation.

There were always short-term fluctuations in prices due to bad harvests or livestock diseases, and sometimes these could be quite severe, as after the wet season of 1224 or the drought of 1226, but the underlying trend of prices after 1200 was consistently upward (see figures 6.1 and 6.2). This represents a drastic change from the previous situation, as prices seem to have been stable during the twelfth century and perhaps from earlier periods. The most dramatic period of inflation was the first

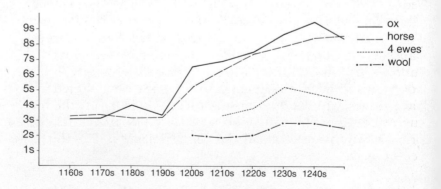

FIGURE 6.2   Livestock and wool prices

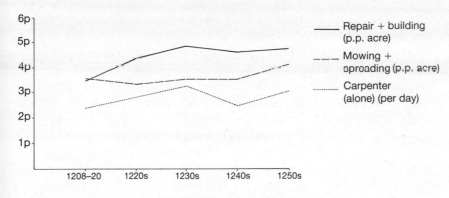

FIGURE 6.3 Piecework wage rates

decade of the thirteenth century, when wheat and livestock prices doubled in ten years. Thereafter inflation was persistent but more gradual. Data on wage rates are less good and a continuous series begins later, but it tells a very different story: thirteenth-century wages remained generally level and sometimes even fell (see figure 6.3). These two sets of figures spell very bad times for the poor, at least for those who had to sell their labour to live. For those with land, who could produce even a little more than they needed themselves, it shows that profits were to be made by producing for the market. Large landlords had an excellent opportunity to make substantial profits, and every incentive to abolish fixed rents.

It is easier to chart the rate of inflation than to explain why it happened – that is true in the modern world, and we need not expect conclusive explanations for the thirteenth century. The great leap after 1200 is the biggest puzzle. Perhaps England was suddenly flooded with silver around 1200 as a consequence of expanded trade in wool with Flanders – an explanation which seems to overrate the size of the export trade as a proportion of the whole economy. Perhaps there was a row of bad harvests, or population growth suddenly outstripped food supplies, or John's war taxation distorted the economy. Inflation does seem to have worsened as the coinage deteriorated and to have slowed after the recoinages of 1205 and 1247; the money supply could possibly have been a factor.[3] Whatever its causes, price inflation underlay all the developments of the thirteenth century.

[3] N. J. Mayhew, 'Money and prices in England from Henry II to Edward III', *Agricultural History Review* XXXV (1987), 121–32.

Agricultural methods constitute another underlying factor. Large areas of the Midlands and central southern England were characterized by 'common field' agriculture. In outline, the peasants held strips evenly distributed among two or three large fields, there was a rotation of winter and spring-sown crops with one field left fallow each year, and common grazing on the stubble of harvested fields and on the fallow. Leaving one field fallow, and folding the village livestock there to manure it, helped to maintain the fertility of the soil. Three fields in this system might appear to be a more efficient use of land than two fields, since more of the area is under crops each year, and a general development from two to three fields has been envisaged. But two fields allow more livestock to be pastured and permit more flexibility in adjusting winter-and spring-sown crops to the weather. Reality was more complicated than the simple outline: how the fields were worked in practice is very difficult to establish. 'Open' fields, unenclosed but not cultivated or grazed in common, were also frequently found. Such sources as we have reveal a situation of bewildering complexity, in which all generalizations are suspect. The cropping units were not the great fields but the furlongs, bundles of strips of which the fields were composed. Fields due to be fallow were sometimes cultivated; private enclosures might exist alongside open fields; the lord's demesne might consist of scattered strips or a consolidated area, which might be enclosed. And above all, the common fields were not the norm over much of the country, and even in the Midlands coexisted with other kinds of arrangement.

The common fields usually accompanied nucleated villages. In other areas there was a much more dispersed pattern of settlement accompanied by private enclosures more like modern fields. There were two types of landscape where this was common. In areas where colonization, or re-colonization, was taking place in the twelfth and thirteenth centuries, often in wooded areas such as Essex, the Kentish Weald and also the Midland forests such as Arden or Feckenham, the work was done by individual peasants or families, who hedged or fenced their clearings. It could be that the common fields themselves had sometimes been extended by piecemeal clearances which then contributed to the common good, but by the thirteenth century at the latest it was more normal for them to be held individually, often for a money rent to the lord. The Statute of Merton in 1235 allowed lords to make clearances for their own use or that of their tenants as long as common rights were not eroded – in other words, it was no longer necessary to put clearances into the common fields, but whether this created a new situation or simply recognized what had long been the case is not easy to say.[4] Nor is it easy to say whether clearances were made wholly on peasant initiative, were organized by the lords, or the lords simply gave the peasants permission.

The upland zone, comprising Cornwall and part of Devon, the hills of the Welsh frontier, and the Pennine mountains and the north-west, was the other region of scattered settlement and individual ownership. Pasture was readily available here so there was no need for communal grazing on the stubble after harvest. Fields tended to be small, the landscape characterized by scattered hamlets and isolated farms. An infield–outfield method of agriculture was widely practised, with the infield, close to the houses, permanently cultivated and manured from barns and stables, and a larger outfield used for pasture, parts of which were brought into short-term cultivation.

Woodland was a vital economic resource: its products provided housing and heating at all levels of society, it supplied raw materials for industries, and it was a crucial source of grazing, often subject to common rights. But the rise in population meant that there was increasing pressure on all woodlands; it has been estimated that 15 per cent of England was wooded in 1086, and barely 10 per cent by 1350.[5] 'Assarting', the clearance of woodland for agriculture and settlement, was under way everywhere; in royal forests it was often permitted in return for a rent. This pressure led to an increasingly close definition of common pasture rights, how many animals, of what type and for how long.

It may also have encouraged the aristocracy to enclose private parks as hunting reserves and supplies of timber and fuel. A great number were created in the thirteenth century as the area under royal forest law began to diminish. They were hedged or walled to keep the deer in, and might be provided with a 'deer leap', constructed to let wild deer in but prevent them leaving. To create a park generally needed royal permission, as did any hunting in the royal forests. It sometimes happened that when the park was enclosed a herd of wild cattle might be trapped inside: there was such a herd at Windsor park in the fourteenth century, and some still survive at Chillingham in Northumberland and elsewhere.[6]

[4] EHD iii, no. 30.
[5] Oliver Rackham, *Ancient Woodland*, London 1980, 126, 134.
[6] Paul Stamper, 'Woods and parks', in Astill and Grant, *The Countryside of Medieval England*, 145.

England thus consisted of a variety of types of countryside jumbled up alongside each other, differentiated by their geography and long history. It was the Midlands that most resembled a textbook medieval society, with large numbers of nucleated villages, many of them consisting of a single manor, surrounded by their open fields. Such villages were concentrated in the river valleys, with newer and less manorialized settlements spreading into the forests and hilly outcrops. A high proportion of the tenant population held a standard size of tenement known as a virgate or yardland, or half of one, in return for services which could vary widely. Such men might be villeins, personally unfree and bound to do as much as five days work a week for the lord as well as owing various other dues. In woodland areas where assarting was taking place there were more freemen paying cash rents – generally in areas of new settlement the burdens of lordship were lighter, the peasants freer though not necessarily richer. Central southern England, the old heartland of the Wessex kingdom from Hampshire to Somerset, resembled the Midlands in its nucleated villages, and forests attacked by clearance. The west Midlands and Wessex contained the great old estates of the churches of Winchester, Glastonbury, Worcester, Evesham and others, with a long continuous tradition of strong lordship.

Eastern England was quite different. Lincolnshire, Norfolk and Suffolk had the highest population density in England in Domesday and throughout this period, and the greatest number of freemen. A numerous, poor peasantry owing comparatively light services continued to characterize the area. The pattern of lordship was very fragmented, manor rarely coinciding with vill. This reflected very complex agricultural methods, with many small fields, strips scattered unevenly, no village-wide crop rotation and much individual cultivation. After the harvest the flocks of the tenants were pastured on the lord's land to increase its fertility. Barley and wheat were the important crops here, and peas and beans were grown extensively – leguminous crops which improve soil fertility.

Kent was different again. Farmland here was wholly enclosed and there were no true villages. Farming techniques were advanced, with leguminous crops introduced early, and grain produced for a prosperous market. Orchards and vineyards were more important than in other parts of the country. Kent had its own body of customary law allowing the free sale of land and partible inheritance. The Wealden forests were being invaded by smallholders carving out their hedged fields and supplementing their income by the numerous crafts of the woodland areas. The effect was to reduce the capacity of the woods for pasture, though pig-herding remained important.

The upland south-west from Dartmoor to Cornwall had a very sparse population in the eleventh century, which increased dramatically in the twelfth and thirteenth. High moorland was colonized for agriculture and there was a great deal of forest assarting. The fields were enclosed and usually held individually. Despite the damp climate, a mixed agrarian economy was practised, with oats as the major crop. A particular local technique was 'beat-burning', where grass was dug up, dried and then burnt on the surface of the field, which would then bear several grain crops before being left to grass over again. The tin industry created a market for food and fuel and must have contributed to the prosperity of agriculture in areas where climate and elevation made it marginal.

It was probably in the north that the greatest increases in population and expansion of settlements took place. Depopulated by William the Conqueror, the vale of York was recolonized in the twelfth century. Here and in Durham there were two- and three-field villages with a population of villeins, but labour services were not onerous and in fact many of the Yorkshire villages had no manorial demesne. Population pressure led to colonization of the moorland and waste rather than the subdivision of existing holdings. Wheat was the main crop here. In the mountains and uplands to the west and in Lancashire and Cumbria new colonization started later. Infield-outfield agriculture was practised, producing mainly oats. Everywhere on the hills were large flocks of sheep. The north was the great area of Cistercian sheep-farming for the wool export trade, leading to a prosperity evident in the vast and splendid abbey ruins at Fountains, Rievaulx, Byland, Furness and elsewhere.

England consisted of regions with their own geographical, economic and social identities. How far this diversity led to regional feeling and loyalty is hard to assess. A few comments can be gleaned from chronicles, such as that of a Rochester cathedral chronicler – 'from the north comes all evil',[7] though to a Kentish writer most of the country could have been the north. There is some sign of local patriotism, notably in the comic list of prejudices put by Richard of Devizes, a monk of Winchester

[7] H. Wharton, *Anglia Sacra*, 2 vols, London 1691, i, 346.

cathedral, into the mouth of a French Jew advising a Frenchman whereabouts in England to go to make his career:

> Rochester and Chichester are mere hamlets . . . Oxford scarcely sustains, much less satisfies her own men. Exeter refreshes with the same food both men and horses. Bath, dumped at the bottom of valleys in thick and sulphurous air, is at the gates of hell. Nor should you go to Worcester, Chester or Hereford, because of the violent Welsh. York is full of filfthy, treacherous, subhuman Scots. The Ely region stinks because of the surrounding fens. In Durham, Norwich and Lincoln there are few powerful people of your sort and you will hear almost no one speaking French. At Bristol there is no one who is not or has not been a soap-maker, and every Frenchman likes a soap-maker as much as a dunghill. . . . In each place there are some good men, but far fewer in all of them together than in one place, Winchester . . . the city of cities, the mother of them all and better than any.[8]

The common law was breaking down the old distinctions in legal practice between different regions. Royal government increasingly intruded into the north, which had hitherto largely escaped close supervision. There was a uniform governmental and legal culture which obscured regional diversity. To a travelling lord differences between regions might have been observable if his estates spanned several of them, but would have had little impact on his way of life. The clergy had other focuses of loyalty: their church or religious order. The views of the labouring population are not known; and the less they travelled, the less their chance of becoming aware of differences. There is little evidence that regional feeling was of any importance in Angevin times.

The inhabitants

Within this complex regionalized society there existed various types of community, overlapping and concentric. A social structure is not defined only by the economic variations and forms of dependence between those comprising it: the bonds between

---

[8] Devizes, 66–7.

individuals and groups, the forms of association and co-operation are aspects of it as well.

The county, the old English shire, was already an old focus of activity. It developed more and more functions in the twelfth and thirteenth centuries: for the royal administration it was an essential unit of government. Its work in taxation and legal matters, centred on the county court and the work of the sheriff and his underlings, proliferated rapidly. This made the suitors to the county court increasingly aware of their common interests, and encouraged a common identity. Counties are found acting as units in their relations with the king, buying freedom from an unwanted sheriff or paying to free an area from the forest law as the men of Devon did in 1204.[9] But the counties do not appear as articulate units expressing grievances when a good opportunity to do so occurred after 1258; these royal administrative organs did not necessarily always act as political units even if they possessed a sense of county identity.[10] Smaller local communities, comprising perhaps a hundred or a large manor, are also found acting together, like the men of Thanet in Kent or Cleveland in Yorkshire.[11] There was a complex web of overlapping local identities.

The geographical unit at the bottom of the hierarchy was the *villa*, the 'vill'. This term is useful in covering both the village as we imagine it, a nucleated settlement with its lands, and areas of the landscape of hamlets and scattered farms normal over much of the country. The vill was the lowest component of royal administration, on which duties ultimately rested: the king's government did not work on the basis of manors. The vill thus came to have many duties in law, taxation and other administration: for example, the Assize of Clarendon of 1166 required four men from each vill to identify malefactors. But it was not only duties imposed from above that created the vill. It also had essential tasks to perform in regulating agricultural practice, though they are not illustrated by surviving documents in the way royal impositions are. In the many places where manor did not coincide with vill there was no other forum which could have organized crop rotations, pasturing and other farming decisions. Vills appointed communal cowherds, haywards and other officers. Where manor and vill coincided, we need not agonize over

---

[9] Foedera I part i, 89.
[10] Prestwich, *English Politics*, 56–8; Reynolds, *Kingdoms and Communities*, 249.
[11] Holt, *Magna Carta*, 67–71.

which one was responsible, but there were no 'vill courts': the courts which performed these functions were manorial. The *villata*, the men of the vill, were presumably illiterate and did not keep records. Their guiding lights would be common sense and custom, but custom cannot have made all the decisions alone. Some vills had sufficient cohesiveness to take their own lands at farm from the lord, as happened with some of the royal demesnes under king John.

An organization covering a defined area which usually coincided with the vill was the church parish. Since Anglo-Saxon times local church organization had been based on 'minsters', churches staffed by a number of priests and serving a wide area. This system was itself often based on a pattern of large estates in which outlying settlements owed their dues to a central collecting point. That ancient pattern of landownership had been breaking down for centuries as the outlying settlements were granted out to minor lords. This process affected the minsters too, outlying settlements acquiring chapels which then gained burial rights, turning into independent churches providing for all the needs of their territory, their parish, but still owing perhaps a small payment to their mother church. The initiative of the lords of the settlements and of the inhabitants worked in the same direction: the creation of local parish churches. The priests of the minster themselves may have split up their responsibility and turned themselves into parish priests.

Thus parish came to coincide with vill, and reinforced its solidarity with an ecclesiastical life and a common meeting-place for all kinds of non-ecclesiastical purposes. The process continued in the twelfth century and was complete over most of England by 1200. The parishioners owed tithes, one-tenth of the increase of crops and stock, to their parish church, which was commonly also given some land in the parish to endow a priest. The villagers were baptized in the font, married before the church door and buried in the graveyard – or so the church would have liked. The agricultural year was sanctified by church festivals, such as Michaelmas when the harvest was in, or Plough Monday when the spring ploughing began, as well as the great festivals of Christmas and Easter. The priest usually needed some laymen to help him in the business of running a parish, and what look like embryonic churchwardens are found in the twelfth century.[12]

[12] Cheney and Jones, no. 65.

The word 'manor' has come up frequently so far, but defining it is not easy. This is because the term covers a great variety of types of estate. The word does not refer to an institution, a system, an area of land or a standard kind of building. Manors are 'management units'[13] and vary with whatever is being managed and how it is being done. It therefore makes better sense to look at the kinds of estate it covers than to try to define the word.

What is sometimes called the 'classical' manor, because historians attempting to reach a definition of the word regarded it as the ideal type, has a home farm, with a manor house, from which the 'demesne' lands were cultivated. To do this there were paid labourers, but an essential source of labour was that provided by the unfree tenants, the 'villeins', who were bound to do a stated number of days' work each week, with extra 'boon' works at harvest or haymaking, and various other services such as carting. The villeins were subject to the lord of the manor, justiciable in his court, and had no access to the king's courts. As well as the villeins there were free tenants, who paid rent and might have to do some more or less token labour services, but who were not subject to the lord in the way the villeins were. Manors of this type were to be found over much of England. They were particularly numerous in the Midlands and south, and on the estates of the great landowners, especially the wealthier churches.

Each of the three elements of the classical manor – demesne lands, villeins and free tenants – could exist singly or in any combination and still be referred to as a manor. Many smaller landowners had one or several manors with just demesne and villeins, or demesne and a few free tenants. Some estates consisted of a classical manor and collections of scattered free tenants, while some comprised solely rent-paying free tenants. Over much of eastern and northern England there survived vestiges of the kind of estate we met when discussing the origins of the parish, called a 'soke' in eastern England and a 'shire' in the north, the extensive lordship with a central collecting point. This might itself be a manor of classical type surrounded by a cloud of rent-paying tenants who might owe light labour services as well. These tenants might then find themselves 'manorialized' under a lord to whom the lord of the whole estate has granted them, and who might set about creating a classical manor on the former outlying estate. The variations on these themes were endless.

[13] Miller and Hatcher, *Medieval England*, 188.

In the law as it developed in the decades around 1200, villeins held all their possessions at the will of their lord. They could be bought and sold, with or without land. They could be subjected to physical punishment. Money could be taken from them at the lord's will in the form of tallage. They could not sell or sublet their holdings without permission, they had no right to inherit, they could not marry without permission and payment for the privilege, and they were not allowed to leave the manor. This was the law as the royal courts saw it. But the law of the manor court to which villeins were restricted was set by custom, and though custom varied, the villein's position there was less unfavourable. Custom was declared by the members of the court, not the lord. The villein's services were fixed, inheritance was possible in return for an 'entry fine' in cash and a 'heriot' or payment of the dead man's best beast, and the villein's goods were assumed to be his own. In practice numbers of villeins did leave their manors and paid 'chevage' to their lords to be allowed to do so. The lord could disregard the custom, and would have the backing of the king's court if he did so, but instances of this are uncommon – the lord's interest was in harmony so that the agricultural routine could continue profitably. But it was very much in the lord's interest to retain control of his tenantry. He needed to be able to set new rents – to put them up, in fact – and he needed the power to prevent the breakup and disposal of holdings. At the same time the royal courts needed clear guidelines on who was to have access to the new forms of litigation available after the reforms of Henry II. The result of these two factors was to firm up the line dividing freedom from villeinage, handing control of those on the wrong side of it to the lords.

The labour services due from the unfree tenants were many and various. Heavy 'week-work', three or more days' work a week on the demesne, was common on large old manors and more frequent in eastern England and the east Midlands than elsewhere. 'Boon' works were commoner, and rent-paying villeins were no rarity. In the twelfth century there was a tendency for works to be 'commuted' for money payments, but this trend was halted as inflation made labour services more valuable than fixed rents. One particularly favoured group of villeins were those who lived on what were or once had been royal manors: the 'villein sokemen'. Their situation was a combination of servility and freedom: though subject to characteristic villein disabilities, these were often limited at a level below that common elsewhere, and they had access to the king's courts.

But the labour of villeins was both insufficient and too irregular for all the jobs that had to be done on the demesne farms. For the continuous work of looking after animals as well as the skilled work of ploughing or blacksmithing, lords kept a permanent pool of paid labourers, the *famuli*. The successors of the slaves of Domesday, they were given small plots carved out of the demesne which they usually held rent-free and which were ploughed by the lord's team. In return they had to work for the lord, and received wages in money or produce, or both. Sometimes villeins could serve as *famuli*, or *famuli* might live on the demesne farm. None of these categories into which we divide people is watertight.

The position of villeins and *famuli* may seem unenviable, but there were still those who might envy them: the landless wage labourers, the 'cottagers'. It is something of a puzzle how they managed to make ends meet, and the suspicion must be that they frequently did not. The most vulnerable members of this society, it was they who died first in famines. There were various possible sources of employment: they could work for the more prosperous peasant farmers of the locality, or on the demesnes of the lords. They could colonize new land if the opportunity offered. They could try their success at some cottage industry if raw materials were available and they could acquire the skill; or they could swell the migration into the towns and hope for employment there.

The free men and women of the countryside may seem to have been at the top of the tree. They could buy and sell free land and their rents were fixed. They could sell up and go where they pleased. Their lives, status and goods were protected by the royal courts if they could afford to use them. There certainly were prosperous freemen who laid acre to acre in the thirteenth century. But in practice freedom itself did not confer prosperity. Prosperity depended on the amount of land held and the balance between it and the service due from it. The lawyers' definition of freedom cut across economic realities. Free and servile people might intermarry, legitimate children taking their father's status and illegitimate children their mother's, but the status of individuals was often a matter of dispute. There were intermediate grades between free and servile: in some places there were rent-paying freemen who owed some light labour services, the 'gavelmen' or 'molmen'. Freedom was not absolute, but existed in greater or lesser degrees; there was freedom from certain dues but not others, to do some things but not others. It could change

over a few generations for individuals and families, being more
a matter of negotiation and economic prosperity than of pure
heredity.

The prosperity or poverty of the rural population is difficult to
assess for a number of reasons. The size of the standard tenement, the virgate or bovate, varied widely from one manor to
the next and even within the manor, and was often assessed in
customary acres which did not correspond to measurements on
the ground. Soil fertility varied enough to make a large tenement
in one area less productive than a small one elsewhere. We
hardly ever know how many people the tenement had to support, relatives or 'undersettled' tenants or labourers and their
families, and size of holding has to be measured against rent and
other outgoings to the lord.

As far as the size of tenements is concerned, it is clear that in
many places the whole virgate had broken down into halves or
smaller fractions. Investigations using rather later sources have
concluded that only a small proportion of the tenants held
anything like a virgate, and the free tenants were even worse off
than the villeins: in a large area of the east Midlands in 1279 29
per cent of the villeins and 47 per cent of the freemen had under
five acres, which without another source of income cannot have
been enough to support even a small family.[14] On the estates of
Westminster abbey in the south-east in the early thirteenth century nearly half of the villein tenants had ten acres or less.[15] In
some areas, notably East Anglia and Kent, the inheritance of
freemen was divided between the sons, making for small subdivided holdings. Another factor working in the same direction
was the land market. The market in free land was very active at
least from around 1200, and earlier too, though evidence is
less plentiful. There was both subletting and outright purchase.
This enabled some to accumulate lands and better their position, while others who had to sell up could do so. The effect was
to make the distribution of land flexible, providing for some
younger sons and going some way to adjusting tenure to the
demands of the population. But as a result some holdings were
uneconomically small. Lords on the whole disapproved, as it
was much harder to assess and collect dues from subdivided
holdings. There was even a market in villein land: villeins were
subletting parts of tenements at least by the early thirteenth

[14] Miller and Hatcher, *Medieval England*, 143.
[15] Harvey, *Westminster Abbey*, 435.

century. Under the pressure of rising population, and the land market, the general trend was for more and more people to have to eke out a living on smaller and smaller holdings. In some areas the situation was worsened by the custom of dividing the inheritance between all the children. Some villagers would have access to common rights for grazing their livestock, and this could have been a lifeline to them. In some places peasants had substantial flocks of sheep. Nevertheless, there was certainly a good deal of poverty in the countryside and a labour force waiting to be hired.

Life as lived by the poorer members of rural society has to be reconstructed largely from archaeological evidence, as the documents from this period provide very little help. No peasant houses have survived: they were generally rather flimsy and were often rebuilt on a slightly different alignment within the plot, or 'toft'.[16] The twelfth and thirteenth centuries saw a general change in construction methods, from the earlier 'earth-fast' houses in which structural timbers were simply inserted in the ground, producing post-holes for the archaeologist, to ones where the timbers rested on low walls or large single 'padstones', relying on jointing for stability. The latter type may well be the work of professional carpenters. Quite why methods changed is unclear: one advantage was that the timbers were better protected from rot and so lasted longer, which may reflect deteriorating climatic conditions or growing shortage of timber. House plans were simple, the one-room cot with central hearth being common. The so-called 'longhouse' had two rooms separated by a passageway, one end supposedly being for animals, though it is usually impossible to prove how the rooms were used. It is hardly ever safe to argue from the form of a building to its function or the tenurial status of its occupants.

Bread was the proverbial staff of life, and could be baked in 'firepits' below the hearth. Mixtures of grains were common, dredge (wheat and rye) and maslin (barley and rye): bread varied in quality and was made from these or from barley – pure wheat bread was not for the poor. Ale could be made from various grains, even oats; it too came in various qualities, and evidence that it was consumed in large quantities does not necessarily imply that paralytic drunkenness was normal. Oatmeal porridge must have been a common peasant dish, likewise pea soup ('pease pottage') with or without meat. Herrings, cured or

[16] J. G. Hurst, 'Rural building in England and Wales', *Agrarian History* ii, 898–915.

salted, were widely available, while those with livestock would have some milk and cheese. The standard of living no doubt varied between households and perhaps between areas, but for many of the poor famine was an ever-present threat. In 1258 in Lincolnshire and East Anglia so many people died of starvation that the coroners were allowed to dispense with inquests.[17]

Lordship in the countryside

The method of estate management inherited from the Anglo-Saxon past and maintained by the Norman conquerors was to let manors to a 'farmer', one who took the manor in return for a 'farm' or fixed rent for a fixed term, which might be for his life. The 'farmer' took over the manor as a going concern with all the lord's rights; he took the risks and made his profit by squeezing more out of the manor than he had to pay the lord. The advantage from the lord's point of view was as secure and predictable an income as he could ever hope for, without the trouble of running the manors himself. This system was ubiquitous on all the larger lay and ecclesiastical estates. It was not wholly inflexible, as when the agreement expired the rent could be put up to give the lord some of the advantage of agricultural expansion. In this way lords had been able to increase their incomes without changing the method of exploitation. The most obvious disadvantage was the tendency for farmers to become hereditary, the lord effectively losing control while deriving only a fixed income from the estate. Generally it was an approach suitable for a period of relatively stable prices, but it left lords very vulnerable to inflation. Different forms of management could be worked simultaneously on the same estate. The Knights Templar, for instance, in 1185 had let Finchingfield (Essex) and Temple Combe (Somerset); at Broadwell (Oxfordshire) they received a pension from the church and rent from five hides of land let in pieces varying from Edward's half-hide to the widow Edith's 'curtilage' (yard), but at Lockridge (Wiltshire) they retained, and even increased, labour services presumably for a home farm, supplemented by dues of grain and chickens.[18]

It was principally the great inflation of the years around 1200 that compelled lords to adopt another form of management if

[17] Cal Cl R 1256–9, 212.
[18] Beatrice A. Lees, *Records of the Templars in England in the Twelfth Century*, London 1935, 12, 54–5, 57, 61–2.

they were not to see their incomes plummet. The method chosen was to take manors into their own hands and run them using a reeve or *minister*, who accounted directly to the lord or his officers. All the receipts from rents and the produce of the demesne farm, which continued to be important in provisioning the lord's household, the labour dues of the villeins and profits from sales of produce would be supervised and accounted for. Under this system the risk and the profit were the lord's. The great landlords became great producers for the market, selling the produce of the demesne farms, especially grain and wool for which demand was buoyant. The change could be very profit-able: the archbishop of Canterbury's income doubled between 1184 and 1204, which kept him ahead of inflation.[19] The change from farming to direct exploitation can be traced on the manors of Peterborough abbey, for example. In 1176 all the manors were farmed; between then and 1193 direct management began to be introduced, and by 1210 all the manors were under direct control.[20]

The resumption of demesne manors brought out some further disadvantages of the old farming system. Farmers with only a temporary interest in the land had no incentive to invest in equipment, and might even sell timber and stock for quick profit when the end of their term approached. Driven by pressure of a land-hungry population and the growing desire of lords for income in cash rather than in produce, they might also allow the home farm to run down, subletting demesne lands and commut-ing villein labour dues to maximize their money income. When lords took over a direct, close interest in production for the market this process was reversed. The resumption of manors sometimes led to the reconstitution of demesne farms, the pur-chase of land and the reimposition of villein services, even the creation of new villein tenements. It was for this reason that the lords developed an interest in the precise definition of villein status. Demesne lands were expanded by purchase from free tenants: this was especially to the lord's advantage if they had been paying no more than uneconomic 'ossified dues'.[21] The profits the new methods brought could also be invested by buying land with rent-paying tenants.

Direct exploitation of estates also created career opportun-ities for managers, professional reeves, auditors of accounts and

[19] Du Boulay, *The Lordship of Canterbury*, 205.
[20] King, *Peterborough Abbey*, 145.
[21] Sandra Raban, *The Estates of Thorney and Crowland*, Cambridge 1977, 65.

inevitably lawyers to fight the legal battles which so often arose
from landownership. The availability of such people was a precondition for this kind of administration, and if it eventually
tended to become bureaucratic and top-heavy this problem was
still in the future. It is the written output of this kind of estate
management, the accounts and court rolls, cartularies and surveys, which tell us so much about conditions on the demesne
manors. Their relative absence from other kinds of estate tends
to distort our view of the overall picture. In the thirteenth
century treatises on estate management were being written to
enlighten managers and their lords: the best known is that of
Walter of Henley.[22]

On the greater estates the principal link between the lord and
the estate administration was usually the steward, who had
general oversight of the bailiffs who looked after groups of
manors. Stewards were generally, but not always, laymen, as
were the lawyers. This kind of work provided a non-clerical,
non-military career for men of a certain social standing by the
thirteenth century. The sprawling nature of most large estates
made it usual to split them up into geographically determined
units, 'bailiwicks', within which a bailiff supervised the reeves of
individual manors. Reeves were usually unfree tenants serving
for remission of rent and services, but increasingly there were
professional reeves better able and more determined to cope
with the onerous managerial responsibilities which might well
make a local man unpopular with his neighbours. The manor
court, often held by the steward or his deputy, was the most
important forum of interaction between the lord, the reeve and
the manor's inhabitants, and played an important part in running the estate. There the tenants formally succeeded to their
holdings, and other transfers of land took place; there they were
punished for their transgressions against each other or the lord,
and had an opportunity to complain about the reeve. But the
adoption of direct demesne management was not universal: on
some estates some manors were always at farm.

The great magnates were far from being the only lords of the
land. Between them and the larger free tenants, in fact shading
off into both categories at the ends, were the middling landowners commonly referred to as 'knights'. In earlier generations
knights had been a group defined by the profession of arms,

[22] *Walter of Henley and other Treatises on Estate Management and Accountancy*,
ed. Dorothea Oschinsky, Oxford 1971.

particularly when exercised on horseback, some of whom were well rewarded with land, others not. With the rise of knightly ideology and the honourable knight, the wealthy and powerful had been happy to take on the trappings of knighthood.[23] By the second half of the twelfth century the term was applied to a horizontal social stratum composed of people who had acquired land in a number of ways – by inheritance, marriage or as a reward for services including military service – and who often held it of several different lords. The social stratum comprised great variations in wealth, from the lords of many manors to those of just one, or even less. Some of them had ancestors going back to the Norman conquest, some perhaps even beyond it, while others were new in their lands. Of course, lords continued to have households, including knights, who could invest their cash rewards in land or rent. Proximity to the powerful was always a source of status.

This was the group that acquired governmental responsibilities, particularly with the legal developments of Henry II's reign: 12 knights were needed for the grand assize and several for the lesser assizes, and even for such purposes as checking that litigants who pleaded illness were not just malingering.[24] It must therefore have been clear, or at least ascertainable, who these knights were. There must also have been an incentive to avoid duties of this kind as well as military service by not taking up knighthood even though sufficiently qualified by wealth and prominence in the locality. The final stage of evolution that need concern us occurred when Henry III's government forced men to take up knighthood, and established financial criteria for this unwanted honour.

Inside the knightly stratum all was not stable. Individuals and families can be seen rising and falling, but examples do not establish a general trend. It is far from clear whether the group as a whole was prospering, standing still or in crisis. There were examples of all three. A number of factors can be seen to have caused strain. For those who seriously intended to fight, or to be prepared to do so, the increasing elaboration of knightly equipment put up the costs, particularly with the introduction of horse armour. As knightly ideology became more elaborate the expense of knighting ceremonies could also be considerable. Ostentation and generosity were part of the lifestyle, expected as well as

[23] See above, p. 26.
[24] See above, pp. 57–8.

accepted, but the cost of even static pretensions was rising. Then the inflation underlying the economy made life more expensive for everyone, and those who depended on relatively inflexible customary rent incomes were at a disadvantage. A small lord could find it difficult and expensive to exert authority over free tenants who were able to invoke the protection of the royal courts. Active lordship was necessary to retain control of the tenants, and lords unable to do this could find themselves in a downward spiral. Then there was taxation: scutage was reckoned on the knight's fee and, particularly in John's reign, was taken heavily and often. A large family could spell difficulties: daughters would need dowries, and younger sons commonly received something from the estate. Gifts of lands to religious houses, whether prompted by piety or ostentation, might have a similar effect. Perhaps the quickest way of all to perdition was to borrow money, and the resentment of those indebted to the Jews found various outlets. But religious houses and acquisitive laymen could also step in with loans secured on land, commonly ending in the impoverishment of the improvident or badly placed and the enrichment of those with cash to lend.

On the other hand, there were avenues of improvement open to those wise or lucky enough to take them. Service as a royal or baronial official enabled some to feather their nests, and an apprenticeship in honorial and county courts gave the knightly class an advantage when a legal profession sprang up. Those who depended on rents in an age of inflation suffered, but those with enough demesne land to create surplus produce and with access to markets would be able to take advantage of the cash economy, on a smaller scale than the great landlords but in the same way. They would then be able to invest the profits in the land market. Then there was the old and very effective aristocratic tool for expansion: marriage. There would in any case be a dowry, but there was always a chance, given human mortality, that a wife who was not an heiress when she married might become one by force of circumstance.

One example of success is provided by Thomas of Moulton. He was a tenant of the honour of Lancaster in Lincolnshire and Suffolk, but held of three other lay lords as well as of the prior of Spalding. He was deeply involved in speculating in offices, buying the shrievalty of Lincoln for 500 marks and five palfreys in 1205, failing to meet his repayments and falling under John's displeasure. He was active in draining and enclosing the fenland on his estates, and in 1213, buoyed up by the profitability of agriculture, he bought the custody of the daughters and heiresses of Richard de Lucy of Egremont in Cumberland,[25] eventually establishing the Moultons as barons there. In later life he was a prominent judge.

The middling landowners who were sometimes the ancestors and in many ways the precursors of the better-defined gentry of the later middle ages were a rather amorphous group. A lesser territorial aristocracy is a persistent feature of English society, and many families of the later twelfth century had held their estates since the eleventh. As new forms of exercising local power became available with legal and governmental reforms, these people took advantage of them. The gentry, so to say, are always with us. But there were gradations within the group, and it could be that the net effect of the factors mentioned above was to shake the poorer stratum out of the knightly class, leading to a greater differentiation between knights and those below them in the thirteenth century. As for their wider political role, it might be said that they had lost the honour and not yet gained the county as the forum of their activity and were left with nowhere to make their voice heard. But the coherence of the twelfth century honour is easily exaggerated, and so is the homogenous political consciousness which would give them a coherent voice in the county. Fairly small landholders had interests widely scattered over several counties, but some areas were dominated by a dense network of interrelated families. Ties of locality smaller than the county were often strong.

[25] Holt, *Northerners*, 56–9, 155–6, 172–3.

7

Towns, Industry and Trade

Towns

A town is defined by having a proportion of its inhabitants engaged in non-agricultural pursuits – trade, manufacture or administration. Medieval towns were enmeshed in the countryside, partly because many of them had fields and some inhabitants who worked them, but mainly because they traded in and processed the products of the countryside. Town soil also had a variety of landlords, including the lords of the countryside. The country would come to town to buy and sell or to attend a court. Towns were an essential part of the life of the countryside, and in turn depended on it. They did not come into existence when they received a charter or had a common seal made – their essence was economic, not constitutional.

Towns were of various types. Some major towns, such as Lincoln, Exeter or London, were of Roman origin, though they had been abandoned and resettled in the Anglo-Saxon period. There were also lesser ones, called 'primary' towns, which occupied the nodal points of ancient routes and had always been there.[1] Such were Banbury (Oxfordshire), Horncastle (Lincolnshire) and Taunton (Somerset). They often had old minster churches, and were the centres of large estates, usually royal or ecclesiastical. Then there were the towns that sat at the gates of wealthy churches, servicing the needs of a static population of clergy and perhaps a flow of pilgrims: Bury St Edmunds, St Albans and Burton-on-Trent, for instance. Some of these towns may actually have been older than the churches, but the churches had the spending power to encourage the town. There were also towns such as Bedford or Cambridge,

[1] Everitt, *Landscape and Community*, 93–107.

which were the seat of the sheriff and centres of royal administration.

But the twelfth and thirteenth centuries also saw the foundation of many wholly new towns. Some were laid out on a fairly grand scale to start with; a famous example is Salisbury, which bishop Richard Poore began in 1219 to house and service his new cathedral built to replace the old one jostled by the castle garrison on the cramped and inconvenient hilltop of Old Sarum. Boston in the Lincolnshire fens had begun earlier in the twelfth century as a trading port with a fair, and its success was rapid and spectacular. It remained in the lordship of the earls of Richmond, who held the manor in which it had been founded. Many other churchmen and lay lords saw opportunities for profit in founding a town on their lands. Baldwin de Freville moved the village of Caxton (Cambridgeshire) on to the main north road from London to Stamford and laid it out anew with a market place; the right to hold the market was granted in 1247. Royston (Hertfordshire) was a point on the boundary of several parishes where an Augustinian priory was founded; in 1189 the prior obtained the right to hold a market and laid out a market place by simply widening the road, and a little town soon sprang up. Not far away the Knights Templar founded a town on their land, and whether out of ambition or irony they named it *Baldac*, medieval French for that urban wonder of the contemporary world, Baghdad. The locals evolved the name to Baldock. These three examples are within a few miles of each other, but they could be paralleled all over England.

Even commoner than new towns were attempts to expand existing villages by giving them a market. It has been estimated that there were over 1200 small markets in England by 1300, which amounts to one for every five or six villages. Founding a market, however, was not quite the same as beginning a successful town, and many of them did not prosper.[2] It could be that there were too many markets by the later thirteenth century. But the proliferation of markets brought everyone within reach of commerce, and must have contributed to economic expansion.

The size of urban populations is even harder to estimate than that of rural ones. The number of people living in a household is barely guessable; mortality rates can be assumed to be high, but how high is unknown, and then there is the problem of

---

[2] Ibid., 109–27; R. H. Britnell, 'The proliferation of markets and fairs in England before 1349', *Econ. Hist. Rev.*, second series 34 (1981), 209–21.

immigration. It would not be surprising if the urban population could not replace its own numbers, and needed to be supplemented – this was normal in medieval towns. There is abundant evidence of immigration, and in the period when townsmen used topographical surnames it is possible to gain an idea of the catchment areas of some towns. York, Norwich and Leicester, for instance, drew migrants from a radius of about 20 miles, Winchester and Bristol from about 40 miles. London was exceptional in having a radius of attraction nearer 60 miles, but the centre of power at Westminster could draw people from as far away as 100 miles.[3] Except Westminster, which was clearly unique, this may give us a rough ranking in size order for the other towns.

The town's inhabitants were a more mixed group than would be found in a rural community, with a wider variety of economic activities and probably even greater contrasts of wealth and poverty. Many towns also contained a resident colony of 'outsiders': the Jews. Communities of Jews had lived in England since the time of William the Conqueror: the most prosperous settlements were at London, Lincoln, York, Canterbury, Nottingham and Norwich. They were under royal protection, enjoying internal jurisdiction under Talmudic law, freedom from most tolls and direct access to royal justice.[4] There seems to have been an influx from northern France during Henry II's reign, probably connected with the temporary expulsion of the Jews from the domain of the king of France in 1182, and by Richard I's reign there were communities in such small places as Dunstable and Devizes. Though links with the French settlements were always closest, Jewish connections were very far-flung and the records show Spanish, German, Italian and even Russian Jews not only in London but also in provincial centres.[5] Moneylending was their principal occupation, but not the only one: they were well known as doctors and some were goldsmiths and other kinds of craftsmen. There were some very big businessmen, such as Aaron of Lincoln, and no doubt many very small ones. Their financial activities certainly extended to trade in wine, wool and corn as well as small-scale peddling and pawnbroking.

It is likely that there was always prejudice against a wealthy, exclusive community benefiting from royal favour, indeed part of an unpopular royal financial system, and to which many influential men were indebted. The Jews were also particularly

---

[3] Rosser, *Westminster*, 182–90.
[4] John's charter in Rot Chart i, 93; Roth, *History of the Jews*, esp. chaps 1–2.
[5] Roth, *History of the Jews*, 12.

susceptible to religious antagonism: abbot Samson's expulsion
of the Jews from Bury St Edmunds was regarded as 'a sign of his
excellence' among the monks.[6] They were at their most vulnerable when the king's authority was distant or weak. The worst
outbreak of popular violence against them occurred in the spring
of 1190, when crusading enthusiasm was at its height and king
Richard was in France preparing for his departure to the Holy
Land. A contemporary describes the crusaders gathered at Stamford as 'indignant that the enemies of the cross of Christ who
dwelt there should possess so much when they had not enough
for the expenses of so great a journey'.[7] Others took the opportunity to wipe out evidence of their indebtedness in attacks at
Lynn, Thetford, Colchester and other places. But the worst tra-
gedy took place at York, where many of the Jewish community
who had survived the sack of their houses took refuge in the
castle, and over 150 committed suicide rather than fall into the
hands of their persecutors.

It was not this kind of exceptional outburst, but arbitrary taxation of extreme severity accompanied by legislation restricting
their activities, driving the Jews to ever more desperate expedients, impoverishing them while increasing their unpopularity,
that brought about the slow demise of the community. England
ceased to be a land where Jews could prosper in security, but
they were forbidden to emigrate. The gradual decline of the
colony was marked by the sack of the London Jewry in 1215, a
succession of heavy tallages and seizures under Henry III, and
the reduction of their internal autonomy, not much relieved by
the king's half-hearted attempts to protect them against increasingly harsh ecclesiastical laws and the hostility of their English
neighbours. It was an impoverished remnant that was finally
expelled in 1290.

Trade and manufacture were the economic basis of the town's
existence. The clergy inherited a strong tradition of hostility to
trade and profit, firmly based on biblical precedent. The theologians of the twelfth century gave close attention to commercial
affairs, the net result of which was to narrow the range of
activities of which they disapproved. For an artisan to add value
to his raw material was quite legitimate, and if a merchant was
involved in labour and expense his profit was morally acceptable. The weight of ecclesiastical censure now fell on two closely

[6] Jocelin, 45–6.
[7] Newburgh i, 310.

defined abuses: usury and Sunday trading.[8] It was partly because of the suspicion of usury that there was ecclesiastical hostility to the Jews, but any moneylender had to go to some lengths to disguise the nature of transactions, which thereby became difficult rather than impossible.

Retailing in a medieval English town was carried on by stall trading, like a modern market, but also in the larger places from permanent shops like warehouses which might be occupied by the craftsman who made the goods. A common type had a lower shop like a cellar and an upper shop slightly above street level. The wealthy merchants in the more important towns built themselves large houses of stone. Southampton had many: the one called 'Canute's Palace' had a hall as large as that at nearby Christchurch castle, a seat of the earls of Devon.[9] Stone houses were not by any means a prerogative of the Jews.

Twelfth-century towns had rising ambitions in the direction of self-government. Most of the larger towns were in direct relations with the king, for whom they were useful sources of cash. They had usually negotiated a fixed sum, a 'farm' like the farm of a manor, which they paid direct into the royal treasury. The king's officials then left the townspeople very much to themselves to run their own affairs. Their status was commonly confirmed by a royal charter which might enumerate some of their legal customs, and they could act together using their common seal to validate agreements. But special charters and privileges were not necessary for a town to function collectively: Oxford acquired a corporate seal in 1191 but had acted corporately long before then.[10] Nor was chartered independence a requirement for prosperity: the burgeoning town of Westminster only had its manor court, with the abbot's steward and bailiff, while Grimsby, which had an impressive collection of royal charters, prospered less than Boston which juridically remained a manor of the earl of Richmond.[11]

In most towns tenements seem to have been held in return for simple cash rents, but in some places the kind of agricultural labour dues which were coming to indicate servile status were only abolished later in the twelfth century. The customs of 'burgage tenure' varied from place to place, but commonly included the right to sell

[8] Baldwin, *Masters, Princes and Merchants*, 261–9.
[9] P. A. Faulkner, 'Medieval undercrofts and town houses' in M. J. Swanton, ed., *Studies in Medieval Domestic Architecture*, Royal Archaeological Inst 1975, 129–131.
[10] Reynolds, *Kingdoms and Communities*, 63.
[11] Rosser, *Westminster*, 245.

and bequeath land freely. The royal charters often granted or confirmed to a town the right to its own court, where alone suits about town property and pleas of debt could be tried, and freedom from trial by battle, but in many places magnates had their own courts in towns for their own men. It is easy to exaggerate the importance of the formal and legal aspects of town government. Regular assemblies going by various names were the normal way of conducting business. The way towns ran themselves is illustrated by events at Ipswich, which in 1200 secured the right to pay its farm directly to the treasury and set about organizing itself like other towns. First 'the whole population of the borough' (*tota villata burgi*) met in the churchyard and unanimously elected two bailiffs. Then 'by common consent' they agreed to meet again and elect 12 'portmen': the bailiffs and coroners chose four men from each parish who elected the 12 from among the 'better and wiser' men of the town.[12] The people who emerge as the embodiment of urban communities are variously described as 'burgesses', 'citizens' or 'men', words which in effect have much the same meaning. They were usually a body of the wealthier merchants, owing their political power to their economic strength, in turn based on their control of the supply of raw materials and their access to profits. Women had no formal political status in the towns, but could still be economically active in their own right. In thirteenth-century Westminster women had a legal right to own property, had their own seals and often kept their maiden names. They were able to join some guilds both as wives and in their own right.[13] It is striking how Jewish women were able to carry on business on their own account, Belaset of Wallingford, Licoricia widow of David of Oxford and Margaret daughter of Jurnet of Norwich being active financiers.[14]

A form of organization which readily grew up in towns was the guild. In origin these were voluntary mutual aid societies, literally 'friendly societies', appropriate among the often uprooted population of towns. They long preserved their sociable and insurance functions, reinforced by oaths, ceremonies and drinking sessions, but they could easily acquire other purposes too, especially religious ones. As towns expanded, guilds grew up devoted to special interests, craft and trade guilds prominent among them. The weavers' guilds of London, Lincoln, Oxford, Winchester, Nottingham and Huntingdon and the fullers' guild

[12] Reynolds, *Kingdoms and Communities*, 188–90.
[13] Rosser, *Westminster*, 196–201.
[14] Roth, *History of the Jews*, 115.

of Winchester existed in the early twelfth century; in London in 1179 there were at least 19 guilds, not necessarily all craft guilds, but all having to pay a fine to the king for recognition of their right to exist.[15] The craft guilds did not always comprise all those pursuing the craft in the town – they were not necessarily mono-polists. Sometimes the guilds of merchants or leading citizens, which in some places went back to the eleventh century or earlier, ran the town in the twelfth century, and though royal charters tended to displace them with mayors and aldermen these may be little more than new names for the same people.

London was unquestionably the largest and richest town in Angevin England. It was a lively place which aroused strong feelings. William fitz Stephen's panegyric of it in his biography of one of its famous sons, Thomas Becket, is well known: 'happy in the healthiness of its air, in its observance of Christian prac-tice, in the strength of its fortifications, in its natural situation, in the honour of its citizens, and in the modesty of its matrons' and so on, for page after page.[16] Less well known, perhaps, is the view expressed in the chronicle of Richard of Devizes: 'If you come to London, pass though it quickly . . . All sorts of men come together from every nation under the sun. Each people brings its own customs and vices to the city . . . Whatever evil or malicious thing is found anywhere in the world you will find in that city . . . If you do not wish to live with wicked people, do not live in London.'[17] To a great extent it differed from other towns in scale only: the provisioning trades were very important, with spe-cialized markets in such places as Bread Street, Milk Street, Candlewick Street and the unfortunately named Old Fish Street (the fish market was later moved). But it was the main mint for the country, the centre of credit operations by Jews and Templars, and it played a vital role in supplying royal needs, thus becoming the centre of luxury trade. The development of pala-tial houses for the aristocracy and greater churchmen is a feature of this period: it was in the 1180s that the archbishops settled at Lambeth, for example. London was also an important craft centre, though the cloth produced was cheap and for the mass market. In 1202 the 'citizens' paid to have a royal charter which destroyed the weavers' guild.[18] This corresponds to ordinances in a number of other towns which declared the weavers and fullers

---

[15] PR 26 Henry II, 153–4.
[16] Mats Becket iii, 2–13.
[17] Devizes, 65–6.
[18] Brooke and Keir, *London*, 285; Rot Obl et Fin, 185–6.

not to be included among the free citizens participating in the towns' privileges, and forbidding them to sell their manufactures. There was clearly conflict between large merchants or industrialists and workers.

London's government and internal politics are rather obscure in this period, though important developments were taking place. The city was the equivalent of a shire, with two sheriffs, elected or appointed but usually Londoners, paying a farm into the treasury. The equivalent of the shire court was the 'husting', and the moots of the wards into which the city was divided corresponded to hundred courts. In 1193 some of the citizens formed a 'commune' and set up a mayor with a council of 'échevins', words betraying the French or Flemish models on which the commune was based; the mayor survived when the commune was suppressed, and his court gradually ousted the husting as the forum for property transactions. London was clearly a centre of constitutional experiment as it was of the legal antiquarianism which fed political ideas at this time; or perhaps it would be truer to say that the social and economic ferment of a large town led to conflicts which issued in political convulsions, in turn leading to new ideas.

Other towns may have been less spectacular, but significant developments were happening in them too. Oxford in the twelfth and thirteenth centuries was a wealthy and expanding town, its prosperity fostered by regular royal visits to Woodstock nearby as well as by the nascent university. It was well situated, at the point where the road from Southampton and Winchester crossed the Thames on the way to Northampton and the Midlands. It had stone houses, generally with the narrow end on to the street and 'entries' leading into the gardens, which were often built on. The four major streets were all markets, the principal commodities being fish, bread, dairy produce, pigs, corn, wood and firewood, straw, earthenware, textiles and gloves. The cattle market was probably outside the gates, where suburbs were growing up. The connections between town and country could hardly be more obvious than in these economic interests. Its two earliest known craft guilds were the weavers and leatherworkers, and by 1200 there was a goldsmith, a vintner, a spicer and an illuminator of books. Life stopped at nightfall, when there was a curfew and the watch patrolled the streets, but only within the gates – the suburbs were unpoliced.[19]

---

[19] Catto, *History of the University of Oxford*, 156–9.

Canterbury still had its Roman walls, but by the twelfth century quite extensive suburbs had grown up beyond them. The king was the lord of the borough, but derived only a modest farm from it through two reeves who collected the dues and carried out various judicial duties.[20] Some of the reeves were local men, and when the citizens took the town at farm from the king in 1234 and elected their own bailiffs the innovation may have been less significant than it seems. There was a borough court, and wards with aldermen. The wards had courts, too, where transactions involving property took place and which also had police functions. Land was held by gavelkind tenure in the same way as in the rest of Kent outside the walls. The economic life of the town had a substratum of ordinary trade like Oxford's, with separate cattle and fish markets and retailers clustering along the streets. There were cloth- and leatherworkers and plenty of mills. But Canterbury was the ecclesiastical capital of England and housed two great Benedictine monasteries and a host of smaller church institutions. The cathedral priory owned about half the town, and St Augustine's abbey another eighth. The local barons and knightly tenants of the archbishop had town property, though the archbishop himself had little but his palace inside the walls. The town was full of servants of the monks, priests, clerks and chaplains, and it was probably conspicuous ecclesiastical consumption that gave rise to a flourishing goldsmithing industry. Moneyers were the other unusual feature, the Canterbury mints being second only to London.

Coventry, unlike Canterbury, is a town of obscure origins. The original nucleus was round the abbey founded before the Conquest, but another grew up in the twelfth century round the earl of Chester's castle. It was thus a double town under two lords, until in 1249 the earl's heirs resigned their half to the prior of what had meanwhile become a cathedral monastery. Though there were burgesses holding by burgage tenure and a town court for the urban tenants of both lords, the burgesses did not have the farm of the borough and the town was integrated into seignorial administration. The cloth industry began to grow later in the thirteenth century, but earlier the economic basis seems to have been much like we saw at Oxford, with provision merchants as the leading citizens. Supplying the church and the castle was the town's basic reason for existence, and the urban elite here included administrators. Relationship with the earl

[20] Urry, *Canterbury*.

was the key to prosperity. Here too a number of out-of-town landowners and knights had burgage property among their other rents, and there was even a townsman, Liulf of Brinklow, who held land outside the town by burgage tenure.[21]

All burgage owners, in other words, were not burgesses. Great magnates could possess useful scatterings of urban property, such as Robert earl of Leicester, Henry II's justiciar, who had houses in London, Winchester, Oxford, Windsor, Southampton and Rouen. He also had the town of Leicester, where his revenues included tolls on the mills and communal ovens, on the market, on goods entering and leaving the town, and a lump sum negotiated with the burgesses.[22]

The importance of the service element in urban prosperity can be seen clearly in the two towns which came nearest to being political capitals, Winchester and Westminster. Winchester declined as the royal bureaucracy moved to Westminster, led by the treasury and exchequer under Henry II. The town of Westminster, most of which was in the abbey's lordship, expanded correspondingly. Winchester's population in the middle of the twelfth century was between 5000 and 8000 but thereafter declined steadily, despite the town having an important fair and continuing as a centre of craft production. The most numerous occupations, after the ubiquitous clerics, were the victualling trades, then cloth- and leatherworkers. But the richest individuals were the royal officials and the moneyers, then the cloth traders and the victuallers.[23] It is not therefore surprising that the transfer of royal officialdom to Westminster made that town's fortune: it never developed a significant craft element, officials and retailers forming its economic backbone.[24]

Some scenes of urban life can be observed at another monastic town, Bury St Edmunds. Here the townsmen owed a rent of £40 to the abbey. The monks were well aware that the value of the town was rising and hoped to put up the rent. They tried to claim more from new shops, and turned down an offer of a £5 increase from the townsmen. But the abbot stepped in and confirmed the town's liberties including the £40 rent, to the anger of the monks, in return for a £40 gift to himself. The abbey sacrist took toll at the market, and ran into trouble with citizens of London who claimed freedom from toll. The Londoners organized a

[21] Coss, *Lordship, Knighthood and Locality*, 25–6, 30–1, 55–6, 62–73.
[22] Crouch, *Beaumont Twins*, 179–83.
[23] Biddle, *Winchester*, 442–5.
[24] Rosser, *Westminster*, 25.

boycott of Bury market and the sacrist's takings fell. The bishop of London patched up a compromise whereby toll was taken but returned to the Londoners; but trouble soon broke out again when the Londoners refused to pay toll on their herrings passing through on the way from Yarmouth.[25] The men of Bury had fields to cultivate and sheep to tend, but there were fullers in the town and flax was brought in for sale. Dung collected in the streets was a valuable commodity: everyone collected it from before their door, and the poor sold it – a useful financial incentive to urban hygiene.[26]

The English towns were not particularly large, rich or independent by European standards, only London bearing comparison with major cities on the continent. There was no distinct class of great merchants in England, or for that matter in France, at this date as there was in Italy. The towns were expanding and some people in them were prospering, but it is doubtful if the urbanized proportion of the population increased. They were so intimately linked to the countryside that they accompanied its expanding economy with growth of their own.

Industry

The society of Angevin England showed a dramatic contrast between rich and poor. The spending power of the aristocracy and the church was a crucial factor in the economy: as we have seen, it could give rise to towns which were largely there to serve them. The other element in the prosperity of towns was industry, or craft production. But these were not just urban pursuits: some were widespread in the countryside, where they helped provide a living for the rapidly increasing population.

Of all the forms of aristocratic ostentation, building must have redistributed wealth most widely among the rest of the population. The sums spent on royal churches and castles were vast and lay lords, bishops and abbots gladly participated in a continuing building boom. The less noticeable but numerous minor buildings – village churches and unpretentious houses and farm buildings – provided work probably adding up to more than the grander buildings, at least for crafts using the cheaper materials. Building work was seasonal, with a dead period in midwinter, parallel to

[25] Jocelin, 76–9.
[26] Ibid., 104.

the agricultural year and so in competition with agriculture for labour rather than complementary to it. Money spent on building found its way into many pockets, benefiting both the skilled and the unskilled, and must have had an enlivening effect throughout the economy. A major building project required stone, both cut 'freestone' and rubble for cores and foundations, lime and sand for mortar – the lime being made by burning limestone or chalk – and wood for roofing and such purposes as scaffolding, centring and the construction of workshops. The floor might be tiled, and tiles needed sand for the moulds and lead for the glaze; the roof would need thatch, tiles or lead, and the windows glass. A great deal of labour would be needed on site, while the materials would sometimes have to be transported considerable distances. Building work gave rise to whole industries.

Quarrying stone and digging clay for tiles were widespread small-scale activities all over the country wherever geology allowed. Unpretentious 'vernacular' buildings are usually made of local materials even when these create constructional difficulties, as do the chalk and flint of which many a small church in East Anglia or the southern English downland is built. Cost was the crucial factor: it has been calculated that a journey of 12 miles overland would double the price of the stone, and even if transport was by water the cost would still mount up.[27] But some of the better stone types were widely used: important quarries were at Barnack near Peterborough, Taynton in the Oxfordshire Cotswolds, Quarr on the Isle of White, and Kentish ragstone was quarried near Maidstone. These competed with Caen stone from Normandy. For architectural details 'Purbeck marble' was popular. It was quarried round Corfe in the Isle of Purbeck, where it gave rise to an industry mass-producing such objects as fonts, grave slabs, tomb chests and altars, as well as the attached columns and bases to be seen at Durham, Canterbury and Salisbury cathedrals, Westminster abbey and many other places. By about 1200 it had driven out the black Tournai marble from Flanders for such purposes. Water transport was essential for delivery, and the successful quarries had access to it.

Roofing slates were being used by the later twelfth century, quarried in Devon and Cornwall and transported along the coast.[28] Roofing tiles were used extensively in London and the

[27] Salzmann, *Building in England*, 119.
[28] Wood, *Medieval House*, 294–5.

south east where stone slates were not available locally, and they have been found archaeologically in large quantities from the twelfth century onwards.[29] Tiled floors could be luxury products of great splendour, as finds at Clarendon and Chertsey and the surviving pavement in Westminster abbey chapter house demonstrate. They were made on the site – at Clarendon the kiln which produced the tiles has been found. Windows were probably made on the site, too, out of material brought to the spot, and glaziers were found in most major towns in the thirteenth century.[30] Glass is made of sand and plant ash fused together by heat, and the centres of production were places where sand and wood, preferably beech, were found together in abundance. The Surrey and Sussex Weald was probably the main English glass-making area throughout the middle ages, Cheshire and Staffordshire also being production centres. Vessels of various kinds and hanging lamps were made, as well as plain window glass. Coloured glass seems to have been imported.[31]

The most important minerals extracted in medieval England were tin and lead. Cornwall and Devon had produced tin since 500 BC, and between 300 AD and 1300 this area was the only significant source of the metal in Europe. In the twelfth and thirteenth centuries it was exported to France, the Low Countries and Germany. It was taken from alluvial deposits, so mining was unnecessary. Devon seems to have been the main source earlier, with Cornwall overtaking it in the thirteenth century. There was a great increase in production over the period, rising from about 70 tons in 1156 to 350 tons in 1171, and from between 400 and 450 tons in about 1200 to 600 tons in 1214. Production at this time was higher than in the fourteenth or fifteenth centuries.[32] It was also a very profitable industry to the king, and was organized to be so. At the first smelting, near the tinfield, the ingot was stamped by royal officers and a toll paid. Later there was a second smelting, the metal being stamped again and a further tax paid. Tin miners had special privileges, confirmed to them by charter of king John in 1201: they had the right to prospect and stake out claims anywhere in Cornwall and Devon except in churchyards, gardens and highways; they could divert streams, and compel landowners to sell them fuel. They came under the

[29] J. Cherry in Blair and Ramsay, *Industries*, 189–200.
[30] Richard Marks in ibid., 275–6.
[31] R. J. Charleston in ibid., 237–64; and fig. 117, a thirteenth-century glass hanging lamp.
[32] Salzmann, *English Industries*, 73–4; Hatcher, *Tin Production*, 18–26.

sole jurisdiction of their own 'stannary' court presided over by a warden. In 1231 the 'stannaries' were granted to Henry III's brother, Richard earl of Cornwall, and the profits of tin-mining no longer occur in the royal records.

Lead was mined in the Pennines, Shropshire and north Wales and in the south-west. Though it had a multitude of uses in domestic implements as well as in building, the economics of mining lead were always uncertain and production was only justified if silver could be obtained from the same ore. Lead and tin were the principal raw materials in the pewter industry, which in the thirteenth century seems mainly to have manufactured mass-produced stamped or cast pilgrim badges in large numbers; the widespread use of pewter for domestic utensils did not begin until after 1300.[33] Silver was produced in significant quantities at Alston Moor in Cumberland and elsewhere where lead was mined, but England also imported precious metals, notably gold which was not produced at home in any quantity. Goldsmithing was widespread in major towns and some monasteries, producing a wide range of luxury articles of which very little has survived from this period.

Coal had been mined in England in Roman times, but not again, it seems, until the late twelfth century. Mining may have started again on the shores of Durham and Northumberland, where seams met the surface and coal could simply be picked up on the beach: this may have helped give it the name 'sea-coal'; but by the thirteenth century there was a coastal shipping trade in coal taking it from the north-east down the east coast and to London. By the mid-thirteenth century coal was being mined, in open-cast pits, in Yorkshire, Nottinghamshire, Derbyshire, Shropshire and the Forest of Dean in Gloucestershire as well as round Newcastle. In 1257 it was being burnt in Nottingham in sufficient quantities for queen Eleanor to dislike staying in the castle there because of the smoke.[34] Its main use was to burn lime for construction purposes, but it was probably used in other industrial processes as well, including iron-smelting.

Iron ore occurs widely in England, but in the middle ages the main sources were the Forest of Dean, the Midlands, south Yorkshire, Durham and Northumberland.[35] Certain types of ore are best for specific uses and it seems that some iron was imported,

---

[33] Ronald F. Homer in Blair and Ramsay, *Industries*, 57–80.
[34] Ann Mon iii, 105.
[35] Jane Geddes in Blair and Ramsay, *Industries*, 167–88.

principally from Spain and the Baltic. Large quantities of charcoal were needed for smelting, though coal could be used in the
later stages of the process. Steel is iron with a higher carbon
content, and ensuring that the carbon was evenly absorbed required a high level of skill; consequently it was more economical
to apply small quantites of steel to sharp edges and tips than to
forge entire steel objects. Iron had a thousand uses, for domestic
and agricultural implements, arms, armour and in building, and
smiths and ironworkers were to be found all over the country.
The commonest surviving ironwork takes the form of grilles and
decorative patterning on doors.

Another metal industry made pots, kettles, candlesticks and so
on out of brass and bronze, both basically copper alloyed with
tin, zinc or lead in various proportions and known in the middle
ages as 'latten'.[36] For this the raw material was imported, copper
not being found in England in significant quantity, though old
objects could be melted down and the material re-used. It may be
that finished objects were imported, too, from the European
centre of this kind of manufacture at Dinant near Liège. The
most impressive products of this coppersmithing industry were
the great church bells, but kitchen ware was the commonest.

Pottery was produced throughout most of the country, often
on a small scale as a part-time occupation, though there were
also urban centres.[37] In late Saxon times Stamford, St Neots and
Thetford produced wheel-made cooking pots, storage jars and
dishes which were quite widely marketed. This industry collapsed
in the twelfth century, perhaps because of competition from
metal products. In the thirteenth century there was considerable
regional variation in pottery products, the industry being more
decentralized. The craft cannot have been very profitable as
potters do not figure among the wealthy townsmen and did not
form guilds. The low status of its practitioners is no doubt
reflected in the often crude quality of their output.[38]

Demand for leather must have been high, as it was used in
clothing, footwear and transport; it was probably produced all
over the country, by tanners using cattle skins and oak bark and
tawyers who treated the skins of sheep and other animals with
alum and oil.[39] Always a malodorous trade, other materials used
in the processes included dog dung, bird droppings, urine and

[36] Blair and Blair in ibid., 81–106.
[37] John Cherry in ibid., 200–8.
[38] See e.g. the illustrations in ibid., figs 93–5.
[39] Ibid., 295–318.

fish oil. The tanners and tawyers sold their output to curriers, who finished it and sold it on to specialized artisans who made it up into shoes, saddles, harnesses, jerkins, scabbards, gloves, bags and so on. Makers of new shoes were called cordwainers, their name deriving from Cordoba in Spain, the source of the most prestigious leather – whether they used Spanish leather or not. Cobblers (*sutores*) mended old shoes. Altogether the leather trades were an important source of employment; in York in the later thirteenth century they accounted for nearly one-third of the freemen, the largest single group. Woodworking was also an important and ubiquitous industry, turning out everything from

Centres of the textile industries, c. 1200   • Sudbury
Other major centres ◉ York
Important fairs ○ St Ives

MAP 7.1   Centres of trade and industry
(*based on Penelope Walton, 'Textiles', in Blair and Ramsay, 1991, 347, fig. 179*)

vast cathedral roofs and huge barns to furniture, plates, bowls, saddles and musical instruments.[40]

But probably the most important industry, if only because of the universal need for its products, was the manufacture of textiles. Even though raw wool was England's most important export, there was a substantial and widespread native textile industry in the period 1150–1250 which also produced some high-quality goods for export (see map 7.1).[41] The value of the wool produced varied markedly by region, the best coming from Lincolnshire and the Welsh borders. A minor industrial revolution took place in the eleventh century, with the introduction of the horizontal loom operated by treadles. Replacing the vertical warp-weighted loom, this enabled longer pieces of cloth to be produced at greater speed, and also affected production methods: from being a domestic task, probably carried out by women, cloth production became the trade of urban craft guilds consisting mainly of men. Domestic production must have continued all over the country for local needs, but certainly by 1150 it was supplemented by professional urban production for the market. The highest quality cloths were produced in Yorkshire and Lincolnshire, the centres being York, Lincoln and Stamford. These were 'scarlet', a finely finished cloth often dyed with expensive red dye, so that its name was eventually transferred to the colour; and 'haberget', a diamond twill which looked rather like mail armour. They also produced 'rayed' or striped cloth, which was unusual because most medieval cloth seems to have been made in single colours. Cheaper cloths such as undyed 'russet' or cheap 'burel' were produced in towns all over the Midlands and central southern England. Plant dyes were used, for instance madder for red, woad for blue and weld for yellow. These were grown in England, though some woad was imported from Gascony and elsewhere. The most expensive dye was vermilion, imported from Mediterranean countries. Not long after 1250 the techniques of production changed again with the introduction of carding, the spinning wheel and the fulling mill, which led to further changes in the geographical location of the industry.

Linen, made from flax or hemp, was probably a widespread industry but there were centres at Winchester, Wilton near Salisbury and Aylsham in Norfolk. The most famous English textile

---

[40] Julian Munby in ibid., 379–405.
[41] Penelope Walton in ibid., 319–54.

product internationally, from Anglo-Saxon times until the end of the middle ages, was embroidery. Church vestments of *opus anglicanum* have survived in various continental cathedral treasuries, and there may have been equally luxurious products made for the laity which have not survived. They make heavy use of gold thread and silk, both imported raw materials. The craft probably originated in nunneries and monasteries, but there were urban commercial practitioners by the thirteenth century.

Trade

The hundreds of markets of rural and urban England were the conduits through which passed the small-scale trade in everyday objects needed by an overwhelmingly rural population. But there were other, wider channels which canalized long-distance trade. The twelfth and thirteenth centuries were the heyday of the medieval fairs. While markets normally took place on one day each week, fairs met for a week or so each year, and attracted merchants and customers from long distances. Europe's greatest fairs were those of Champagne in northern France, but England had its fairs too. Most of them were already old in 1150. In the early thirteenth century they formed a circuit: the fair at St Ives in Huntingdonshire was held at Easter, and Boston fair in June. Then there was Winchester in August, St Edward's fair at Westminster in October and Northampton in November.[42] The trading centre of gravity thus oscillated between the south-east and the east Midlands. Much of the point of a fair was the availability of luxury goods, and the big spenders used them to make important puchases of wine, furs and wax for candles, while foreign merchants probably bought wool.

But international trade was not confined to a round of annual events, though much of it was focused on them; it was a continuous process taking place in the principal ports. It is not until about 1300 that the sources exist which give us an overall picture of this trade, and we have to reconstruct the earlier picture from scraps of information. The most important English export was wool, and the market for it was in Flanders where the great medieval weaving industry was already well established. There was, as we have seen, an English textile industry too, which exported some of its products, but it seems to have collapsed in

---

[42] Rosser, *Westminster*, 99.

the face of Flemish competition in the thirteenth century. The Low Countries, mainly the area of modern Belgium, were a hive of industries in this period: as well as Flemish weaving there was an important metal industry in the Meuse valley further east, and the towns of both areas were large and populous. This created a market not only for wool but also for food products, and grain and cheese were exported to Flanders from the east coast ports of Ipswich, Yarmouth and Lynn, and from east Kent. Yarmouth was also a fishing port, and herrings were exported to Flanders too. The finished cloth was then imported. England thus appears as a supplier of primary raw materials and foodstuffs to an industrialized area, whose products it then buys.

Trade with Scandinavia was of long standing in 1150, and continued thereafter though the Baltic trade fell increasingly into the hands of the north German Hanse. Furs and timber were the principal imports from this region. The valuable furs were white ermine, from the Arctic stoat, and black sable from the marten. Gris was grey and vair was grey and white, both from species of squirrel.[43] Trade with Germany was largely with the citizens of Cologne and other Rhinelanders, who brought wine, metalwork and spices. But north Germany was rising in importance, merchants of Bremen and Münster joining the Rhinelanders in the thirteenth century.

The second most valuable import, after cloth, was probably wine. The largest single consumer of imported wine must have been the royal household, and the chief source of supply was western France, increasingly Bordeaux. King John ordered Geoffrey fitz Peter to pay the Poitevin and Gascon wine merchants well for the wine taken from them for the king's use, so that they should be pleased and bring their wines freely, 'for if not we may suffer a shortage of wine because of them'.[44] Other commodities traded down the western seaways from Southampton and Bristol were salt, woad, grain, hides from Ireland and Spanish iron. Metals were another significant English export: lead from the Pennines and especially tin. There was also an import trade in small edible luxuries: nuts and dried fruits from the Mediterranean and the Middle East – figs, dates, raisins, almonds and also sugar. From exotic places of which contemporary Englishmen knew nothing came pepper, cumin, ginger, cloves and other

[43] Brooke and Keir, *London*, 258–61.
[44] Rot Lib, 60.

spices, probably traded through the Champagne fairs or the Flemish towns.

England, though right at the end of the Eurasian landmass, was plugged into trading networks covering all of western and northern Europe and the Mediterranean, which brought in some commodities from as far as India, China and south-east Asia. Its place within this network was generally the rather humble one of a supplier of raw materials and an importer of manufactured goods and luxuries, but this did not preclude a good deal of prosperity among merchants and conspicuous consumption among the landowners, to whom an expanding economy delivered a standard of living comparable to that of their peers on the continent. This occurred against a background of generally worsening peasant poverty. The surplus was being creamed off by the lords, and much of it spent on luxury imports. No mass market was able to grow up for non-agricultural produce beyond basic necessities, and in consequence diversification and long-term growth were stultified.

8

Learning, Literature and the Arts

Language and education

Three languages were used in Angevin England. Latin had to be learned at school. It was for church services, academic writing and business documents, and might occasionally be spoken by the clergy. French had been the language of the upper classes since the Norman conquest, and bore a cachet of social distinction. It was the language of the law courts, of instruction in the schools and of contacts abroad. Norman to start with, the French spoken in England had tended to develop local characteristics which made it an identifiable dialect looked down upon by those who spoke the French of Paris. It nevertheless had a life of its own, and spawned a vigorous culture. Because of its high status it was a necessary accomplishment for those who wished to rise in society, and by the middle of the thirteenth century manuals were available to help English-speakers to learn it. English was the speech of the despised rustics and of many who despised them. Since the Anglo-Saxon period its inflections had become simpler and its vocabulary was in the process of changing, with French loan-words gradually creeping in. When English began to resume its role as a written literary language, which seems to have been in the decades around 1200, it re-emerges in a different guise – Middle English has replaced Old English.

In practice, bilingualism, or even trilingualism, must have been common: lords picked up English from their nurses and their servants, and English-speakers acquired French in their lord's household. Though Henry II needed an interpreter when addressed in English,[1] Gilbert Foliot was fully at home in all three

---

[1] Gerald of Wales vi, 64–5.

languages.[2] The usefulness of the languages in communicating with a general audience was in inverse proportion to their learnedness: better than a pretentious sermon in Latin, thought abbot Samson of Bury, was one in French or, best of all, English.[3] Each language had its own area of appropriate use, and its speakers were largely defined by the social group to which they belonged; nevertheless twelfth- and thirteenth-century England was a polyglot society.

Much elementary learning was taught at home: social and domestic skills, a trade, and perhaps reading and writing. It was a common practice to send children to another household for education. Boys were sent to the households of craftsmen and merchants to learn a trade, and higher up the social scale magnate households took in boys as pages, to be trained for the life of the aristocracy, and other children for menial work. King John as a young man had received part of his education in the household of the justiciar Rannulf de Glanville, where he may have acquired an interest in law and administration and certainly met men who were to be useful to him later. Some households had a master to teach the children, and upper-class boys might have both knightly and academic masters. Though boys were destined for careers at an early age, they did not begin to specialize in knightly or clerical education until the middle or late teens, by which time they had acquired a range of skills including in many cases basic literacy. Hence there were both literate laymen and hunting and fighting clerics. There is evidence that some members of the higher aristocracy could read Latin in the twelfth century and that literacy spread downwards in the thirteenth, but with the growth of a literature in French, skill in reading the vernacular appears to have replaced Latin. For those lower down the social scale elementary schooling in reading Latin and the plainchant that went with basic literacy could also be learned from parish priests and clerks, who were ordered to hold schools by pope Gregory IX in 1234.[4] Monasteries and the cathedrals continued to teach children, as they always had done, almonry and choir schools becoming more visible to us in the thirteenth century.

But the educational monopoly of the household was breaking down: by the mid-twelfth century a network of schools with

[2] Map, 37. M. D. Legge, 'Anglo-Norman as a spoken language', *Proceedings of the Battle Conference* ii (1979), 110–11.

[3] Jocelin, 128.

[4] Orme, *English Schools*, 60–7.

professional schoolmasters had grown up, widely scattered over the country. In the late twelfth century 22 are known, 32 in the early thirteenth, but this certainly underestimates the real total.[5] They were to be found in all the major towns and in such small places as Helmsley (Yorkshire), Arundel (Sussex) and Stratford (Warwickshire). A few school textbooks have survived from this period to show that the teaching of children was of concern to the learned: the Latin poem *Stans puer ad mensam*, attributed to Robert Grosseteste, deals with table manners and serving etiquette, while a group of friars including Bartholomew de Glanville wrote treatises on the education of children. But the schools were all-male and charged fees: girls and the poor were not catered for.

The education of girls is not well documented, which does not necessarily mean there was little to document. But girls' education was less formal than boys' and much less written about, though some, especially the highly born, were taught in convents. Nuns must have been able to cope with the Latin liturgy, but it is possible to say prayers without understanding the language, and much material written by or for women is in French and English. There may have been a thirteenth-century switch from Latin to vernacular literacy for women as there was for laymen. Upper-class girls were apparently also sent to other households, and as well as dress, needlework, music and proper behaviour some girls were certainly taught reading. Writing was a different matter: in a large household there would be a clerk or two for the menial business of actually setting pen to parchment. With men, too, the ability to read does not necessarily imply skill in writing.

The higher studies of canon law and theology were taught in many centres. Schools in Exeter, Lincoln and other cathedral cities and at Northampton taught law, theology and the liberal arts, and they continued to do so until later in the middle ages. But it was in the 1190s that the Oxford schools began to establish a lead over the others. At first the canon and Roman lawyers showed the way, but by 1200 Alexander Neckham was teaching theology and others were active in the liberal arts. Though the interdict and trouble with the townsmen in 1209 resulted in a temporary exodus of scholars, to Cambridge among other places, a settlement reached in 1214 under the aegis of the papal legate established a chancellor and a common fund – the institutional rudiments of corporate existence. The masters of the

[5] Orme, *English Schools*, 168–80, 294.

Oxford schools became in effect a guild like other urban trades-men. In 1231 Henry III ordered that the rents of scholars' dwellings should be fixed by a panel of masters and townsmen, and gave the chancellor the use of the king's prison and the help of the sheriff in dealing with riotous students, thus increas-ing the chancellor's power over both town and gown. In 1254 the 'university (*universitas*) of masters and scholars of Oxford' gained confirmation of its liberties and customs from pope Inno-cent IV. Unmistakable proof of its standing is provided by the appearance of high-born students: Aymer de Valence, Henry III's half-brother, went to Oxford in the 1240s, and the sons of the earl of Gloucester a decade later.[6] By then Oxford was attracting students from all over England, Wales, Scotland and Ireland: in 1252 there was a riot between the 'northerners' and the Irish-men, reflecting the tendency of compatriots to lodge together and stay together, as they did in a more organized way at the schools of Paris.

But before the mid-thirteenth century no English school could rival the great continental centres in technical excellence: from the 1140s Paris led Europe in theology and Bologna in canon law, a situation facilitated by the universality of Latin. A period of study in one or both was part of a recognized career path leading, for some, to high office in the church. A young English scholar would go in his late teens to the schools of northern France to study rhetoric, logic and grammar for anything from two to seven years. He would return to England a young 'master of arts' (*magister*), and hope for employment in the rapidly developing administration of a magnate, a bishop or even the king. Much would depend on his connections. The greatest prize was appointment to a rectory or other benefice which would provide an independent income. He might then undertake study in theology or canon law, which would mean a further six or seven years abroad. He would then be a strong candidate for any high ecclesiastical office. Such careers were followed by many of the outstanding churchmen of the period: Gerald of Wales, Edmund of Abingdon, Stephen Langton – the path was open to young men from quite humble backgrounds, though for them it was more arduous, and might lead to the security of a wealthy monastery rather than the competitive world of the secular church or the royal court. The estate administration of the great

[6] Orme, *Childhood*, 67.

abbeys provided as much scope for a career as any but the wealthiest of magnates.

Academic education was thus remarkably cosmopolitan, more so perhaps than in any other period of English history. Many English clerics stayed on the continent, making a career there – Stephen of Lexington, abbot of Cîteaux, and Hamo of Faversham, minister general of the Franciscan order, for instance, while John of Salisbury ended his days as bishop of Chartres. A reverse movement, though less than under the Norman kings and diminishing further in the thirteenth century, produced Frenchmen in England, amongst others Hugh of Avallon, bishop of Lincoln, and Hugh du Puiset, bishop of Durham. But alongside that of the cosmopolitans there was another career path entirely within England, leading from the parish priest to a local monastery and perhaps a magnate household. The level of learning acquired was not of the highest, but quite sufficient to draft a lord's charters and cope with his finances.

The decades around 1200 witnessed one of the most fundamental changes of the middle ages: the growth of a widespread habit of documentation. It was an age in which much that had been customary, dependent on memory and oral testimony, was written down, codified and thus made more fixed. A massive increase in surviving written documents covering transactions of all kinds reflects the realization, constantly stressed in charter preambles, that writing supplements the brief memory of man. It was not that writing replaced human memory, as written documents were still read aloud to those who had to hear them and oral testimony was still crucial in law; but the new documentary habit required a new professionalism in administration, both reflecting and furthering the availability of literate and numerate clerks. The educational expansion that marks the late twelfth and thirteenth century served this revolution. Not least, it dramatically increases our sources of information, which now include quantities of standardized business documents. After about 1200 we begin to have, at least in some places, for the first time in European history, an embarrassment of quantity in our sources.

These changes may also have been accompanied by an increase in lay literacy, but here we are on less firm ground. Vernacular literary works as well as Latin business documents were intended to be read aloud to an audience. Literacy was therefore not necessary for the enjoyment of literature. Business documents in Latin appear to have been translated for the benefit of lay audiences, so literacy and latinity were also unnecessary for following business in a fairly simple but effective way. Even learned Latin works were read out to audiences: this is how the schools proceeded, public readings being accompanied by running commentaries by the master, though here the audience would have to be familiar with Latin and therefore be literate. Both literary and scholarly writings were thus performances, events rather than texts.

It is not easy to envisage the nature of intellectual activities in the centuries before printing could fix a standard text and multiply it beyond all imagining. Once written down, a work in the manuscript age might be given to a patron – who may simply put it away and never look at it or listen to it again, as Gerald of Wales feared might happen to one of his productions.[7] Or it could be tried out on several patrons, with a dedication to each; or if successful, texts could be multiplied and circulated round groups of friends. In this way works came to be associated with circles of acquaintances, and might soon pass out of the author's control. Thus there was no profit for the writer other than patronage and reputation, and then only as long as the work was associated with him. And once written down a work developed a life of its own: an author could recopy it with alterations, and others might do the same. A popular work might evolve, and never take a definitive form. Chronicles in particular could circulate among monasteries and be added to in several places. These basic conditions of book production underlie all the intellectual activity of the middle ages.

Learning

Throughout its history much of European culture can be seen as a dialogue between the Christian religion and the civilization of classical antiquity. The sudden increase in intellectual activity often called the 'twelfth-century renaissance' was a stage in the long process of recovering the thought and writings of the ancient world, and reconciling their often very different presuppositions and attitudes with the basic tenets of Christianity. It was translations of works of Aristotle which had not previously been available, made either directly from Greek or from Arabic accompanied by Arab commentaries, which provided the thinkers

---

[7] Gerald of Wales vi, 161: preface to *Description of Wales*.

of the twelfth and thirteenth centuries with their agenda. By 1150 Aristotle's works on logic were available, and scientific works by Aristotle, Ptolemy and Avicenna, called the 'libri naturales', were coming in. A further revelation was provided by the commentaries of Averroes which became available about 1230, but revisions and new translations of philosophical and scientific works continued all through the thirteenth century. The 'twelfth-century renaissance' did not simply stop with the century: but the literary approach based on the study of rhetoric, popular in the twelfth century, gave way to logic and philosophy. It is true that the scholar who in the twelfth century 'had wandered at large in the fields and woods of noble literature', in the thirteenth 'was bound to service in the mill of scholastic logic';[8] but logic had an important place in the twelfth century, and as the foundation of scholastic theology it became dominant.

The most prominent representative of the 'humanist' trend in the twelfth century was John of Salisbury. Educated at Paris in the 1130s and 1140s, he was employed in the households of archbishops Theobald and Thomas Becket as a lawyer and administrator, probably as an expert on appeals to Rome. He was in Canterbury cathedral when Becket was murdered, and in 1176 his association with Becket brought him the bishopric of Chartres. His importance is less as a philosopher or classical scholar – the basis of his education was a thorough knowledge of set texts and the cultivation of a good Latin style, but he treated his classical sources very freely – than as a window into the scholarly world of his time. His Policraticus is a treatise on political ideas; the Entheticus, written at Becket's request, is an introduction to the doctrines of the ancient philosophers, and the Metalogicon investigates the role of logic in education and the arts of language. All these works contain criticisms, now satirical, now moralizing, of contemporary trends; his descriptions of his own education and his teachers, and his criticisms of the futility of logic-chopping have become famous. His letters were much appreciated by his contemporaries, and were collected as models of style.

Scholastic philosophy was not at this time the dead hand of outmoded system that it became to later generations, but an exciting, invigorating pursuit of new knowledge of universal importance, applying rigorous techniques of rational criticism to

---

[8] Powicke, Henry III and the Lord Edward, 327–8.

authoritative texts in order to clarify the basic principles of religion, ethics and human behaviour, and then applying these principles to social organization. The main types of scholastic writing emerged from the teaching activity of the masters. The principal task of a theologian was to lecture on the Bible. A verse was read out and then commented on. Biblical commentaries survive in large numbers, outstanding among them those on the entire Bible except for the Psalms by the English master Stephen Langton, the future archbishop of Canterbury. Another form of intellectual activity was the disputation, the written form of which was called a *questio*; a master's *questiones* might be assembled into a *summa*. Masters also preached sermons, and might write independent treatises. The main scene of this activity was Paris, a genuinely European intellectual centre, including among its leading luminaries in the twelfth and thirteenth centuries Albertus Magnus from Germany, Peter Lombard and Thomas Aquinas from Italy, as well as the Breton Peter Abelard. It is noticeable how many of the leading figures, though less eminent than those just named, were of English origin. Throughout the twelfth and thirteenth centuries English students went to Paris to study, some achieving eminence and staying to teach, from Robert Pullen and Adam of Le Petit Pont in the twelfth century, through Robert Courson, Stephen Langton and Thomas of Chobham around 1200, to Alexander of Hales in the thirteenth century.

There were two strands in theology: one highly technical developed from Peter Lombard's *Sentences*, the other characterized by a strong concern with practical morality and the problems posed by the priest's position as shepherd of his flock. It was particularly the latter category that interested the English scholars. Their concerns were expressed most clearly by the writing of 'penitentials', or guides for confessors. Robert of Flamborough, a canon of the Parisian abbey of St Victor, wrote a penitential at the request of Richard Poore, then dean of Salisbury. But the most influential of such works was the *Summa Confessorum* by Thomas of Chobham, probably the son of the village priest of Chobham in Surrey. There are indications that he studied at Paris, but for most of his life he was associated with Salisbury cathedral, of which he was a canon. The desire to instruct the clergy in morality and the sacraments also led Gerald of Wales to compile his *Gemma Ecclesiastica*. Another English member of this Parisian group, Robert Courson, had the opportunity, or rather the onerous duty, of putting his principles into practice. He was suddenly catapulted to prominence in 1212 when Innocent III made him a cardinal and in the following year sent him as papal legate to France. Cardinal Robert toured France holding provincial councils at which was enacted legislation inspired by his and his colleagues' views first expounded when they were teachers at Paris. He remained English enough for the French to suspect him of activity in favour of king John in his conflict with Philip Augustus. Recalled to Rome for the Lateran council of 1215, Robert was later sent as a preacher on the Fifth Crusade, and died of sickness at the siege of Damietta in Egypt in 1219.

The best-known member of this group is Stephen Langton. He is also the best represented by surviving writings, including a mass of biblical commentaries, several collections of *questiones*, and over a hundred sermons including even his inaugural lecture as a theology master, the earliest such lecture extant. Born around 1160 at Langton by Wragby in Lincolnshire to a family of small freeholders, nothing is known of his education before his Paris years: he was certainly teaching there by 1193. He was one of the leading masters of the schools when Innocent III made him a cardinal in June 1206. Not long afterwards he was elected archbishop of Canterbury.[9] Unable to take up his see, he spent much of his time to 1218 in exile, when he had opportunities to write. His views on political theory are of particular interest, though it is difficult to trace the relationship of ideas to actions. Nevertheless, the outline is clear: he was an upholder of the 'dualist' view which regarded both the church (*sacerdotium*) and the state (*regnum*) as divinely instituted, the superiority of the church not implying the state's complete subordination. In this he contrasted with some other commentators, such as Alan *Anglicus* ('the Englishman'), who espoused the 'hierocratic' position which claimed complete superiority for the church, with authority flowing from God to the pope and only thence to lay potentates. Stephen Langton defined the church as not only the prelates but the whole congregation of the faithful; power was transmitted to princes by the church in the sense of both clergy and laity, and it rested on the consent of both; the archbishop in crowning the king acted as representative of all the faithful. These views explain why he was never a mere papal agent, but sided with the barons of Magna Carta to the extent of incurring the pope's wrath. However, he was not prepared to resist the

---

[9] See above, pp. 120–1.

pope, and was willing to revise his views to accomodate changing papal doctrine. The common view that the king should not
make decisions without a judgment of his court, which led to an
important principle enshrined in Magna Carta, is to be found in
his academic writing. His limitation of the power of the king
was, however, counterbalanced by his restricted view of those
the king needed to consult: if the prince's court decided to wage
war the people outside the court, who were not summoned to the
deliberations, had no right to discuss the decision even if it was
unjust.[10]

Canon law, the law of the church, was another important area
of intellectual activity. A disproportionate number of decretals –
papal rulings on specific points of law – in the twelfth century
collections are addressed to English recipients. This reflects exceptional activity by English canon lawyers, perhaps stimulated
by the need to seek accomodation with the rapidly developing
law of the royal courts. Much of this work is anonymous, but a
number of eminent canon lawyers are known by name: Alan
Anglicus, the author of a decretal collection and other works,
taught at Bologna in the first decade of the thirteenth century;
Richard *Anglicus*, also of Bologna, wrote a number of surviving
works in the 1180s and 1190s and may later have become prior
of Dunstable. The stream runs dry as the thirteenth century
progresses: although canon law was taught at Oxford, the school
seems to have been rather dim. The nearest thing to a legal
luminary there was William of Drogheda, who taught and wrote
about Roman law which served as an adjunct to canon law.
Apart from the work of the earlier canonists the major achievement in the legal field was the development of the common law
of the royal courts.

It was contact with Arabic learning in the twelfth century that
set European science going again. The centre of this learning was
not northern France but Spain; it was to Toledo that Daniel of
Morley (d. *c.*1210) went after rejecting the learning of the Paris
schools, 'to hear the wisest philosophers in the world'.[11] Alfred
of Shareshill also studied in Spain, learning enough Arabic to
translate versions of Greek scientific works into Latin. The work
of scholars such as these and Roger of Hereford, who drew up
astronomical tables for the latitude of Hereford about 1178,
demonstrates the absorption of this material by about 1200. An

[10] Baldwin, *Masters, Princes and Merchants*, 209–10.
[11] Southern, *Robert Grosseteste*, 89 n7.

important motive for such curiosity was the desire for improved astrological prediction: 'since the astronomer knows about future events', wrote Daniel of Morley, 'he can repel or avoid disasters such as civil wars or famine, earthquakes, conflagrations, floods and general pestilences.'[12]

An older tradition of science as an aid to biblical exposition, which went back to Bede, continued with Alexander Nequam. Sometime student and teacher at Paris, master of the schools at Dunstable and St Albans, and the first known scholastic theologian to lecture at Oxford, Alexander felt a vocation for the monastic life and entered the Augustinian house at Cirencester, of which he became abbot before his death in 1217. More than half his surviving work is biblical commentary, and the *De Naturis Rerum*, the work for which he is remembered, a moralized encyclopedia of the natural world, is an introduction to a commentary on Ecclesiastes.

But the most important English thinker to concern himself with scientific matters was Robert Grosseteste. First master of the Franciscan school at Oxford, though not a friar himself, he was bishop of Lincoln from 1235 until his death in 1253, and one of the most influential religious and intellectual leaders of his time. His works covered astronomy, meteorology, physics, optics and linguistics, as well as theology. His special contribution lay in giving equal weight to observation and doctrine; this 'observation' did not take the form of deliberately created, repeatable 'experiments', but of close attention to phenomena observable in nature which could reveal the action of a general law or allow a glimpse of a previously hidden pattern. To this he joined a belief in the importance of mathematics: 'all the causes of natural effects should be reached by lines, angles and figures',[13] and his works on optics and the rainbow are copiously illustrated with them. He saw matter as inherent in light: to create the world God needed only to create a single point of light, which instantly expands to form a sphere of indefinite size – the physical universe is attributable to the workings of light. The legacy of his thought was especially influential at Oxford for the rest of the middle ages, forming an independent, non-Aristotelian scientific and philosophical system which marked Oxford out.

One of the most solid intellectual achievements of Angevin England was in the writing of history. Most appreciated by

[12] Southern, *Robert Grosseteste*, 105.
[13] Quoted in Gordon Leff, *Medieval Thought*, Harmondsworth 1958, 189.

modern historians are the writers who cover contemporary affairs, but many of them also edited earlier material and wrote lengthy histories in the modern sense. Few writers were active in the early years of Henry II, but there was an efflorescence in the late twelfth century and the thirteenth is the great age of the monastic annalist.

The chronicles of Roger of Howden and Ralph Diceto have a semi-official character: Roger was a royal clerk and Ralph was dean of St Paul's from 1180 to his death in about 1203. Both had access to official documents and incorporated many of them in their work, and they are both very favourable to Henry II and Richard. In fact, Roger may be the author of a biography of Henry, the *Gesta Henrici*, which he condensed when writing his main chronicle. Ralph's work runs from the Creation to 1200, and is a very ambitious attempt at world history. Two interesting monastic chronicles, both starting in 1066, are those of William of Newburgh, a Yorkshire Augustinian, and Ralph of Coggeshall, a Cistercian from Essex. William was not taken in by Geoffrey of Monmouth's *History of the Kings of Britain*: he compares its statements with Bede's, tests for internal consistency and sense, and finds it wanting. His horizons and views were wide; he is unusual as a monastic writer in not being obsessed with his own institution. Ralph of Coggeshall is rather the opposite, having a love of the picturesque story: the merman fished up from the sea at Orford, or the green children who appeared in Suffolk.[14]

As well as general histories, there were also biographies of individuals, usually saints or holy men. Many were written at such places as Canterbury and Durham which already had a strong historiographical tradition. Such are the lives of Godric the hermit of Finchale, and the quantity of Becket lives – there were at least ten by 1200. The most vivid example is the life of St Hugh of Lincoln by Adam of Eynsham, which tells with unforgettable details the life of the saintly monk from the foothills of the Alps who was head of Witham priory in Somerset, the first and for long the only Carthusian house in England. Hugh's wit and charm won over Henry II, who made him bishop of Lincoln, and by his death in 1200 he had become something of a legend. Another minor masterpiece is Jocelin of Brakelond's life of abbot Samson of Bury St Edmunds, which throws a unique and revealing light on life inside a great abbey.

[14] Coggeshall, 117–20.

In the mid-twelfth century in a number of the older, wealthier Benedictine monasteries – Abingdon, Ramsey, Ely, Peterborough and Battle, amongst others – histories of the house were written incorporating earlier documents whose aim was to establish and defend the traditions, privileges and property of the community. Written proof of title was becoming more and more necessary; this led to the improved organization of archives, the creation of cartularies or registers of deeds, and this group of cartulary-chronicles. With the ever-increasing flow of documentation the archival and narrative functions gradually diverged, though some documents were still copied into later chronicles. In the thirteenth century many houses deputed a succession of monks as chronicler, and so chronicles become continuous over long periods unlike the earlier individual productions. They also tend to be drier, with less personal comment. Southwark, Merton, Dunstable, Worcester, Waverley and others are examples; the 'Barnwell' annalist, who in fact wrote somewhere in Lincoln-shire, is an exceptionally perceptive commentator on political affairs.

Justly the most famous of the later chroniclers is Matthew Paris of St Albans, whose *Chronica Majora* covers world history from the Creation to 1253. This was 'the most comprehensive history yet written in England'.[15] Generations of historians have seen the mid-thirteenth century through Matthew's eyes, making allowance for his prejudice against foreigners, his carelessness, his hostility to the activities of royal and papal government, and his outrageous bias in favour of his own house and order, while demonstrating their respect for his encyclopedic curiosity, his interest in people and his sheer voluminous liveliness. He based his work on that of his predecessors at St Albans, Roger of Wendover and others; he was much given to rewriting and produced abbreviations and expurgations of his great chronicle, as well as illustrated saints' lives – he was a considerable artist – a book of documents and a history of his monastery. One of his more unusual interests was cartography: he produced the earliest detailed maps of England and Scotland in existence, and others of Palestine and the road to Italy, as well as a map of the world.

Angevin England was not a place of narrow horizons: its inhabitants could find out a good deal about the world if they wanted. Political relations with the Celtic lands, France, Italy and to some extent Germany and Spain were close enough to

---

[15] Gransden, *Historical Writing*, 359.

ensure constant coming and going and a flow of information, while Richard's crusade attracted a lot of interest to southern Europe and the Holy Land. The important French educational connection meant that many clerics had lived abroad. While studying at Paris Walter Map met Luke of Hungary, who later became archbishop of Esztergom; in later years Walter heard about Luke's adventurous life from a mutual acquaintance.[16]

As well as travel, foreigners staying in England were a source of information. Without going outside his cloister Matthew Paris met a group of visiting Armenians and the bishop of Beirut. Archbishop Augustine of Trondheim stayed at Bury St Edmunds for a while, and information supplied by him found its way to Roger of Howden and William of Newburgh. The international connections of the Cistercian order kept Ralph of Coggeshall supplied with news, but he heard about king Richard's capture in Austria from the king's chaplain, Anselm, one of the very few who had been there at the time.[17] Matthew Paris's 'almost unlimited curiosity'[18] has resulted in the best account anywhere of the 1245 Council of Lyons, and he is an important source for the Mongol invasion of eastern Europe. Robert Grosseteste wanted to study Greek writings in the original, and as bishop of Lincoln he invited a group of Greek scholars to come and live there – those with sufficient resources have always been able to follow up their curiosity.

There was also a permanent colony of 'outsiders': the Jews. The culture of the English Jews was an offshoot of that of the larger and older communities of Germany and northern France, with which they remained in close contact. Their principal intellectual interest was in religious law and practice, but they are known to have written liturgical poetry and grammatical works, while the books looted during the York massacre of 1190 were much admired by the Jews of Cologne when brought there for sale. There was a certain amount of interest in Hebrew among English clerics, Herbert of Bosham having a creditable knowledge of it, and the Franciscans took the study further in the thirteenth century. But intellectual interest in the Jews was inspired largely by polemical motives, and a series of written disputations with Jews has survived, ending not unexpectedly in victory for the Christians.

---

[16] Map, 143.
[17] Coggeshall, 53–4.
[18] Gransden, *Historical Writing*, 361.

But the most original explorer of the peoples of the world around him was Gerald of Wales. Born in 1146 into the Norman-Welsh aristocracy of the Pembroke region, his cousins were closely involved in the conquest of Ireland, his uncle was bishop of St Davids and his mother's mother was a Welsh princess. After he had been sent to Gloucester abbey for elementary education and to Paris for more advanced learning, his uncle the bishop gave him an archdeaconry and used his energies in the administration of the diocese. By about 1184 he had taken another step on the ladder of promotion and become a royal clerk. He now grew familiar with the court and its personalities. He seems to have been used as a specialist on Welsh and Irish affairs, accompanying John to Ireland in 1185, and archbishop Baldwin on his tour of Wales preaching the crusade in 1188. It was now that Gerald began writing his Welsh and Irish works. But the court was a place of rivalry and envy, and the vain, pompous cleric made enemies. Precisely what happened is unclear, but by the middle 1190s he had retired disillusioned from the court. He seems to have nursed the misjudged hope that literary achievement would gain him such royal favour as would lead to a wealthy English bishopric, not the poverty-stricken Irish ones that John offered him and that he turned down. His Welsh connections also made him something of an outsider, or feel like one; he recalls in his writings some of the jibes the other courtiers aimed at him.[19] It was after he had withdrawn from court that he was elected bishop of St Davids. His heroic but unsuccessful attempts to have his election confirmed, against the fixed opposition of the English government led by archbishop Hubert Walter, and to establish St Davids as an independent archbishopric recognized by Rome, occupied the next five years and consumed the rest of his life in retrospective rage. He lived on until 1223, pouring out a stream of vituperation against all those he had quarrelled with – and they were many, English and Welsh alike.

Gerald's fame is based principally on his early works, the *Conquest of Ireland*, the *Topography of Ireland*, the *Journey through Wales* and the *Description of Wales*. These reveal his very wide interest in the natural world – birds, animals, fish, climate, natural wonders of all kinds – and even more remarkably, in people. The *Description of Wales* is a fully fledged ethnographic monograph, 'a form that had not been attempted

[19] Gerald of Wales viii, lviii.

for over a thousand years',[20] and all the more remarkable for being written in ignorance of its classical precursors. His great strength is in intelligent observation, often remarkably accurate if sometimes obscured by preconceptions, and in his omnivorous interests: he discusses dress, military methods, Welsh choral singing, Irish instrumental music, the similarities between languages – Indo-European, though he does not call them that – marriage and inheritance customs and much else. But he is discursive and unmethodical; he fits into no school and had no real successors. Gerald's works have long been quarried for his descriptions of his contemporaries, especially of the Angevin kings, on whom his comments range from the eulogies of the hopeful courtier to the invective of his embittered old age. It was perhaps his in-between position, not fully Norman, not quite Welsh, certainly not English, that lay behind both his failure and his success. The Welsh princes and the government in England alike distrusted him as too close to the other side. On the other hand, he was able to observe Welsh and Irish society, and much of the world about him, with considerable detachment.

Literature

Latin could only be acquired by study, and Latin grammar and rhetoric were the staple diet of the schools. Much surviving work in Latin is the product of school exercises, was composed by masters as a means of instruction or was collected to provide examples of style. John of Garland, an English grammar master who taught at Toulouse and Paris, where his pupils included Roger Bacon, wrote versified textbooks for the use of his students. But the best-known English rhetorician was Geoffrey de Vinsauf, whose treatise *Poetria Nova*, written about 1210, was one of the most popular handbooks on poetics of the whole middle ages, its teaching of rhetorical devices influencing much later poetry in vernacular languages too.

Rhythmic metres and rhyme are a feature of twelfth- and thirteenth-century Latin poetry, unlike classical Latin which reckoned metres according to vowel quantity. Rhythmic verse had begun to be used in liturgical compositions several centuries earlier, and it was liturgical forms which provided models of regular versification for non-religious works, some of them scur-

---

[20] Bartlett, *Gerald of Wales*, 181.

rilous parodies of the originals. Hymns were composed in considerable quantity throughout the period. Many such pieces are anonymous and their provenance and date impossible to establish with certainty, but it is reasonable to assume that much of the outpouring of liturgical poetry and music in praise of St Thomas Becket was of English origin. Alexander Neckham turned his hand to composing sequences in honour of the Virgin Mary and the Magdalen, while *Veni, Sancte Spiritus*, one of the most famous hymns of the middle ages, has been attributed to archbishop Stephen Langton.

As well as liturgical writing, longer, meditative pieces on religious themes were written by a number of authors. Serlo of Wilton, a master in the Paris schools and author of didactic and *risqué* poems, experienced conversion to the religious life, becoming abbot of a French Cistercian monastery in 1171. In his pious phase he wrote a poem on contempt of the world (*De contemptu mundi*), and other pieces on his conversion. John of Garland's *De mysteriis ecclesie* dwells on the symbolism of the church's buildings, furnishings and services, and his *De triumphis ecclesie* is a call to the crusade against Saracens and heretics, particular interest attaching to it as John was with Simon de Montfort the elder on the Albigensian crusade. John of Howden, chaplain to queen Eleanor of Provence, composed lengthy meditations on the divine love as revealed in the Incarnation and Passion of Christ, and praises of the Virgin Mary.

Despite this list of writers, it was in secular rather than religious material that the English contribution to Latin literature was greatest. The great prose histories have already been mentioned. Joseph of Exeter, a clerk of archbishop Baldwin who accompanied his master on the crusade but lived to tell the tale, wrote an epic poem about king Richard's crusade, the *Antiocheis*, lost apart from a few fragments, and a six-book reworking of the classical epics, *De Bello Trojano*, which has survived. In this he shows an impressive knowledge of the Latin classics which led him to a genuine feeling for them. His technical virtuosity is remarkable, his formal mastery complete: 'he had no peer in his own time ... The middle ages produced only one Joseph of Exeter'.[21]

But it is the satirists who are the strongest suit in English Latin literature. This genre, looking principally to Juvenal for its classical prototype, enables the author to combine entertaining

[21] Raby, *Secular Latin Poetry*, 137.

storytelling with social and moral comment and denunciation. John of Salisbury's *Entheticus* can be regarded as a satire in this sense, but the most famous example is *Courtiers' Trifles (De Nugis Curialium)* by Walter Map. He was a Welsh Marcher of cosmopolitan background who had studied at Paris before attracting the patronage of Gilbert Foliot when bishop of Hereford. From the early 1170s he was a royal clerk, but after Henry II's death he pursued a career in the cathedral and diocese of Lincoln, eventually becoming archdeacon of Oxford. He died in 1209 or 1210. His years at court are the background for *Courtiers' Trifles*, an entertaining jumble of personal anecdotes, ghost stories, history, gossip, thumbnail sketches, longer stories and serious moralizing. Its purpose was to amuse and instruct, but it was never made public and survives in a single manuscript. It provides a fascinating glimpse into the mental world of a twelfth-century clerk with his wit, humour, pretentious classical learning and chronic misogyny, illustrating yet another aspect of the court, its moments of relaxation. His denunciation of the monastic orders, especially the Cistercians, is bitter but fundamentally moral, despite his occasional scurrility, and is directed at the gap between the ideal and the reality.

The *Mirror of Fools (Speculum Stultorum)* by Nigel Longchamps or Wireker, a monk of Canterbury cathedral priory, is the adventure of an ass called Burnellus who is unhappy with his tail. A physician gives him a prescription for lengthening tails, and the ass sets out for Salerno to obtain the ingredients. The events of the journey provide opportunities to denounce monks, students, bishops, kings – the laity and clergy generally. Unlike Map's work it has a consistent storyline based on a quest. So too has *Architrenius*, the 'Chief Mourner', an allegorical poem dedicated to Walter of Coutances, a royal clerk from Cornwall recently promoted to the archbishopric of Rouen, by John de Hauville, a poet who may, however, have been French. Related to the English satirists is the work of Gervase of Tilbury, a clerk of king John's nephew, the emperor Otto IV. His *Otia Imperialia* are a miscellany of history, geography and folklore.

The Latin *Comedie* of the twelfth century are versified tales, entertainments with amorous intrigue, sometimes written as dialogue: some at least of them could be performed, which is not quite to say that they ever were. They are anonymous, and it is not certain that any of them come from an English milieu, though some could, among them *Baucis and Thraso*, the comedy of a soldier and a prostitute. *Babio*, also possibly English, is cast as continuous dialogue: Babio is an absurd figure who, defeated in every plot, fails to gain his love and is fooled by his servant and his wife. *De clericis et rustico*, sometimes attributed to Geoffrey de Vinsauf, tells how two wise clerks are tricked by the rustic they despise.

There is nothing strikingly original about the Latin literary productions of Angevin England; rather, a full participation in the European mainstream. The genres of satire and history are notably strong and, to judge by what survives, lyric poetry is rather weak. Many of the writers are known to have studied or worked in France: the cosmopolitanism of contemporary education is well reflected in the Latin literature.

Down to 1204 the royal courts, particularly that of Henry II, regularly crossed the Channel and attracted suitors, hopefuls and hangers-on from all over north-west Europe, among them writers and entertainers. The Latin poet Walter of Châtillon worked in Henry II's chancery for a while, as did the letter-writer Peter of Blois, while Walter Map and Gerald of Wales came and went. The question of royal patronage of literature is complicated by the likelihood that works were written, not in response to the king's commission but in the hope of attracting his attention and reward. The royal court was the centre of power, its lord the richest of all, the rewards greater, the competition keener. The king did not need to attract entertainers, poets or storytellers – they would come to him. Even so there are few works which can definitely be associated with Henry II or Eleanor of Aquitaine, and none that they certainly commissioned rather than simply received, though 'court' connections can be suspected in a number of cases.

But the royal court was far from being the only centre of cultural life and literary patronage in England. It is in its contribution to literature in French that the vitality and originality of twelfth-century England is most evident, even though it is not always clear on which side of the Channel a work was written. Anglo-Norman culture produced

> the first adventure narrative . . . in French literature; the earliest example of historiographic writing in French; the first eye-witness history of contemporary events in French; the earliest scientific texts in French; the first administrative texts in French; the first Biblical translations into French; the earliest French vernacular versions of monastic rules; the first scholastic text to be translated into French; the

earliest significant examples of French prose . . . the first
named women writers in French; the earliest named and
identifiable patrons of literature in French . . .[22]

Some of these works date from before 1150, but of the others
very little can be unequivocally attributed to the courts of Henry
and Eleanor. What is known of the patrons points to interest
from a variety of social backgrounds: the higher aristocracy,
quite minor landholders, and a strong current of religious writing in the monasteries. The literature is the product of a society
well described as multicultural and polyglot.[23]

It was Geoffrey of Monmouth's *History of the Kings of Britain*
that launched king Arthur on his European career, and an interest in British history is prominent in works in French as well as
those in Latin. Whether because they felt they were parvenus in
a world of older peoples, or whether as part of a process of
settling down in a conquered country whose natives spoke a
different language, the French-speakers of England set about
appropriating, or inventing, the English and British past. This is
clearly visible in the work of Wace, a Channel Islander whose
two surviving works, the *Roman de Brut* and the *Roman de Rou*
cover British and Norman history down to the recent past; he is
unusual in being directly associated with Henry II's court. The
Brut was finished in 1155, but *Rou* was left unfinished when
Wace was replaced in royal favour by Benoît de Ste-Maure, the
author of the *Chronique des Ducs de Normandie*. Recent history
might also form the basis of epic-style recitations in which lords
could listen to their own prowess and adventures or those of
their fathers recounted in more or less dramatized form. Such are
the chronicle of the rebellion of 1173–4 composed soon after the
events by Jordan Fantosme, the *Song of Dermot and the Earl*,
which covers the invasion and conquest of Ireland and was
probably written for the Anglo-Norman colony there, and – the
most famous example – the *Histoire de Guillaume le Maréchal*,
a biography of William Marshal, earl of Pembroke and regent of
England, written for his son the younger William. All three are
invaluable both for their version of events and, more interestingly, as windows into the material and emotional world of the lay
upper class.

[22] Ian Short, 'Patrons and polyglots: French literature in twelfth century England',
Anglo-Norman Studies xiv (1991), 229.
[23] Ibid.

There was also a taste for adventure of a more frankly fictionalized kind. Straightforward tales of male action against a background of partly real topography and including some real historical characters, with an admixture of love interest, the 'ancestral' romances are the equivalent of the French *chansons de geste* even if technically their form is different. Examples are the *Romance of Horn* by Master Thomas, or *Waldef*. *Boeve de Haumtone* was ostensibly intended for recitation to an audience – the poet threatens to stop in the middle unless he is paid.[24] It recounts violent adventures which take place all over Europe and the Middle East but which end in the castle of Arundel, built by Sir Boeve and named after his horse, one of the main characters in the story.

The Anglo-Norman *Tristan* romance by another Thomas is among the most important in French literature, probably the earliest surviving version of the famous Tristan and Iseut story, also told by the Norman Béroul. Thomas's work, in which some of the motifs of the troubadours are to be found, is often supposed to have been written for Eleanor of Aquitaine, but definite proof is lacking. It is an example of the 'courtly' romance, in which relations between men and women are the focus of interest. Another example is *Amadas et Ydoine*, in which a young squire is smitten with love for a lady of much higher rank who rejects him and marries someone more suitable. Amadas falls ill with unrequited love, but the same arrow of love later pierces Ydoine, who has to keep her husband at bay by witchcraft. Complicated adventures ensue, including the seizure of Ydoine by a demon knight whom Amadas has to defeat in battle in a graveyard before the hero and heroine can be united, the husband having finally agreed to a separation. This is the kind of story parodied in the works of Hue de Rotelande, a Welsh Marcher – Rotelande is probably Rhuddlan in north Wales – who wrote *Ipomedon* and *Protheselaus* between 1174 and 1190, the latter for Gilbert fitz Baderon, lord of Monmouth. The interest is less in the plots or the characters, which are conventional, than in Hue's flippant, witty and cynical attitude to them.

In a class of her own stands Marie, a continental poet whose identity is unlikely ever to be established, though she was probably associated in some way with Henry II's court. She was an educated lady who knew Latin and English and wrote in French a collection of the short narrative poems known as *Lais* and

24 Legge, *Anglo-Norman Literature*, 157.

some rhymed *Fables* translated from English. She is unusual in being only the second known female poet in French; the *lai* form is itself uncommon.

The earliest known woman writer in French introduces us to the strong religious theme in Anglo-Norman literature. She was Clemence, a nun of the wealthy and aristocratic convent at Barking near London, who in the 1160s wrote a life of St Catharine which she prefaced with an apology for her poor English French: 'Un faus franceis sai d'Angletere',[25] an interesting admission that already continental French was recognized as more authoritative than the insular version. Nunneries were centres of vernacular culture: a large collection of saints' lives comes from the Suffolk nunnery of Campsey Ash, while it may have been a nun who wrote the early thirteenth-century life of St Etheldreda, a female saint of much greater antiquity. Even so, more hagiography in French can be attributed to the monks, especially those of Bury St Edmunds and St Albans. Denis Pyramus was a lay poet who repented of his life, became a monk of Bury and versified the life and miracles of the patron saint. Also from Bury come a large collection of Mary legends and Simon of Walsingham's life of St Faith, while the undoubted star of the St Albans school is Matthew Paris, the chronicler, who produced elegantly illustrated French verse lives of St Alban, Edward the Confessor, Thomas Becket and St Edmund to circulate among the ladies of Henry III's court. But the list of French saints' lives composed in or associated with England is very long, as is that of the surviving French sermons.

A number of more meditative religious works have survived in French, including the *Romaunz de Temtacioun de Secle* by Guichard de Beaulieu from about 1200, on the shortcomings of the world, the pains of hell and the delights of paradise. A poet called Chardri wrote the only surviving French version of the well-known story of the Seven Sleepers of Ephesus, and a popular philosophical dialogue between a young man and an old man called *Le Petit Plet*. The emphasis on improving the religious life of the laity, a feature of the thirteenth century and often attributed to the stimulus of the 1215 Lateran Council, resulted in a series of manuals and treatises on religious knowledge in French. Such are the *Merure de Seinte Eglise* by Edmund of Abingdon, later archbishop of Canterbury, the *Manuel des Péchés*, an aid to confession, and Robert Grosseteste's *Château*

---

[25] Ibid., 63, line 7.

d'Amour, which provides a rapid outline of Christian doctrine. Two religious dramas have survived, the *Mystère d'Adam* of about 1140, and the *Seinte Resureccion* of uncertain date. Both are early and important landmarks in the history of drama in England and France – these and the Latin comedies mentioned above could well be the earliest known dramas written in England.

It is hard to say whether it was interest from the laity or from uneducated clergy that led to the translation of some works of theology and even the pagan classics into French. These include a rhymed adaptation of Boethius's *Consolation of Philosophy* by Simund de Freine, and the *Dialogues* of Gregory the Great by Angier, a canon of St Frideswide's, Oxford. *La Petite Philosophie* is a treatise on the nature of the world translated from Latin, and there were various versions of parts of the Bible.

Enough has been said to show that French literature in England was extensive, varied and original. There are no English *chansons de geste,* but the action-packed romances take their place, and in fact the earliest and best surviving text of the most famous medieval epic, the *Chanson de Roland,* is probably Anglo-Norman. There are very few surviving lyrics, nothing to compare with the works of the *trouvères* of northern France who flourished in the thirteenth century. England was important in introducing and popularizing the Arthurian and Tristan stories, but played little part in their subsequent development. There is a strong religious bent to the surviving work, reflecting the importance of the monasteries as centres of French-speaking culture and the activity of the church in evangelizing the lay upper classes. But there is no lack of courtly romance and historical works to show the interests of the laity. The survival of so much is all the more remarkable in a country where French has not been the dominant language for six hundred years.

There must have been a great deal of ephemeral music and song that escapes us entirely. Singers could be hired to spread political propaganda. This type of entertainment shaded off into others of which no trace remains except in the works of the clergy who condemned them. Reading between the lines of Thomas of Chobham's *Summa Confessorum* we can gain a vivid idea of the kind of entertainers available: those who transformed their bodies with costumes and masks, practising shameful dancing and wanton disrobing; those who circulated among aristocratic households spreading abuse and scandal; and musicians who sang bawdy songs at drunken gatherings. Other clerical denunciations mention jongleurs (*joculatores*) and actors (*histriones* or *mimi*). Thomas distinguished good jongleurs, who sang of the edifying deeds of saints and princes, from wicked, lascivious ones: the former should be rewarded, as long as they refrained from obscenities.[26]

There is no doubt that the century after the Norman conquest represents the lowest point in the whole history of English literature. The language lost its prestige, and writing in it was largely confined to a few old-fashioned monasteries. The Anglo-Saxon chronicle ceased in 1154, the year of Henry II's accession to the throne. The re-emergence at the end of the twelfth century of works in English is therefore highly significant, suggesting that English-speaking patrons may have appeared. Exactly who these patrons were is not known, but a certain amount can be guessed.

Most of the surviving secular writing consists of translations or adaptations from French. As well as a version of the bestiary, there survive two romances in English from the first half of the thirteenth century. The earlier is *King Horn*, in which the hero is turned adrift by an invasion of Saracens and on his wanderings falls in love with the king of Westernesse's daughter, Rymenhild, with whom he eventually lives happily. Its date and that of the Anglo-Norman version are not precisely known, though the Anglo-Norman is earlier, and they could both derive from a common original. *Floris and Blancheflour*, of about 1250, takes a French original, strips down the story and leaves out the analysis of love.

The interest in history which is such a marked characteristic of Angevin England is represented in the native language by Layamon's *Brut*, derived from Wace's poem and dating from around 1200. At 16,000 lines the second longest poem in the English language, it sets out to tell the noble deeds of Englishmen – an epic in scale and purpose. As well as rhyme, it uses the alliterative techniques which had been characteristic of Anglo-Saxon poetry. In fact, alliteration is very evident throughout Middle English literature, and raises the possibility that linking the Old English and Middle English literatures as we know them there was a continuous oral tradition.

The work generally regarded as the nearest thing to a masterpiece in English from this period, and with no known French source, is *The Owl and the Nightingale*. It takes the form of a

[26] Baldwin, *Masters, Princes and Merchants*, 199–203.

debate between the two birds as to their respective merits, each comically abusing the other and defending itself. A work of considerable sophistication and lightly borne learning, it is wide open to symbolic interpretation. It probably dates from the early thirteenth century.

The specifically religious contribution is strong in English too. A large number of homilies and sermons survive, and the Anglo-Saxon homilies of Aelfric were still being copied in the twelfth century. The *Ormulum* is the work of a Lincolnshire canon called Orm: 'Thiss boc is nemmned Orrmulum forrthi that Orrm itt wrohhte', it begins. A lengthy commentary on the Gospels in long lines of verse to be chanted or intoned, it is characterized by the author's very idiosyncratic spelling and Scandinavian-influenced English.[27] The audience for such pieces could have been monastic or lay, or both. The remaining religious works were directed at nuns, a group of them perhaps composed for a nunnery in the Hereforshire area. A group of lives of virgin martyrs, Saints Margaret, Juliana and Katherine, present constancy and chastity as the key virtues. The *Margaret* was extremely popular, several Latin and six Anglo-Norman versions being made before 1300. Associated with the lives are two religious tracts: *Sawles Warde*, an allegorical work on the soul derived from a Latin work attributed to St Anselm, and *Hali Meithhad*, 'Holy Maidenhood', in praise of virginity. More devotional advice for nuns written by their chaplain can be found in *Ancrene Wisse*, sometimes known as *Ancrene Riwle*. The women addressed were 'anchorites', recluses; they were ladies, and had maids and servants who ran errands for them so as to keep them secluded in their anchor-holds. There is also a contemporary French version of the work, but it is interesting to find at least some of these ladies addressed in English. The work consists of eight sections, one on devotions to be recited, one on domestic arrangements, then on the senses, the heart and emotions, temptations, confession, penance and love. It contains quite traditional monastic spiritual teaching, in the manner of St Bernard and other twelfth-century writers.

Literary productions in this period are seldom datable very precisely, and different authorities will often give widely varying dates for a piece. The exact chronology of the resurgence of English as a literary language is never likely to be agreed. Our view is also dependent on the chance survival of texts, a rather

---

[27] Bennett, *Middle English Literature*, 30–3.

slender chance with a language of relatively low status in a form which later ages found incomprehensible or even uncouth. But the fact remains that there was a resurgence, and that it happened in the later twelfth or early thirteenth century. It may have to do with the growing tendency, observable in other spheres, to write things down, in which case there need have been no revival of creativity. Or it could be that by 1200 people whose grandparents had listened to French now wanted entertainment or instruction in English. The audiences must have been happiest in English, or there would have been no need to adapt so much French and Latin writing. It is suggestive that this revival occurs at roughly the time when a sense of Englishness becomes observable in other spheres.

Religious culture

We have seen something of the strength of religious culture in the output of theologians and spiritual writers in the three languages of Angevin England. Academic writings were largely the product of the secular clergy and, by the middle of the thirteenth century, of the friars. But until the 1220s at least, leadership in the religious life of the country belonged to the monks and canons, the 'religious' *par excellence*. Monasteries led the way in liturgical observance, and lay devotions tended to copy monastic patterns. As we have seen, the monasteries were important centres of vernacular writing, particularly the hagiographical and homiletic branches, and Latin history. The great ancient Benedictine abbeys, such as Glastonbury, Bury St Edmunds, St Albans and Westminster, and the cathedral priories such as Winchester and Canterbury owned whole tracts of countryside and had extensive judicial privileges. Many of them guarded the body of a saint or a great collection of relics in their vast churches, all had splendid libraries and palatial monastic buildings. The Cistercians, founded in austerity as a reaction against the splendours of the Benedictines, had discovered that the untamed wildernesses to which they fled could become highly profitable sheep farms, and they were constructing magnificent buildings of their own.

But splendid though the outer shell was, there were suspicions that it concealed a hollow or even a rotten interior. Criticism of the religious was widespread. Too fond of their stomachs, Rannulf de Glanville, the justiciar, thought of the Benedictines, while the

Cistercians' strictures on the laxity of others combined with their own growing wealth earned them an unenviable reputation for hypocrisy.[28] The downfall of religious orders, thought Walter Map, came from abandoning humility in the attempt to remedy their poverty.[29] In every generation there were those who pointed out that the wealth of the church was contrary to the Gospel teachings, and some who set about devising new institutions to fulfil the mission without encumbering themselves with property. The great irony of such attempts was that the more effective their renunciation and the higher their reputation, the more the laity pressed donations on them in return for their prayers. The higher the aspirations, the harder the fall from them. The Cistercians had already failed; the next to try were the followers of Francis of Assisi. More successful in avoiding this fate were the Augustinians, whose mission was more modest and practical, and the Carthusians, who avoided excessive popularity.

The spiritual life of the majority of the population was expressed most visibly to us in the cult of saints and pilgrimages. In his role as the judge of the Last Judgment, Christ was conceived rather as a contemporary baron or king, with a few intimates whose advice He seeks and who can intercede for their own clients. The saints were conceived as personalities with varying talents and interests, and their special characteristic was the production of miracles. Papal canonization was just becoming necessary in this period, but miracles could easily happen without it – in fact, they were a precondition for it. English saints canonized at this time were Edward the Confessor, Wulfstan of Worcester and William archbishop of York who were long dead, and among contemporaries Thomas Becket, Gilbert, the founder of the order of Sempringham, Hugh, bishop of Lincoln and archbishop Edmund Rich, while Richard Wych, bishop of Chichester, was sainted in 1263. Six bishops, one monk and one king: a rather official group, and of them only Becket gave rise to a substantial cult. William of Norwich, the boy allegedly murdered by the Jews, and the holy hermit Godric of Finchale had local cults but were never canonized: William's was notably urban, perhaps encouraged by local anti-semitism, and Godric's drew at first on the women of the north-east, extending to the men later. The saints had their own clientele. A cult of a long-dead saint could start after a translation of the relics, as hap-

[28] Gerald of Wales iv, 244–5.
[29] Map, 111–13.

pened with Wulfstan of Worcester after 1198 and Frideswide of Oxford, who had been dead for over 400 years, in 1180. Becket's, of course, was the greatest of all English cults, the only one of Europe-wide appeal.

Signs of heresy, in the sense of organized disbelief, were very few and soon stamped out. But doubt, or qualified belief, was not by any means impossible though it is rare to find written evidence. Baldwin of Ford was anxious to reassure doubts about that notorious faith-stretcher, the doctrine of transubstantiation. The Hebrew scholar Herbert of Bosham at one point began to wonder whether the Jews might not be right after all, that Jesus was not the Messiah – would God accept the faith of Christians? He mentioned his doubts to archbishop Thomas, who told him to pull himself together.[30]

The visual arts

The century after 1150 witnessed the development of a distinct English school of gothic architecture. Two great churches were built, at Canterbury and Westminster, under very strong French influence, but the forms introduced there were interpreted by English architects and patrons in the light of their own tastes and traditions. As has often happened, English architects took over the decorative elements of a continental style without adopting the structural system behind it. It was not a question of a predefined style being exported, in this case from northern France, or misunderstood if not reproduced exactly; it was more as if certain features were selected by practitioners of an art which had its own impulse towards development. The great rebuilding of all the major English churches that followed the Norman conquest was virtually over by 1150, and thereafter churches were rebuilt only in response to a particular need. Usually only a part was reconstructed: often the east end was extended and given a flat eastern termination instead of the apses normal in romanesque churches. With less building going on, development was rather slow, a situation contrasting with that in the Île-de-France where virtually all the major churches were rebuilt in this period.

Anglo-Norman romanesque architecture had been inventive and technically precocious, and some of its features were never

[30] Smalley, *Becket Conflict*, 75–6.

wholly abandoned: thick wall construction with a passage at clerestory level; a love of rich mouldings and profuse ornament, especially blind arcading; and a pronounced horizontal emphasis going with the extreme length of English churches. As the style aged it became more elaborate, a phase represented by the

PLATE 3   Wells cathedral: nave interior from the west, *c.*1180–*c.*1230
The 'scissor arches' are fourteenth-century additions
(*courtesy of the Courtauld Institute of Art, Conway Library, London*)

'Galilee' chapel at Durham from the 1170s. A new influence came from the Yorkshire Cistercian monasteries, which set about building large churches strongly influenced by the pointed-arched, barrel-vaulted style current in parts of northern France. Some elements of this new style were taken on at non-Cistercian churches such as Hexham and Ripon, giving rise to a local school of skin-deep gothic which continued into the thirteenth century.

Another regional school developed in the west and south-west, still rather mongrel in effect in the west bays of the nave at Worcester, rebuilt after 1175, where broken arches coexist with romanesque ornament. But the major monument of early gothic in the south-west is the new cathedral built at Wells from 1180 (see plate 3). With pointed arches and ribbed vaults throughout and a fine array of 'stiff-leaf' capitals, all romanesque decoration banished, the visual effect is completely gothic. Yet the method of construction is still thick-walled Anglo-Norman complete with clerestory wall passage. The difference from contemporary French work could hardly be greater: the rich arch mouldings, facilitated by the thicker walls, the extreme horizontality emphasized by the triforium stage which disregards the bay divisions, and the low proportions are all symptomatic of English gothic. The screen-like west front at Wells, which is treated as a gallery for the all-over display of figure sculptures, and the tiny doorways are quite unlike the cavernous porches of French cathedrals.

When the monks of Canterbury cathedral came to rebuild their choir destroyed by fire in 1175, they turned to a French architect, William of Sens. The monks insisted he retain the undamaged outer walls and crypt, which determined the plan and width of the new work, and under William's successor, William the Englishman, the opportunity was taken to add an extra eastern chapel to house the shrine of St Thomas Becket. The sexpartite vaults, the correlation between vault ribs and supporting shafts, and the use of alternating round and octagonal columns all derive from northern French gothic, as does the use of different-coloured marbles for shafts, but at Canterbury they produce a much more elaborate effect than their prototypes (see plate 4). The exterior boasts the first exposed flying buttresses in England.

This rush of French ideas, displayed in the metropolitan cathedral and the most frequented pilgrimage centre, could not but be influential, and many thirteenth-century southern churches took on Canterbury-derived features. Its influence was also felt at

PLATE 4   Canterbury cathedral: presbytery from the north, 1175–c.1180
The archbishop's throne is at the head of the steps
(courtesy of the Courtauld Institute of Art, Conway Library, London)

Lincoln cathedral, rebuilt from 1192. Here the richest features
of Canterbury become normal, especially the use of Purbeck
marble, while the stiff-leaf capitals are like those of Wells. The
vaults of Lincoln are an interesting study in assimilation and
innovation: those in the eastern transept are sexpartite, but sit on

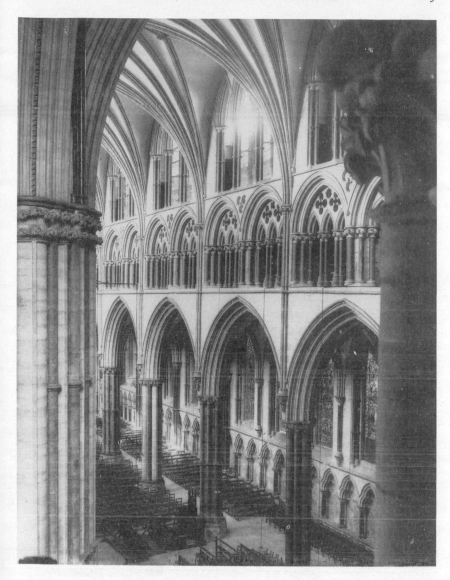

PLATE 5   Lincoln cathedral: north side of the nave from the east, c.1225
(courtesy of the Courtauld Institute of Art, Conway Library, London)

single bays, rather than on double bays as they do at Canterbury
and generally in France. The unique asymmetrical 'crazy vaults'
of the choir lack a centre, but introduce a rib along the ridge. In
the nave the aesthetic problem has been solved: a sheaf of vault
ribs leads up to a thick ridge rib, but two from adjacent sheaves
meet and unite before reaching the ridge, the first 'tiercerons' in

gothic architecture. The result is to increase the horizontal effect and dissolve the distinction between the bays, as the eye perceives the vaults not as units corresponding to the bays below, as is normal in French gothic, but as a succession of fronds emerging from between the bays in an off-beat rhythm (see plate 5). Another Lincoln innovation, much copied in the north of England, is the two-layer blind arcade along the wall of the choir aisle, which also fails to respect the bay divisions by ending at the apex of an arch. The structural vocabulary of gothic is redeployed to make rich surface patterns.

The influence of Lincoln was felt widely, at Ely, York and Beverley for example; the choir of Worcester takes over the ridge

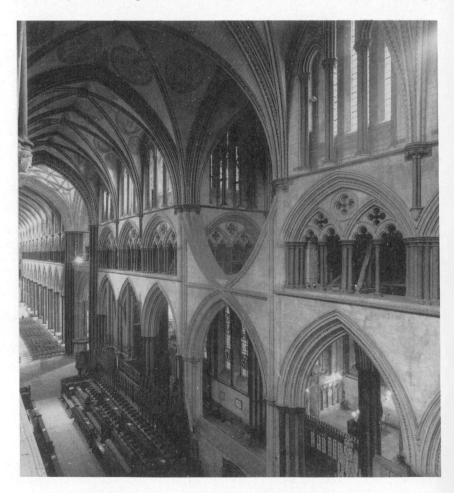

PLATE 6   Salisbury cathedral: interior from the east, 1225–58
(*courtesy of the Courtauld Institute of Art, Conway Library, London*)

PLATE 7 Westminster abbey: east end from the choir screen, 1246–59
The altar screen is from the fifteenth and nineteenth centuries
(reproduced by kind permission of The Dean and Chapter of Westminster)

rib and boasts the richest of all arch mouldings. But meanwhile
the far south had developed a more austere style of broad, simple
forms, restrained use of Purbeck marble, moulded capitals with
no stiff leaf, simple quadripartite vaults and graduated lancet
windows. The finest example is the new cathedral built at Salisbury from 1220 by bishop Richard Poore and his successors (see

plate 6). The double transept plan derives from Canterbury and the square ambulatory with three parallel chapels leading off it, which was widely copied in southern England, may reproduce that of the cathedral's predecessor. The architect and patron had a completely free hand; they produced a long, low, compartmented building of rare stylistic unity and lucidity.

Salisbury cathedral was dedicated in 1258. Before it was finished the next new wave of French ideas had been imported by Henry III in his rebuilding, from 1245, of the eastern arm and transepts of Westminster abbey (see plate 7). It was highly unusual, if not unique, for a single patron to foot the entire bill for a church of cathedral size, but Henry knew what he wanted: an up-to-date symbol of his kingship, a coronation church and a shrine for England's premier royal saint which would stand comparison with anything available to his main rivals, the kings of France. Henry was buried at Westminster, and after his death it became the royal mausoleum as well. The French coronation church, Reims cathedral, was an important source of motifs, and the first architect, Henry 'of Reyns', either came from Reims or had been trained there. He built an apse with radiating chapels, a plan new to English gothic though there were romanesque precedents. Other French features are the tall proportions, the thin clerestory walls with no suspicion of a passage, the highly visible flying buttresses, and especially the window tracery. It was already becoming apparent that the possibilities of groups of lancet windows and circles, called 'plate tracery', had largely been exhausted. The answer was bar tracery. English architects might have arrived at it anyway, since it is found in the west window of Binham priory in Norfolk which could predate Westminster, but it was the great royal church at the administrative capital of the kingdom that set the fashion. The patterns in the clerestory windows come from Reims; the great rose windows in the transepts are in the latest Parisian fashion from St Denis. The beautiful carved angels in the transepts derive from Louis IX's Sainte Chapelle in Paris. Compared to any major English church Westminster is a very foreign-looking building, yet there is much about it that is English, including basic structural techniques such as the way the vaults are built. There is lavish use of Purbeck marble, the arch mouldings are rich and complex, the interior walls are covered with all-over surface enrichment, the vault boasts a longitudinal ridge-rib and in the choir vault there are even tiercerons. Westminster does not look like a French church either.

As well as the abbey church, Henry III rebuilt the chapter house at Westminster. This fitted into a tradition of centrally planned chapter houses going back to the circular building at Worcester of the early twelfth century, and taken up in the octagonal room built at Lincoln in the early thirteenth. The Westminster chapter house is a large octagonal room with a tall, slender central shaft bearing vaults designed to allow the inclusion of huge traceried windows. Unlike the clerestory windows of the abbey, these take up the full width of the wall. It was the huge window and the effect of all-over tracery that subsequent English architects took from Westminster, forgetting about most of its other French innovations. In the 'Angel Choir', the eastern extension added to the choir of Lincoln cathedral from 1256, richly encrusted arcading finds its translucent counterpart in the vast window filling the whole east wall.

The design of castles also developed and changed in the Angevin period, though change was erratic and there was no simple stylistic evolution. So dense was the network of castles, mostly of earthwork and timber, built during and after the Norman conquest that a completely new castle was a rarity, the new works generally being on old sites. As castles were both residence and fortress, the choice of sites was dictated by the pattern of landowning and tended to be tactical rather than strategic – a defensible site on the lord's land, near the bulk of his estates for which it could act as an administrative centre. Even with royal castles and even where there was a land frontier there was no planned system of national defence, but a thick scattering of castles under various ownership.

The main development was the replacement of wooden structures with stone. The old motte-and-bailey type of castle, easy and quick to put up and very common in lowland England, could simply have its palisades replaced by walls, as at Pickering (Yorkshire) or Berkhamstead (Hertfordshire). On top of the motte this proceeding gave rise to the circular stone 'shell keep', within which lean-to wooden buildings provided accomodation. Walls could be given projecting towers to provide covering fire, such as we find at Framlingham castle (Suffolk), built by Roger Bigod about 1190, and in the thirteenth century such towers became very common. The gate was the weakest place in the defences, and stone gatehouses are a feature of some very early castles, such as Exeter where the entrance way penetrates through a tower. In Henry II's inner bailey at Dover castle we find two mural towers placed on either side of the entrance passage with a projecting outwork or 'barbican', a plan which became common in the thirteenth century. A very fine later gatehouse is the Constable's Gate, also at Dover, part of Henry III's work there. Henry II's Dover had an outer line of walls which probably covered the whole site, forming with the inner bailey two concentric rings of walls – the principle of concentricity is thus found as early as the 1180s (see plate 8).

The dominant feature of many castles is the great stone tower or keep, which is both the last refuge and the principal residence. Two of the grandest were built for Henry II, at Newcastle (1172–7) and Dover (1181–5). The latter has extra suites of rooms in the thickness of the walls, a chapel and a forebuilding to protect the entrance. Both these are rectangular, as is the particularly massive keep built by Robert fitz Ralph, a leading tenant of the honour of Richmond, at Middleham in Yorkshire.

PLATE 8 Dover castle from the north
In the centre is Henry II's keep (1181–5); in front of it is Henry II's inner bailey wall, at the right of which two towers close together form a gatehouse. In front of this is the outer curtain wall, the left of it of Henry II's time, elsewhere the work of John and Henry III, including, on the right, a gatehouse blocked after the siege of 1216. On the extreme left are the Anglo-Saxon church of St Mary in Castro and the Roman lighthouse of the second century AD
(reproduced by permission of RCHME Crown Copyright)

But in the later twelfth century polygonal keeps are also found, such as the eleven-sided one at Tickhill, the curious irregular polygon with three projecting buttress-towers at Orford (also built by Henry II, in the 1160s), and the cylindrical tower with polygonal buttresses built at Conisbrough by Henry's illegitimate half-brother Hamelin, earl Warenne c.1180. The plain cylindrical keep was fashionable in France at this time; the form was not so popular in England, but examples are to be found in the Welsh Marches: at Pembroke, built by William Marshal c.1200; at Longtown, Tretower, Skenfrith and other places. Great towers continued to be built in the thirteenth century, Henry III erecting, for instance, the quadrilobed Clifford's Tower at York from 1245.

In book production and manuscript painting, too, Norman England had produced some remarkable achievements. The wealth of the English church and the desire of its leaders for display continued unabated into the Angevin period, but changing fashions in devotion, the increase of academic study and an expansion of the market for decorated books all had an impact on the methods and products of scribes and painters.

Missals and Gospels are service books used in church, and some psalters and Bibles served that purpose too. Bibles and psalters were also used for meditative reading, and fine Gospels could be made simply to reside on an altar. There survive a number of very large and magnificent lectern Bibles, the biggest and finest being the Winchester Bible, which was created by a number of artists over some 20 years. Each type of book has its own appropriate illustration: Bibles typically have a large initial to each book, Gospels have portraits of the evangelists, while many manuscripts have decorative borders and initials. Psalters, which contain the psalms, were the main texts used as private prayer books; they are often prefaced by pictures of Old and New Testament stories. The production of psalters increased considerably in the thirteenth century, as more lay people began to use them as aids to private prayer. From about 1240 comes the earliest surviving English book of hours, a form which was to become the most popular illustrated private devotional book of the later middle ages: they consist of psalms, prayers, and Bible readings to be recited at the times of the liturgical 'hours', often lavishly and beautifully illustrated. The format of Bibles changes too, with smaller, less-expensive copies accompanied by glosses and running commentaries becoming common in the later twelfth century: these were for academic study, requiring textual analysis rather than the meditative approach practised in the monasteries. The only non-religious type of book to receive much painted decoration was the bestiary, an encyclopedia of moralized natural history with pictures of animals, both real species and the strange creatures believed in the middle ages to inhabit the remoter parts of the world.

The centres of production in the twelfth century were the greater monasteries, such as Bury St Edmunds, St Albans, Canterbury and Winchester. The *scriptoria* or writing offices in these institutions had long histories behind them; they were responsible for the large-format lectern Bibles and the copies of the works of church fathers which were the staple products in the twelfth century. The artists may have been monks, but in the second half of the twelfth century it is clear that there were professional artists who moved from place to place carrying out commissions. Such artists could cross and re-cross the Channel, and might pick up new techniques or tricks of style as they went. They could also form themselves into groups, or 'workshops', and might settle down somewhere for a period. In the thirteenth century there seems to have been an increase in the production of luxury psalters for lay patrons: the book trade which grew up then led to centres of production developing in towns – London, Oxford and Salisbury are known to have been the most important. The best-known workshop of the period is that of Walter de Brailes, who was active at Oxford from about 1230 to 1260, some of whose products have survived. The monasteries gradually faded out as artistic centres: Matthew Paris, the most famous monk-artist of all, was exceptional in his own time.

The style of painting evolved, too, though the architectural terminology – gothic and romanesque – often applied to it is not particularly appropriate. The style of wall-painting and sculpture evolved parallel to that of manuscript painting. This could be the result of simple copying, or it could be the effect of using pattern books which have not survived, or because artists worked in several media. The 'damp fold' drapery patterns and inventive decoration of late 'romanesque' painting and sculpture were superseded from c.1170 by a more restrained, naturalistic, almost classicizing style often compared with Byzantine work and in at least one case influenced by Greek Sicilian art. From around 1220 this again changes: figures are elegantly posed and gesticulating, composition becomes rather more small-scale and fussy, and the decorative repertoire begins to expand again. This last phase shows relatively little influence from France, which, how-

ever, becomes important again after 1250 as Henry III's patronage
begins to develop.

Did Angevin England have a distinctive culture? With French the
language of the upper classes, a spell in Paris an important part
of higher education, and French influence in the arts, was England not simply a cultural colony of France? For much of the
period it was, after all, only a province in a larger empire, and
even when the empire broke up the English kings bent most of
their energies to reconquering it. Writing the history of art as a
web of influences makes it seem as if impulses diffuse from a
centre or centres, and stylistic evolution can appear self-driven.
French and other art historians frequently find the radiating
centre in northern France. But impulses are not only transmitted,
they are also received, and in reception they can be modified and
combined with pre-existing local ways of thought and action.
The result will be an original synthesis, not just a failed copy of
a misunderstood model. The history of literature is sometimes
approached as if infinite comparisons were possible across all
human culture, and the historical context of a work can be dis-
regarded. If we attempt to put the cultural products of Angevin
England together, does any pattern emerge to lend significance to the obvious fact that they are all products of the same
society?
   We have mentioned education abroad as a powerful contribu-
tor to the cosmopolitan character of contemporary English culture, but the rise of universities in England went some way to
diminish that. In 1250 it was possible, as it had not been in 1150,
to obtain an education at, or very nearly at, the highest level
without leaving England. The minority of people thus affected
was small but influential. It would not be surprising if England
was less cosmopolitan by 1300 than it had been in 1200. In
some subjects, notably Latin literature, canon law and theology,
the English contributed to a Europe-wide mainstream, but the
centres of European law and theology were not in England. In
history and science the work of English scholars was much more
distinctive, while the French literature of Angevin England is a
surprisingly original and impressive creation. With the rise of
the common law we have the beginnings of a completely independent intellectual tradition. It is noticeable that there is a
thread of practicality running through these subjects, especially

science and law; and if the preference of English theologians for
the more practical world of pastoral theology is real and not
just the result of some writers being more studied than others,
then perhaps we can suspect that the English bias towards the
concrete and empirical was present already. In architecture the
'Englishness' of the early gothic cathedrals is very obvious as
soon as they are compared to cathedrals elsewhere: they conform
neatly to what Pevsner defined as long-term characteristics of
English architecture: horizontality, a love of over-all pattern-
making, a tendency to extract decorative rather than structural
methods from foreign models.[31] In many ways the culture of
Angevin England was distinctive, and in some ways, as it turned
out, distinctively English.

[31] N. Pevsner, *The Englishness of English Art*, London 1956.

9

England and the Angevin Empire

What was the 'Angevin empire'? The term was not used by contemporaries; are we justified in using it? How far was the 'empire' a united whole, in economic and social structure and government? Did it have anything approaching a common culture or an awareness of itself?

Parts of it certainly supported a common aristocracy: we have seen the number and importance of cross-Channel estates linking England with Normandy and to a lesser extent Brittany, and how some at least of the Anglo-Norman baronage and their followers ramified across the British Isles. But between Normandy and the lands to the south there was much less connection. The great lords of Poitou and Aquitaine did not become English landholders. Henry III's patronage of his relatives created a few Anglo-Gascon lords in the different environment of 'English Gascony', but Henry II and his sons did not set out to bind their lands together by creating a single aristocracy spread across them. There were certainly economic links between all the constituent parts of the empire which grew as the whole economy grew and formed some important connections, such as that between England and Gascony. But trading links bound all of Europe together, England with Flanders as much as with France, and they cannot be expected to define a political entity.

In governmental structure once again England and Normandy were very alike, and the Anglo-Norman pattern was exported to Brittany and Ireland by the Angevin kings. But it was a matter of replication, not integration; the structures were parallel and separate, not a single organization even though, for example, funds could be transferred from one province to another, from one treasury to another. Personnel could be transferred as well as goods, and here we begin to find some connections across the empire as individuals were drafted into posts away from their home province. Instances of this can also be found in the church, but there it was largely a matter of royal clerks being rewarded with preferment or, like some of the archbishops of Dublin, sent to govern a province. Again, this common feature did not often extend to Aquitaine.

It was the person of the king which gave the empire such unity as it possessed. It had a single supreme political authority, even when provinces had been given to Henry II's sons. The way Henry II treated his lands as a family estate, endowing younger sons with parts of it, has always attracted the attention of historians concerned principally with politics, and discussion has often concentrated on his intentions. Though he always intended to provide for his sons with the provinces of the empire, he intended the younger ones to do homage to the eldest in what amounted to a family federation. What actually happened was the result of bad family relations and mortality. It was on this highest of political levels that the empire existed: it supported the royal dynasty and provided them with the resources to play a leading role in European politics. In this light it can be described as 'the dominant polity in western Europe'.[1]

The French language was common to the empire's aristocracy, but as the empire straddled the divide between northern and southern French, between *oc* and *oui*, the differences may have seemed more obvious than the similarities. In the British Isles the aristocracy spoke the same kind of French, closest to that of Normandy though gradually diverging from it, but in some regions French-speaking culture was probably rather thinly spread. There are difficulties in attributing individual cultural products to the royal court, as we have seen, though it did have a cultural life; no 'court style' can be discerned in any art which might have unified the artistic and intellectual lives of the various provinces, and there is no evidence of the attempt being made. The provinces had vigorous artistic traditions of their own and continued to go separate ways. Itinerant craftsmen might wander across political boundaries as well as within them, drawing influences from many sources: they were not a unifying factor either.

It is therefore not surprising to find that the 'Angevin empire' as such attracted little or no notice from contemporaries. The focus of political loyalties, and indeed of disloyalties, was the king, not his collection of lands. While the 'empire' existed its lord was powerful, but in the event not powerful enough to

[1] Gillingham, *Angevin Empire*, 1.

ensure the survival of the empire. English expansion within the British Isles was guaranteed by the monarchy, but its English base provided sufficient power for that – as became clear after 1204. Within the wide and disparate empire individual provinces had a life and feeling of their own. They were the blocks from which it was created, and they survived it. When the empire's heartland was cut out, England emerged more clearly as the focus of a British 'empire'.

In many ways Angevin England demonstrated a growing distinctiveness, even a growing Englishness. This was primarily an underlying cultural matter. It is observable in language, where English French was differentiated from other dialects, and the native language re-emerged as a literary medium. The growth of high-level schools in England meant that there was less need to go abroad for study in youth, a change which could have far-reaching consequences; and academic careers could now be pursued in this country. In intellectual and literary activity, despite the uneven survival of different types of work, it seems that English writers had specific priorities and preferences for certain types of enquiry. A distinctiveness can be seen too in architecture, despite continental influences. The widespread interest in history, serious or fictionalized, represents the rehabilitation and repossession of the native past by poets, historians, churchmen and their audiences.

Observant contemporaries noticed that the English and Norman elements in society were no longer distinguishable except at the lowest level (which of course was all English). Walter Map thought it was Henry I who 'federated the two peoples in firm amity' by arranging marriages between them.[2] This may be 'memorable history', like much else in Walter's work, for instance the stories of the heroic Edric the Wild, a guerrilla leader who fought the Normans after 1066,[3] but contemporaries knew that times were changing. A certain amount of pride in Norman descent can still be found in the later twelfth century. Battle abbey, founded on the site of the famous victory, had obvious reasons to cultivate *Normanitas*: its chronicler puts into the mouth of the justiciar Richard de Lucy, actually the abbot's brother, a speech on the wiles of the English,[4] but such views were becoming rarer. They are to be found in heroic poetry, a somewhat backward-looking genre; but where Jordan Fantosme

---

[2] Map, 437; cf. Dialogue, 53.
[3] Map, 155–61.
[4] Battle Chronicle, 182, transl. in Holt, *Feudal Society and the Family* i, 207.

in the 1170s can still say 'Normans are great conquerors, there are none like them',[5] by the time of William the Marshal the note has become more elegiac: 'then they were grain and now they are straw, since King Richard died'.[6] Normandy had been conquered twice, by the Angevins in the 1140s and again in 1202–4 by the French. None the less old habits of obedience were long in dying: still after 1200 it was thought desirable to have an abbot 'Norman by nation', and fluent in French.[7] Equally 'English' could still be used by Gerald of Wales to mean the rustics, 'the most worthless of all peoples under the sun', slaves in their own land.[8] But England and Normandy were drifting apart in various ways, and within the island the two peoples had to a great extent merged. An English identity was becoming clearer.

English identity is inevitably aided by island geography – 'our island, that is, England'[9] – but it is a product of human feeling and social processes, not of geography. It is helped along by attributing common qualities to the group. The poet Chardri in *Le Petit Plet* wrote 'England surpasses all the kingdoms there are, and do you know how? In all pleasures and in nobility. If the women there are well brought up you should not wonder, for so are the knights. . . .'[10] Interestingly, he wrote that in French. Attributed qualities do not always have to be positive: the English were notorious for their drunkenness, and native as well as foreign writers notice and condemn it. To cite only two examples of this widespread opinion, the author of the *Dialogue of the Exchequer* attributes the prevalence of robbery to 'the untold riches of the kingdom and the natural drunkenness of its inhabitants', while William fitz Stephen felt that the only things that spoilt London were 'the immoderate drinking of fools and the frequency of fires'.[11] What is important is not whether this was true, though it may have been, but that it was believed. It is harder to be sure whether the same applies to another well-known attribution, that Englishmen had tails. This turns up in Richard of Devizes' description of king Richard's activities in Sicily, when 'the little Greeks and Sicilians' called all Richard's followers 'Englishmen and tail-wearers'.[12]

[5] Jordan, ll. 169–70.
[6] Marshal, ll. 4648–9.
[7] Jocelin, 129.
[8] Bartlett, *Gerald of Wales*, 14.
[9] Map, 166–7.
[10] Legge, *Anglo-Norman Literature*, 198.
[11] Dialogue, 87; Mats Becket iii, 8.
[12] *Anglos et caudatos*, Devizes, 19.

Alongside a growing sense of identity went a propensity to stereotype and belittle foreigners. Even quite distant peoples receive unfavourable comment: 'the Greeks are soft and womanly, voluble and deceitful, of no constancy or valour against an enemy', wrote Walter Map.[13] He is also the source of the famous gazetteer of royal resources which topples over into national stereotypes, and which he attributes, rightly or not, to Louis VII of France. The king of Sicily and the emperor of the Greeks, Louis allegedly says, have gold and silks 'but no men who can do anything but talk'; the emperor of the Germans has warriors, but no gold, silk or splendour; the king of England wants for nothing – men, horses, gold, silk, jewels, fruit, game; while we in France have nothing but bread, wine and gaiety.[14] Ecclesiastical politics and taxation dominate attitudes to Italians, and there is no lack of disparaging comments about the Italian bureaucracy at Rome. Cardinal John of Anagni, according to a monk of Canterbury, was 'a man in whom we have confidence as far as his nationality allows'.[15]

The French, meaning the people of the Île-de-France, attracted a good deal of hostility. Prolonged and ultimately unsuccessful war must have been a factor here, and their position at the metropolis of northern French-speaking culture laid them open to charges of arrogance. 'The French are by nature fierce and arrogant', wrote William of Newburgh, 'especially when they are superior in numbers and equipment.'[16] Gerald of Wales in his old age adopted a francophilia influenced by nostalgia for his student days, and John of Salisbury always loved France: but they were from a generation that had spent its youth in Paris, and here too times changed. Richard of Devizes loses no opportunity to belittle Philip Augustus, contrasting him with king Richard's power and glory, and to show his dislike of the French, whom he pictures spreading lies all over Europe about Richard's conduct of the crusade. The passage of Chardri's *Le Petit Plet* cited above gains its point by proving both English knights and English women superior to French: but the moon shines everywhere, and even in France a few good women are to be found.

It is particularly revealing to find the inhabitants of Henry II's other lands belittled. The Poitevins were regarded as faithless

---

[13] Map, 175.
[14] Ibid., 451.
[15] Epp Cant, 286.
[16] Newburgh, 174.

and treacherous by the Gascons as well as by the English.[17] Gerald of Wales even has hard words for the Normans: he claimed William Longchamps's alleged verbosity and homosexuality were both typically Norman. The Normans, he said, had originally learnt homosexuality from the French but had soon made it their own.[18] Fawkes de Bréauté was tarred with the same brush as John's hated Poitevin mercenary captains despite coming of respectable Norman ancestry: he was 'the first layman of Norman extraction to be damned as such'.[19]

The Celtic peoples were easy targets for such comments, the Welsh and Irish having distinctive identities and cultures noticeably different from the English. It was in the twelfth century that these differences of culture and behaviour became so marked as to enable English writers to depict the Welsh, Scots and Irish as barbarians. Their marital customs were regarded as bestial, and their violent family feuds as inhuman. Their slave-raiding and technologically backward methods of warfare, together with the general failure of their leaders to adopt the norms of French-speaking culture, disqualified them from the club of knighthood.[20] Gerald of Wales sometimes showed a little sympathy for Welsh dispossession, but mostly regarded them as barbarous and backward. Walter Map adopts a generally patronizing attitude to 'our Welshmen', and characterizes them as violent, fickle, warlike and prone to anger, but also brave and hospitable.[21] The same view of them as faithless, bloodthirsty and barbarous is found in William of Newburgh, who adds the interesting comment that they are 'filled by nature with hatred of the English people'.[22] The Scottish aristocracy came to conform to Anglo-Norman models – many were in fact Anglo-Norman lords – and were accepted, but the rest of the population was unfavourably characterized, and the dislike of the wild inhabitants of Galloway found in earlier chroniclers remained vivid. Jordan Fantosme expresses it so strongly that it cannot be merely a literary cliché.[23]

The situation that developed in Ireland after 1169 was of great complexity and interest. The leaders of the conquerors normally

[17] Stacey, *Politics, Policy and Finance*, 169–70.
[18] Gerald of Wales ii, 348, iv, 423.
[19] Holt, *Feudal Society and the Family* iv, 27.
[20] John Gillingham, 'Conquering the barbarians: war and chivalry in twelfth-century Britain', *Haskins Society Journal* 4 (1993), 67–84.
[21] Map, e.g. 145–7, 183, 189–91.
[22] Newburgh, 107.
[23] Jordan, ll. 684–8.

spoke French – an epic poem, *The Song of Dermot and the Earl*, was composed in French about Strongbow's exploits – and French was understood in the towns.[24] But the lower-class settlers spoke English, and by the fourteenth century a distinctive dialect, drawing on various English dialects, had come into existence in Ireland. The settlers were of mixed origin, the leaders partly Welsh and partly Norman, and modern historians sometimes call them 'Cambro-Norman'. But to the Irish annals they were all 'English' (*Saxain*) and, revealingly for their self-image, the *Song of Dermot and the Earl* simply calls them *Engleis*.[25] Political and cultural pressures in the thirteenth century were leading to the creation of a separate people, the Anglo-Irish, as their interests and even their language differentiated them from the English of England while the threat of absorption made them ever more keen to mark themselves off from the Irish.

The re-emergence of English national feeling is therefore visible in the twelfth century, and it certainly gained momentum in the thirteenth: dislike of the 'aliens' is to be found in Ralph of Coggeshall, who commented on the defeat of Louis of France's invasion in 1217 that 'God struck the heads of his enemies who had come to destroy the English people' – God was on the side of the English as early as that.[26] The Stanley, Dunstable and Worcester annalists all show bias against foreigners in John's reign, while the Barnwell chronicler's dislike of the papacy and foreigners can be seen growing.[27] Matthew Paris's prejudices are certainly the most all-embracing and vividly expressed, but he wrote the longest chronicle. He detested especially the French, Poitevins, Welsh and Greeks, though not apparently the Jews. The Flemings were 'filthy and ignoble', the Poitevins 'wily traitors', the queen's Savoyard relatives 'the scum of a terrible rabble'.[28]

These attitudes of the chroniclers are not quite automatic xenophobia: they accompany specific grievances. John's mercenaries are foreigners and terrorize the population, Louis brings a French army. Envy of the political success of incomers, of their harvesting of royal favour and patronage, is a prominent grievance, especially under Henry III, though it is to be found earlier. There was a strong feeling that the people of the country, the king's 'natural subjects', should be consulted and make the

[24] A. Bliss and J. Long in Cosgrove, *New History of Ireland*, 708–18.
[25] F. X. Martin in ibid., lii–liii.
[26] Coggeshall, 185.
[27] Gransden, *Historical Writing*, 334, 344.
[28] Vaughan, *Matthew Paris*, 33, 142–3 and refs.

profits. This view is found in the 1170s with Jordan Fantosme, who says of king William of Scots that 'he never had much affection for his own people, whose right it was to counsel him and his realm',[29] and in the 1190s Richard of Devizes showed dislike of 'unknown incomers' getting the 'custodies' which should have gone to 'the legitimate men of the kingdom'.[30] In John's reign the English baronage was said to dislike the appointment of Peter des Roches as justiciar because they regarded him as a foreigner.[31] It was the Poitevins and Savoyards under Henry III who attract most attention, then and now;[32] there was also opposition to Italian clerks in English church benefices and resentment of papal taxation developed an anti-Italian and anti-French tinge. This is not quite nationalism as a motive for political action, not yet; being foreign was a lightning-conductor for other dislikes, and would always come up in denunciation. But it is significant that foreignness was noticed and included in the reproach. National identity had become part of the self-definition of individuals and of the identification of others; a national unit had developed, with a common awareness, capable of adopting nationalism.

The emergence of an English national feeling is visible before the French conquest of Normandy and Anjou. It was not therefore a consequence of that loss, though it gained momentum after it. This consciousness grew up when England was part of a larger political grouping and shared its monarch with other lands. It was therefore not the product of the monarchy, though later kings were able to harness the strength of national feeling and to emerge as its embodiment. But it was older than they, and did not depend on them for its vitality. The symbols of identity are not to be confused with the identity itself. An English identity emerged irrespective of the cross-border activities of many lords, whose sense of identity is harder to penetrate than that of the chroniclers, though some of the evidence just cited attributes the same feelings to them. The feeling grew up at a time when the culturally dominant language in England was French, and some of its early manifestations were written in that language. So it is not to be identified with the English language. There was a distinct English identity even when the upper classes spoke French.

[29] Jordan, ll. 640–2.
[30] Devizes, 31.
[31] Coggeshall, 168.
[32] See above, pp. 99–100.

An English ethnicity began to emerge in the twelfth century and, once rolling, it gradually gained pace. The fusion of Norman and English was the precondition which made a single national awareness possible. The England of the Angevin kings was becoming a more complex, many-layered society, with an expanding economy, increasingly strong and self-conscious local social communities, and a political life of increasing sophistication. There were growing opportunities for education, proliferating career openings, and a lively intellectual, literary and artistic life. This provides the context for the emergence of ethnicity: success and growing self-confidence visible in many fields may well produce a greater self-awareness. Being intimately connected with developments of all kinds on the continent did not impede its growth, in fact the opposite was more likely the case: awareness of the existence of other groups furthered English self-definition. The foundation of ethnicity had been laid on which political nationalism would be built.

Bibliography

A Sources

This section is arranged alphabetically by the abbreviated forms that are used in the footnotes.

Acta: *Acta of Henry II and Richard I: Hand-list of documents surviving in the original in repositories in the United Kingdom*, ed. J. C. Holt and Richard Mortimer, List and Index Society, special series, 21, 1986.

Ann Mon: *Annales Monastici*, ed. H. R. Luard, 5 vols, Rolls Series, London 1864–9.

Battle Chronicle: *The Chronicle of Battle Abbey*, ed. Eleanor Searle, Oxford 1980.

Béroul: *Romance of Tristan*, trans. Alan S. Fedrick, Harmondsworth 1970.

Bracton: *Bracton on the Laws and Customs of England*, ed. G. E. Woodbine, trans. and rev. Samuel E. Thorne, 4 vols, Cambridge, Mass. 1968–77.

Cal Cl Rolls: *Calendar of Close Rolls*, 67 vols, London 1902– .

Cal Lib Rolls: *Calendar of Liberate Rolls, 1226–72*, 6 vols, London 1917–64.

Cal Pat Rolls: *Calendar of Patent Rolls*, 60 vols, London 1901– .

Cheney, C. R. and Jones, B. E. A., *English Episcopal Acta ii, Canterbury 1162–1190*, Oxford 1986.

Cheney, C. R. and John, Eric, *English Episcopal Acta iii, Canterbury 1193–1205*, Oxford 1986.

Chron Maj: *Matthaei Parisiensis Chronica Majora*, ed. H. R. Luard, 7 vols, Rolls Series, London 1872–84.

Coggeshall: *Radulphi de Coggeshall Chronicon Anglicanum*, ed. Joseph Stevenson, Rolls Series, London 1875.

Councils and Synods i: *Councils and Synods with other docu-*

ments relating to the English Church I part ii, 1066–1204,
ed. Dorothy Whitelock, Michael Brett and C. N. L. Brooke,
Oxford 1981.

Councils and Synods ii: *Councils and Synods with other documents relating to the English Church II, 1205–1313,* ed.
F. M. Powicke and C. R. Cheney, Oxford 1964.

CRR: *Curia Regis Rolls,* 15 vols, London: HMSO 1923– .

Devizes: *The Chronicle of Richard of Devizes,* ed. J. T. Appleby,
London 1963.

Dialogue: *The Course of the Exchequer by Richard son of Nigel,*
ed. Charles Johnson, with corrections by F. E. L. Carter and
D. E. Greenway, OMT 1983.

Diceto: *The Historical Works of Master Ralph de Diceto,* ed.
William Stubbs, 2 vols, Rolls Series, London 1876.

EHD ii: *English Historical Documents ii, 1042–1189,* ed.
D. C. Douglas and George W. Greenaway, 2nd edn, London
1981.

EHD iii: *English Historical Documents iii, 1189–1327,* ed.
Harry Rothwell, London 1975.

Epp Cant: *Chronicles and Memorials of the Reign of Richard I,
ii, Epistolae Cantuarienses,* ed. William Stubbs, Rolls Series,
London 1865.

Flores Hist: *Chronica Rogeri de Wendover qui dicitur Flores
Historiarum,* ed. H. G. Hewlett, 3 vols, Rolls Series, London
1886–9.

Foedera: T. Rymer, *Foedera, conventiones, litterae et cuiuscunque generis acta publica,* ed. A. Clarke and F. Holbrooke,
4 vols in 7 parts, London: Record Commission 1816–69.

Gerald of Wales: *Giraldi Cambrensis Opera,* ed. J. S. Brewer,
J. F. Dimock and G. F. Warner, 8 vols, Rolls Series, London
1861–91.

—— *The Journey through Wales, The Description of Wales,*
trans. Lewis Thorpe, Harmondsworth 1978.

Gervase: *The Historical Works of Gervase of Canterbury,* ed.
William Stubbs, 2 vols, Rolls Series, London 1879–80.

Gesta: *The Chronicle of the reigns of Henry II and Richard I
commonly known under the name of Benedict of Peterborough,* ed. William Stubbs, 2 vols, Rolls Series, London 1867.

Glanvill: *The Treatise on the Laws and Customs of the Realm of
England commonly called Glanvill,* ed. G. D. G. Hall, NMT,
London 1965.

Howden: *Chronica Magistri Rogeri de Houedene,* ed. William
Stubbs, 4 vols, Rolls Series, London 1868–71.

Huntingdon: *Henrici Huntendunensis Historia Anglorum*, ed. T. Arnold, Rolls Series, London 1879.

Jocelin: *The Chronicle of Jocelin of Brakelond*, ed. H. E. Butler, NMT, London 1949.

Jordan: *Jordan Fantosme's Chronicle*, ed. R. C. Johnston, Oxford 1981.

Magna Vita: *The Life of St Hugh of Lincoln*, ed. Decima L. Douie and Hugh Farmer, 2 vols, NMT, London 1961–2.

Map: *Walter Map, De Nugis Curialium*, ed. M. R. James, C. N. L. Brooke and R. A. B. Mynors, OMT, 1983.

Marshal: *Histoire de Guillaume le Maréchal*, ed. Paul Meyer, 3 vols, Paris 1891–1901.

Mats Becket: *Materials for the History of Thomas Becket*, ed. J. C. Robertson, 7 vols, Rolls Series, London 1875–85.

Newburgh: *Chronicles of the Reigns of Stephen, Henry II and Richard I*, ed. R. Howlett, vols i and ii, Rolls Series, London 1884–5.

NMT, Nelson's Medieval Texts.

OMT, Oxford Medieval Texts, Oxford.

Peter of Blois: *Petri Blesensis Bathoniensis Archidiaconi Opera Omnia*, ed. J. A. Giles, 4 vols, Oxford 1846–7.

PR: Pipe Rolls, published by the Pipe Roll Society, cited by regnal year of the king.

Red Book: *The Red Book of the Exchequer*, ed. Hubert Hall, 3 vols, Rolls Series, London 1896.

Rot Chart: *Rotuli Chartarum in Turri Londinensi asservati, 1199–1216*, ed. T. D. Hardy, Record Commission, London 1837.

Rot Lib: *Rotuli de Liberate ac de Misis et Praestitis*, ed. T. D. Hardy, Record Commission, London 1844.

Rot Litt Claus: *Rotuli Litterarum Clausarum in Turri Londinensi asservati*, ed. T. D. Hardy, 2 vols, Record Commission, London 1833–4.

Rot Litt Pat: *Rotuli Litterarum Patentium in Turri Londinensi asservati, 1201–1216*, ed. T. D. Hardy, Record Commission, London 1835.

Rot Mis: *Rotuli de Liberate ac de Misis et Prestitis, regnante Johanne*, ed. T. D. Hardy, Record Commission, London 1844.

Rot Obl et Fin: *Rotuli de Oblatis et Finibus in Turri Londinensi asservati tempore regis Johannis*, ed. T. D. Hardy, Record Commission 1835.

Select Pleas in Manorial Courts, ed. F. W. Maitland, Selden Society ii, 1888.

Torigni: *Chronicles of the Reigns of Stephen, Henry II and Richard I*, ed. R. Howlett, vol. iv, Rolls Series, London 1889.
TRHS: Transactions of the Royal Historical Society.

B   General and narrative works

This section includes the abbreviations used in the footnotes for journal titles.

Baldwin, John W., *Masters, Princes and Merchants: The Social Views of Peter the Chanter and his Circle*, 2 vols, Princeton 1970.
BIHR: Bulletin of the Institute of Historical Research.
Carpenter, D. A., *The Minority of Henry III*, London 1990.
Chibnall, Marjorie, *The Empress Matilda*, Oxford 1991.
Clanchy, M. T., *England and its Rulers, 1066–1272*, 2nd edn, Oxford 1993.
Coss, P. R. and Lloyd, S. D., *Thirteenth Century England*, Woodbridge: i (1985), ii (1987), iii (1989), iv (1991).
EHR: English Historical Review.
Gillingham, John, *The Angevin Empire*, London 1984.
—— *Richard the Lionheart*, London 1978.
Holt, J. C., *Magna Carta*, 2nd edn, Cambridge 1992.
—— *The Northerners*, Oxford 1961.
Ormrod, W. M., *England in the Thirteenth Century: Proceedings of the 1984 Harlaxton Symposium*, Harlaxton 1985.
Painter, Sidney, *The Reign of King John*, Baltimore 1949.
Poole, Austin Lane, *From Domesday Book to Magna Carta*, Oxford 1955.
Powicke, F. M., *King Henry III and the Lord Edward*, Oxford 1947.
Prestwich, Michael, *English Politics in the Thirteenth Century*, London 1990.
Reynolds, Susan, *Kingdoms and Communities in Western Europe, 900–1300*, Oxford 1984.
Stacey, Robert C., *Politics, Policy and Finance under Henry III, 1216–1245*, Oxford 1987.
TRHS: Transactions of the Royal Historical Society.
Vale, Malcolm, *The Angevin Legacy and the Hundred Years War, 1250–1340*, Oxford 1990.
Warren, W. L., *Henry II*, London 1973.
—— *King John*, London 1961.

C   Chapter bibliographies

This section lists titles cited more than once in the footnotes and not included in sections A and B, and also suggestions for further reading. Details of references which are cited only once are included in the relevant footnotes.

Chapter 1:   The Background to Politics
Astill, Grenville and Grant, Annie (eds), *The Countryside of Medieval England*, Oxford 1988.
Barlow, Frank, *Thomas Becket*, London 1986.
Blair, J. and Ramsay, N., *English Medieval Industries*, London and Rio Grande 1991.
Duby, Georges, *A History of Private Life ii: Revelations of the Medieval World*, trans. Arthur Goldhammer, New Haven, Conn. 1988.
—— *William Marshal, the Flower of Chivalry*, London 1986.
Gillingham, John and Holt, J. C., *War and Government in the Middle Ages*, Woodbridge 1984.
Given, James B., *Society and Homicide in Thirteenth-Century England*, Stanford, Cal. 1977.
Herlihy, David, *Medieval Households*, New Haven, Conn. 1985.
Holt, J. C., 'Feudal society and the family in early medieval England', *TRHS* 5th ser.: i, 'The revolution of 1066', 32 (1982), 193–212; ii, 'Notions of patrimony', 33 (1983), 193–220; iii, 'Patronage and politics', 34 (1984), 1–25; iv, 'The heiress and the alien', 35 (1985), 1–28.
Jolliffe, J. E. A., *Angevin Kingship*, 2nd edn, London 1963.
Orme, Nicholas, *From Childhood to Chivalry*, London and New York 1984.
Pollock, Sir Frederick and Maitland, Frederic William, *The History of English Law before the Time of Edward I*, rev. S. F. C. Milsom, 2 vols, Cambridge 1968.
Poole, A. L., *Obligations of Society in XII and XIII Centuries*, Oxford 1946.
Powicke, F. M., *The Loss of Normandy (1189–1204)*, 2nd edn, Manchester 1961.
Smail, R. C., *Crusading Warfare (1097–1193)*, Cambridge 1956.
Stenton, F. M., *The First Century of English Feudalism, 1066–1166*, Oxford 1932.
Stringer, K. J., *Earl David of Huntingdon, 1152–1219*, Edinburgh 1985.

Verbruggen, J. F., *The Art of Warfare in Western Europe during the Middle Ages*, Amsterdam 1977.

Wood, Margaret, *The English Medieval House*, London 1965.

Chapter 2: The King's Government

Barlow, Frank, *Thomas Becket*, London 1986.

Bartlett, Robert, *Trial by Fire and Water*, Oxford 1986.

Beeler, John, *Warfare in England, 1066–1189*, Ithaca, N.Y. 1966.

Brand, Paul, *The Making of the Common Law*, London and Rio Grande 1992.

Brown, R. Allen, Colvin, H. M. and Taylor, A. J., *History of the King's Works i: The Middle Ages*, London 1963.

Chaplais, Pierre, *English Royal Documents, King John–Henry VI, 1199–1461*, Oxford 1971.

Cheney, C. R., *Hubert Walter*, London 1967.

Crouch, David, *The Beaumont Twins*, Cambridge 1991.

Gillingham, John and Holt, J. C., *War and Government in the Middle Ages*, Woodbridge 1984.

Harding, Alan, *The Law Courts of Medieval England*, London 1973.

Harriss, G. L., *King, Parliament and Public Finance in Medieval England to 1369*, Oxford 1975.

Holt, J. C., 'The assizes of Henry II: the texts', in D. A. Bullough and R. L. Storey, *The Study of Medieval Records*, Oxford 1971, 85–106.

Hoyt, Robert S., *The Royal Demesne in English Constitutional History, 1066–1272*, Ithaca, N.Y. 1950.

Hunnisett, R. F., *The Medieval Coroner*, Cambridge 1961.

Jolliffe, J. E. A., *Angevin Kingship*, 2nd edn, London 1963.

Keefe, Thomas K., *Feudal Assessments and the Political Community under Henry II and his Sons*, London 1983.

Milsom, S. F. C., *Historical Foundations of the Common Law*, London 1969.

—— *The Legal Framework of English Feudalism*, Cambridge 1976.

Mitchell, Sydney Knox, *Studies in Taxation under John and Henry III*, New Haven, Conn. 1914.

—— *Taxation in Medieval England*, New Haven, Conn. 1951.

Morris, William Alfred, *The Medieval English Sheriff to 1300*, Manchester 1927.

Palmer, Robert C., *The County Courts of Medieval England, 1150–1350*, Princeton, N.J. 1982.

Pollock, Sir Frederick and Maitland, Frederic William, *The History of English Law before the Time of Edward I*, rev. S. F. C. Milsom, 2 vols, Cambridge 1968.

Poole, Austin Lane, *Obligations of Society in XII and XIII Centuries*, Oxford 1946.

Poole, Reginald L., *The Exchequer in the Twelfth Century*, Oxford 1912.

Roth, Cecil, *A History of the Jews in England*, 3rd edn, Oxford 1964.

Sanders, I. J., *Feudal Military Service in England*, Oxford 1956.

Stenton, Doris M., *English Justice between the Norman Conquest and the Great Charter*, London 1965.

Turner, Ralph V., *The English Judiciary in the Age of Glanvill and Bracton, c.1176–1239*, Cambridge 1985.

—— *Men Raised from the Dust: Administrative Service and Upward Mobility in Angevin England*, Philadelphia, Pa 1988.

Van Caenegem, R. C., *Royal Writs in England from the Conquest to Glanvill*, Selden Society 77, 1959.

Verbruggen, J. F., *The Art of Warfare in Western Europe during the Middle Ages*, Amsterdam 1977.

Warren, W. L., *The Governance of Norman and Angevin England*, London 1987.

West, Francis, *The Justiciarship in England, 1066–1232*, Cambridge 1966.

Young, C. R., *The Royal Forests of Medieval England*, Leicester 1979.

Chapter 3: The King and the Aristocracy

Altschul, Michael, *A Baronial Family in Medieval England: The Clares 1217–1314*, Baltimore, Md 1965.

Brand, Paul, *The Making of the Common Law*, London and Rio Grande 1992.

Brown, R. Allen, Colvin, H. M. and Taylor, A. J., *History of the King's Works i, The Middle Ages*, London 1963.

Coss, Peter R., *Lordship, Knighthood and Locality: A Study in English Society, c.1180–c.1280*, Cambridge 1991.

Crouch, David, *The Beaumont Twins*, Cambridge 1986.

—— *William Marshal: Court, Career and Chivalry in the Angevin Empire*, London 1990.

Davies, R. R., *The British Isles*, Edinburgh 1988.

Denholm-Young, N., *Seignorial Administration in England*, Oxford 1937.

Duby, Georges, *William Marshal, the Flower of Chivalry*, London 1986.

Greenway, D. E., *Charters of the Honour of Mowbray, 1107–1191*, London 1972.

Keefe, Thomas K., *Feudal Assessments and the Political Community under Henry II and his Sons*, London 1983.

Miller, Edward and Hatcher, John, *Medieval England – Rural Society and Economic Change, 1086–1348*, London and New York 1978.

Milsom, S. F. C., *The Legal Framework of English Feudalism*, Cambridge 1976.

Painter, Sidney, *Studies in the History of the English Feudal Barony*, Baltimore, Md 1943.

Stenton, F. M., *The First Century of English Feudalism, 1066–1166*, Oxford 1932.

Stringer, K. J., *Earl David of Huntingdon, 1152–1219*, Edinburgh 1985.

Warren, W. L., *The Governance of Norman and Angevin England*, London 1987.

Wightman, W. E., *The Lacy Family in England and Normandy, 1066–1194*, Oxford 1966.

Young, C. R., *The Royal Forests of Medieval England*, Leicester 1979.

Chapter 4: The King and the Church

Adams, Norma and Donahue, Charles Jnr (eds), *Select Cases from the Ecclesiastical Courts of the Province of Canterbury, c.1200–1301*, Selden Society 95, 1981.

Barlow, Frank, *Thomas Becket*, London 1986.

Brooke, Rosalind, *The Coming of the Friars*, London 1975.

Cheney, C. R., *From Becket to Langton*, Manchester 1956.

—— *Pope Innocent III and England*, Stuttgart 1975.

Cheney, Mary G., *Roger, Bishop of Worcester, 1164–1179*, Oxford 1980.

Gibbs, Marion and Lang, Jane, *Bishops and Reform, 1215–1272*, Oxford 1934.

Knowles, David, 'Archbishop Thomas Becket – a character study', *Proceedings of the British Academy* 35 (1950), 3–31.

—— *The Episcopal Colleagues of Archbishop Thomas Becket*, Cambridge 1951.

—— *The Monastic Order in England*, 2nd edn, Cambridge 1962.

—— *The Religious Orders in England, i*, Cambridge 1948.

Knoles, David, *Thomas Becket*, Stanford, Cal. 1970.

Lawrence, C. H., *St Edmund of Abingdon*, Oxford 1960.

Powicke, F. M., *Stephen Langton*, Oxford 1928.

Sayers, Jane E., *Papal Government and England during the Pontificate of Honorius III (1216–1227)*, Cambridge 1984.

—— *Papal Judges Delegate in the Province of Canterbury, 1198–1254*, Oxford 1971.

Smalley, Beryl, *The Becket Conflict and the Schools*, Oxford 1973.

Whitelock, D., Brett, M. and Brooke, C. N. L., *Councils and Synods with Other Documents Relating to the English Church, i part ii, 1066–1204*, Oxford 1981.

Chapter 5: England and its Neighbours

The Continent

Baldwin, John W., *The Government of Philip Augustus: Foundations of French Royal Power in the Middle Ages*, Berkeley and Los Angeles, Cal. and London 1986.

Bautier, R. H., *La France de Philippe Auguste – Le Temps des mutations*, Paris 1982.

Cuttino, G. P., *English Medieval Diplomacy*, Indiana 1985.

Dunbabin, Jean, *France in the Making, 843–1180*, Oxford 1985.

Gillingham, John, *The Angevin Empire*, London 1984.

—— *Richard the Lionheart*, London 1978.

Le Patourel, John, *Feudal Empires, Norman and Plantagenet*, London 1984.

Pacaut, Marcel, *Louis VII et son Royaume*, Paris 1964.

Powicke, F. M., *The Loss of Normandy (1189–1204)*, 2nd edn, Manchester 1961.

The British Isles

Barrow, G. W. S., *The Anglo-Norman Era in Scottish History*, Oxford 1980.

—— *Kingship and Unity: Scotland 1000–1306*, London 1981.

Cosgrove, A. (ed.), *New History of Ireland ii: Medieval Ireland, 1169–1534*, Oxford 1987.

Davies, R. R., *The British Isles, 1100–1500*, Edinburgh 1988.

—— *Conquest, Coexistence and Change: Wales, 1063–1415*, Oxford 1987.

Davies, Wendy, *Wales in the Early Middle Ages*, Leicester 1982.

Duncan, A. A. M., *Scotland: The Making of the Kingdom*, Edinburgh 1975.

Flanagan, M. T., 'Henry II, Strongbow and the Conquest of

Ireland' in John Gillingham and J. C. Holt, *War and Government in the Middle Ages*, Woodbridge 1984.

Frame, Robin, *The Political Development of the British Isles, 1100–1400*, Oxford 1990.

Simms, Katharine, *From Kings to Warlords*, Woodbridge 1984.

Stones, E. L. G., *Anglo-Scottish Relations, 1174–1328*, London 1965.

Stringer, K. J., *Earl David of Huntingdon, 1152–1219*, Edinburgh 1985.

—— *Essays on the Nobility of Medieval Scotland*, Edinburgh 1985.

Chapter 6:   Rural Society

Astill, Grenville, and Grant, Annie (eds), *The Countryside of Medieval England*, Oxford 1988.

Aston, Michael, Austin, David and Dyer, Christopher (eds), *The Rural Settlements of Medieval England*, Oxford 1989.

Blair, John, ed., *Minsters and Parish Churches: The Local Church in Transition, 950–1200*, Oxford 1988.

Du Boulay, F. R. H., *The Lordship of Canterbury*, London 1966.

Dyer, Christopher, *Lords and Peasants in a Changing Society*, Cambridge 1980.

Everitt, Alan, *Landscape and Community in England*, London and Ronceverte 1985.

Hallam, H. E. (ed.), *The Agrarian History of England and Wales ii: 1042–1350*, Cambridge 1988.

Harvey, Barbara, *Westminster Abbey and its Estates in the Middle Ages*, Oxford 1977.

Harvey, P. D. A., *A Medieval Oxfordshire Village: Cuxham, 1200–1400*, Oxford 1965.

——, 'The Pipe Rolls and the adoption of demesne farming in England', *Economic History Review* xxvii, 1974.

—— (ed.), *The Peasant Land Market in Medieval England*, Oxford 1984.

Hyams, Paul R., *Kings, Lords and Peasants in Medieval England: The Common Law of Villeinage in the Twelfth and Thirteenth Centuries*, Oxford 1980.

King, Edmund, *Peterborough Abbey, 1086–1310*, Cambridge 1973.

Miller, Edward, *The Abbey and Bishopric of Ely*, Cambridge 1951.

—— and Hatcher, John, *Medieval England – Rural Society and Economic Change, 1086–1348*, London and New York 1978.

Postan, M. M., *The Famulus: The Estate Labourer in the XIIth and XIIIth Centuries, Economic History Review* Supplement 2, 1954.

—— *The Medieval Economy and Society*, London 1972.

Raban, Sandra, *The Estates of Thorney and Crowland*, Cambridge University, Department of Land Economy, Occasional Paper 7, 1977.

Rackham, Oliver, *The History of the Countryside*, London and Melbourne 1986.

Searle, Eleanor, *Lordship and Community: Battle Abbey and its Banlieu, 1066–1538*, Toronto 1974.

Chapter 7: Towns, Industry and Trade

Ballard, Adolphus, *British Borough Charters, 1042–1216*, Cambridge 1913.

—— and Tait, James, *British Borough Charters, 1216–1307*, Cambridge 1923.

Beresford, Maurice, *New Towns of the Middle Ages*, London 1967.

Biddle, Martin (ed.), *Winchester in the Early Middle Ages*, Winchester Studies i, Oxford 1976.

Blair, J. and Ramsay, N., *English Medieval Industries*, London and Rio Grande 1991.

Brooke, C. N. L. and Keir, G., *London, 800–1200: The Shaping of a City*, London 1975.

Catto, J. I., *History of the University of Oxford i, The Early Oxford Schools*, Oxford 1984.

Coss, Peter R., *Lordship, Knighthood and Locality: A Study in English Society, c.1180–c.1280*, Cambridge 1991.

Crouch, David, *The Beaumont Twins*, Cambridge 1986.

Everitt, Alan, *Landscape and Community in England*, London and Ronceverte 1985.

Hatcher, John, *English Tin Production and Trade before 1500*, Oxford 1973.

Holt, Richard and Rosser, Gervase, *The Medieval English Town*, London and New York 1990.

Reynolds, Susan, *An Introduction to the History of English Medieval Towns*, Oxford 1977.

Rosser, Gervase, *Medieval Westminster, 1200–1400*, Oxford 1989.

Roth, Cecil, *A History of the Jews in England*, 3rd edn, Oxford 1964.

Salzmann, L. F., *Building in England*, Oxford 1952.

—— *English Industries of the Middle Ages*, London 1913.

Urry, William, *Canterbury under the Angevin Kings*, London 1967.

Wood, Margaret, *The English Medieval House*, London 1965.

Chapter 8: Learning, Literature and the Arts

Alexander, Jonathan and Binski, Paul, *Age of Chivalry: Art in Plantagenet England, 1200–1400*, London 1987.

Bartlett, Robert, *Gerald of Wales, 1146–1223*, Oxford 1982.

Bennett, J. A. W., *Middle English Literature, 1100–1400*, ed. and completed by Douglas Gray, Oxford 1986.

British Archaeological Association, Conference Transactions: i (1975), *Medieval Art and Architecture at Worcester Cathedral*; viii (1982), *Medieval Art and Architecture at Lincoln Cathedral*.

Brown, R. Allen, *English Castles*, London 1976.

Catto, J. I., *History of the University of Oxford i: The Early Oxford Schools*, Oxford 1984.

Clanchy, Michael, *From Memory to Written Record*, 2nd edn, Oxford 1993.

Finucane, Ronald C., *Miracles and Pilgrims: Popular Beliefs in Medieval England*, London 1977.

Gransden, Antonia, *Historical Writing in England c.550 to c.1307*, London 1974.

Hunt, R. W., *The Schools and the Cloister: The Life and Writings of Alexander Nequam (1157–1217)*, ed. and rev. Margaret Gibson, Oxford 1984.

Kauffman, C. M., *Romanesque Manuscripts, 1066–1190*, London 1975.

Kibler, W. W., *Eleanor of Aquitaine, Patron and Politician*, Austin, Tx and London 1976.

Legge, M. D., *Anglo-Norman Literature and its Social Background*, Oxford 1963.

Macready, Sarah and Thompson, F. H., *Art and Patronage in the English Romanesque*, London 1986.

Morgan, Nigel, *Early Gothic Manuscripts i: 1190–1250*, Oxford 1982.

Norton, Christopher and Park, David, *Cistercian Art and Architecture in the British Isles*, Cambridge 1986.

Orme, Nicholas, *Education and Society in Medieval and Renaissance England*, London and Rio Grande 1989.

—— *English Schools in the Middle Ages*, London 1973.

—— *From Childhood to Chivalry*, London and New York 1984.

Pepin, Ronald E., *Literature of Satire in the Twelfth Century*, Lewiston, Queenston and Lampeter 1988.

Raby, F. J. E., *A History of Christian-Latin Poetry from the Beginnings to the Close of the Middle Ages*, Oxford 1927.

—— *A History of Secular Latin Poetry in the Middle Ages*, Oxford 1957.

Smalley, Beryl, *The Becket Conflict and the Schools*, Oxford 1973.

Southern, R. W., *Robert Grosseteste: The Growth of an English Mind in Medieval Europe*, Oxford 1988.

Vaughan, Richard, *Matthew Paris*, Cambridge 1958.

Warren, Ann K., *Anchorites and their Patrons in Medieval England*, Berkeley and Los Angeles, Cal. and London 1985.

Wilks, M., *The World of John of Salisbury*, Studies in Church History Subsidia 3, Oxford 1984.

Wilson, Christopher, *The Gothic Cathedral*, London 1990.

Chapter 9: England and the Angevin Empire

Bartlett, Robert, *Gerald of Wales, 1146–1223*, Oxford 1982.

Cosgrove, A. (ed.), *A New History of Ireland ii, Medieval Ireland 1169–1534*, Oxford 1987.

Gransden, Antonia, *Historical Writing in England c.550 to c.1307*, London 1974.

Holt, J. C., 'Feudal society and the family in early medieval England', *TRHS* 5th ser.: i, 'The revolution of 1066', 32 (1982), 193–212; iv, 'The heiress and the alien', 35 (1985), 1–28.

Legge, M. D., *Anglo-Norman Literature and its Social Background*, Oxford 1963.

Vaughan, Richard, *Matthew Paris*, Cambridge 1958.

Index